What Is Film Noir?

William Park

Lewisburg
Bucknell University Press

Published by Bucknell University Press
Co-published with The Rowman & Littlefield Publishing Group, Inc.
4501 Forbes Boulevard, Suite 200, Lanham, Maryland 20706
www.rowman.com

10 Thornbury Road, Plymouth PL6 7PP, United Kingdom

Copyright © 2011 by William Park
First paperback edition 2013

All images courtesy of the Film Noir Foundation

All rights reserved. No part of this book may be reproduced in any form or by any electronic or mechanical means, including information storage and retrieval systems, without written permission from the publisher, except by a reviewer who may quote passages in a review.

British Library Cataloguing in Publication Information Available

Library of Congress Cataloging-in-Publication Data
The hardback edition was previously cataloged by the Library of Congress as follows:

Park, William.
  What is film noir? / William Park.
    p. cm.
  Includes bibliographic references and index.
  1. Film noir—History and criticism. I. Title.
  PN1995.9.F54P38 2011
  791.43'6552—dc23   2011021230

ISBN 978-1-61148-362-8 (cloth : alk. paper)
ISBN 978-1-61148-521-9 (pbk. : alk. paper)
ISBN 978-1-61148-363-5 (electronic)

∞™ The paper used in this publication meets the minimum requirements of American National Standard for Information Sciences—Permanence of Paper for Printed Library Materials, ANSI/NISO Z39.48-1992.

Printed in the United States of America

Dedicated to my parents
Dorothea Louise Jordan and William John Park, Jr.

Contents

Acknowledgments		ix
Introduction		1
1	Theory of Genre	11
2	Film Noir: The Genre Defined	19
3	Objections	31
4	Style	55
5	Period Style	65
6	Alfred Hitchcock	89
7	Meanings	115
8	Last Words	133
Appendices		135
Appendix A: Within the Genre		137
Appendix B: Borderline		173
Appendix C: Period Pieces		179
Works Cited		185
Index		193
Index of Cited Films		205
About the Author		213

Acknowledgments

I could never have completed this book without the aid and support of my late wife, Marlene Park. I owe a great debt to my colleague, Gilberto Perez, who, from the time this book was a mere unpublished article until its conclusion offered astute criticism and insight into the nature of film and film noir. William Gerdts lent his encyclopedic knowledge of noir and its players. Professor Thomas Leitch of the University of Delaware gave an extraordinarily accurate critique of an earlier version of the book, without which it would never have made it into print. Eddie Muller, as ever generous in his knowledge and love of film noir, provided invaluable help, as did Ted Whipple to whom I am indebted for the images, and Gary Deane. And special thanks go to Greg Clingham and Kate Parker of Bucknell University Press and to Brooke Bascietto, Liliana Koebke, and Gwen E. Kirby at Rowman & Littlefield. All the images in the book come from the archives of the Film Noir Foundation, whose help in preserving the films and assisting critics and scholars cannot be overestimated. Finally, I wish to thank Sylvia Thompson Park for her helpfulness during the final stages of bringing this book into the light.

Introduction

"Is film noir a genre or a style?"

—Rick Altman[1]

What is film noir? Most commentators agree on the essential films that make up the category, films such as *Double Indemnity* (1944) and *Out of the Past* (1947).[2] They also agree that the "movement" began in earnest in 1941 with *The Maltese Falcon* (the third Hollywood version), that it peaked in the late 1940s and early 1950s, that it included a semi-documentary phase, and that its classic period ended in 1958 with *Touch of Evil*. Every writer acknowledges the same sources of noir: German expressionism, pre-Code Hollywood, French poetic realism, the pulp fictions of Dashiell Hammett, Raymond Chandler, James M. Cain, and Cornell Woolrich. As to "causes," there too we find the usual suspects, most of them the result of World War II: wartime gloom; reduced production budgets, angst-ridden veterans disoriented by their experiences in combat and threatened by working women; a post war boom that as it created new suburbs also destroyed the city and turned it into a dark wasteland; a new war that threatened atomic annihilation; various responses to Communism at home; a simmering dissatisfaction with the restrictions of the Production Code, and the decline of the studio system of film making.

In addition, everyone seems to know what film noir means. As Nathaniel Rich puts it:

> Coined by French film critic Nino Frank in 1946 and popularized by French critics Raymond Borde and Etienne Chaumenton in their 1955 study *Panorama du film noir americain*, the term describes, in its most narrow application, a series of American films made during World War II and in the years following,

punctuated by violence and pervaded with a profound sense of dread and moral uncertainties. The heroes tend to be cynical, tough, and overwhelmed by sinister forces beyond their control. Stylistically, film noir is distinguished by its stark chiaroscuro cinematography, influenced in large part by German expressionism (many of film noir's greatest directors, including Fritz Lang, Otto Preminger, Billy Wilder, Robert Siodmak, and Edgar Ulmer had emigrated from Germany and Austria in the 1930s). Films are shot in black and white, lit for night, favor oblique camera angles and obsessive use of shadows, and, most importantly, take place in a city. Film noir tries to make sense of the complexities and anxieties of the postwar urban experience by exploring the rotten underside of the American city, the place where the American dream goes to die.[3]

Yet, despite this accurate summary of received opinion about film noir, no agreement has yet been reached about what exactly it is. As Rich said in the preface to his statement: "'Film noir' is itself an amorphous, foggy term." In common usage, for instance on the Internet Movie Data Base, film noir means any black and white crime film of the 1940s and early 1950s.[4] But the scholars and film critics most knowledgeable about film noir have reached no such agreement. Some consider film noir a genre; others think it a style. Robin Wood sees it as "occupying an indeterminate space between a style and a genre"[5] and still others refer to it variously as a "movement," a "cycle," a "hybrid," some kind of "generic field"[6] or "transgeneric phenomenon"[7] which defies classification. For Thomas Elsaesser it's a "conceptual black hole,"[8] and Steve Neale denies that it even existed.[9]

The fog generated by discussions of film noir results from arguments about genre and the relationship between it and style. By style, the critics usually mean the look of the films, in this case a number of visual motifs that bind the films together, such as night scenes, expressive camera work, and chiaroscuro. Movement is less clear to me, but I think it means a group of films having similar outlooks, such as the Italian "Neo-realist" films following World War II, or the French New Wave of the 1960s, films that have some influence on the historic development of cinema. Cycle is even less clear, but it probably means not something that goes round but a series of films with the same subject, such as Tarzan or James Bond, and in this case the hundreds of gritty crime films of the 1940s and 50s. By hybrid the critics mean a cross between two genres, in the case of film noir between detective stories and melodramas or women's films. And as to film noir not existing, that comes from critics who complain that the name film noir was a historic afterthought, that there is nothing new in film noir, or that creating categories of this nature will get you nowhere. Left to choose between a vulgar and nondiscriminating everything and an unresolved and sophisticated ontological dispute, one is tempted to throw up one's hands and exclaim like a character in *Out of the Past* "I always say everybody's right."

By far the most thorough and knowledgeable book on film noir is James Naremore's *More than Night: Film Noir in its Contexts*.[10] Convinced that film noir has "no essential characteristics" (5), Naremore turns away from an examination of genre and what film noir might be in its own right and looks instead at some of its contexts.[11] In its relation to the world from which it arose, he considers modernism, post-war France, and the post-war United States, in particular McCarthyism. In its relation to the people who created it, he considers Dashiell Hammett, Raymond Chandler, and Graham Greene, as well as the studio system and left wing Hollywood screenwriters and directors. In its relation to the forms on which it is based, instead of discussing crime films in any detail, he concentrates on early film noirs such as *The Maltese Falcon* and *Double Indemnity*. He speaks of the popularity of the films, but does not spend much time on the audience. And to these basic contexts, he adds the history of this genre, which has no essentials, from the 1940s up to the late 1990s when he first published his book. In the expanded and updated edition of 2008, he continues his history into the twenty-first century.

Given his dismissal of generic questions, it does indeed seem odd that he makes reference to "classic film noir" (97, 103, 139), to "the noir category" (136), to the evolution of film noir "like any other genre or style" (219) and to *The Manchurian Candidate* (1962) as "operating on the margins of film noir" (135). These and numerous other usages throughout the book would seem to contradict his notions about film noir's nonexistence as a genre. Aware of the problem, Naremore says:

> It may seem odd, however, that after questioning most of the usual generalizations about film noir in my first chapter, I go on to use the term in a familiar way and to employ a more or less conventional historiography. I would explain the apparent contradiction by pointing out that film noir functions rather like big words such as romantic or classic. An ideological concept with a history of its own, it can be used to describe a period, a movement, and a recurrent style. Like all critical terminologies it tends to be reductive, and it sometimes works on behalf of unstated agendas. For these reasons, and because its meaning changes over time, it ought to be examined as a discursive context. It nevertheless has heuristic value, mobilizing specific themes that are worth further consideration (6).

This is a strange statement coming from someone who says in the Acknowledgements that his wife endured the process of writing the book "because she likes film noir as much as I do" (xiv). How can one like something that has no essential characteristics? Classic has thousands of applications, but film noir refers to a limited body of movies in what he himself refers to as "a fully developed noir canon" (160). How can something devoid of essentials provide so many contexts as well as an "important legacy" (11)? How can one deny the existence of something and then talk about it in a "familiar way" as though after all it exists? There's more than an apparent contradiction here.

That a writer as intelligent and well informed as Naremore could breezily dismiss these problems in itself deserves some further consideration. To explain Naremore's apparent contradiction in usage, it may help to place him in one of his own contexts. He belongs to the first generation of academic film historians. Before the late 1960s, the best writing on film came from reviewers and contributors to magazines, authors such as André Bazin, Otis Ferguson, Robert Warshow, William Pechter, Barbara Deming, and Manny Farber. But with the establishment of film history as a bona fide academic subject and the university departments that supported it, a new generation of film lovers, now with the time and money for archival research, inevitably took over the field. Most of these academicians earned their own advanced degrees in departments of English, French, or Comparative Literature, and they concentrated in the more welcoming Midwestern Universities, such as Wisconsin, Iowa, and Indiana. The Ivy League was slow to pick up the new beat, and traditional film departments such as USC, UCLA, and NYU remained more heavily committed to production than to history or theory.

The rise of academic film study also coincided with the powerful influx of French theory on all aspects of culture. Semiotics and deconstruction ruled the day, and not to be familiar with Foucault, Derrida, Barthes, and Lacan, among others, marked one at the very least as ill-informed. Joining the liberating spirit of Rousseau and Marx to the iconoclasm of Nietzsche, these critics concerned themselves not so much with absolutes such as "Truth" but with disclosing the "unstated agendas" (6) and oppressive ideologies behind such concepts. Needless to say they provided strong ideological support for all 1960s and 1970s radicalism, but they also struck at an older generation of critics, most of them politically liberal, who came to be known as "structuralists," writers such as Claude Lévi-Strauss and Northrop Frye. Whether in anthropology or literary criticism, these writers had discovered what they claimed to be basic human structures, core myths, and archetypal plots which underlay all cultural projects. Such thinking proved anathema to the new school, which far preferred historic relativism and individual self determination. As a result such structuralist thinking came to be labeled as "essentialism," a term that had the stench of other negative terms such as sexism and racial profiling.

Nothing was sacred; every received opinion came under scrutiny.[12] If the world were not so imperfect, one might see the whole era as characterized by a kind of intellectual paranoia, but suspicion and skepticism are better terms, and deeper readings became the order of the day. Such is the milieu which formed Naremore and other important writers on film such as Rick Altman. Thus instead of defining a term such as film noir, Naremore finds "problematizing" it (2), that is to say deconstructing it or examining its various discourses, a much more useful and sensible project. As he says:

> Perhaps the very word genre, with its etymological links to biology and birth promote a kind of essentialism. . . . The fact is, every movie is transgeneric or polyvalent. Neither the movie industry nor the audience follows structuralist rules, and movie conventions have always blended together in mongrelized ways (6).

That is true. Yet another fact is that moguls, audiences, and critics place movies in genres and discuss them as belonging to genres, which is what Naremore himself does throughout the book. Genre is not simply an either/or between the alleged structuralist who is too rigid and reductive and the more sophisticated critic who favors discursivity.

Reductive as they may be, we cannot think or discourse without such categories. One notices that the films Naremore chooses to discuss in some detail—*The Maltese Falcon*, *The Third Man* (1949), *Double Indemnity*, *The Blue Dahlia* (1946), *Crossfire* (1947), *Detour* (1945), *Kiss Me Deadly* (1955), and *Out of the Past*—all fit snugly into the "fully developed noir canon." When he points out that *Clash by Night* (1952) has "nothing specific in common with *Laura* (1944), even though both have been called noir" (6), I cannot help thinking that he knows that *Clash by Night,* lacking even a crime, has very little in common with any canonized film noir.[13]

Of course any film can be perceived in multiple genres. The Internet Movie Data Base, for instance, classifies *Double Indemnity* as "Crime—Film Noir—Thriller" and *Out of the Past* as "Drama—Film Noir—Thriller." But you needn't be a PhD to see which category is more specific and best describes it. Then, too, any critic can create genres according to subjects, themes, politics, characters, technologies, production levels, studios, stars, and dozens of other possibilities. Thus we can speak of circus films, Freudian films, radical films, biopics, early Technicolor films, B movies, Warner Brothers films, and Elvis Presley or Esther Williams films, to name but a few. Yet over time, the discussion of films has centered on what André Bazin in his famous essay, "L'Evolution du Langage Cinematographique," called Hollywood's "grands genres."[14] He names seven: American comedy (*Mr. Smith Goes to Washington* [1939]); burlesque (the Marx Brothers); the musical (Fred Astaire and Ginger Rogers; *The Ziegfeld Follies* [1946]); police and gangster films (*Scarface* [1932], *I Am a Fugitive* [1932], *The Informer* [1935]); the psychological and social drama (*Back Street* [1932], *Jezebel* [1938]); the fantasy and horror film (*Dr. Jekyll and Mr. Hyde* [1932 and 1941], *The Invisible Man* [1933], *Frankenstein* [1932]); and the Western (*Stagecoach* [1939]). Bazin wrote the earliest version of this essay in 1950. Looking over the history of Hollywood since, to these we would add science fiction, a subdivision perhaps of fantasy and horror, war films, and most importantly film noir, as witnessed by the many articles, books, and contexts it has generated.

Were the critical fashion not so prejudiced against defining genres, the complexity of film noir and the diversity of films and techniques attributed to it present still further difficulties. As Rick Altman exclaims, "Is film noir a genre or a style?" (70). The answer is that it is both, the only Hollywood genre that is also a style, a period style no less. My colleague Gilberto Perez has remarked that genre is like grammar and style like rhetoric. Or to borrow terms from Altman, genre has two aspects, the "syntactic," that is "plot structure and relationships," and the "semantic," "key scenes," "character types," and "recognizable shots" (89). In the case of film noir, the syntactic perspective enables us to see the genre more clearly, while the semantic gives us a better view of the style and its period. In this case the genre depends more on the situation and actions of the protagonist, while the style consists of dark

Figure I.1. Humphrey Bogart in *The Maltese Falcon*

cities, night clubs, detectives, femme fatales, expressionist camera work and chiaroscuro. When a writer refers to film noir, he may be referring to the genre or the style, for of course in the classic period the two accompany one another and cannot be easily separated.

If conventional historiography sees the genre commencing in 1941 with *The Maltese Falcon*, the most astute observers have recognized *Citizen Kane*, released earlier in the same year, as the origin of the style. In one of his last essays, André Bazin remarked on the connection between the two:

> Bogart is without doubt, typically the actor/myth of the war and post-war period. I mean the period between 1940 and 1955. True, his filmography signals some seventy five films since 1930, of which forty or so predate *High Sierra* and *The Maltese Falcon* (1941). But those were only supporting roles, and it is beyond question that his character emerged with what is commonly called the noir crime film whose ambiguous hero he was to epitomize. In any case for us it was after the war and especially through the films of Huston that Bogart won such popularity. Now one is aware that the years 1940–1 remark precisely the second major state in the evolution of the American talking picture. 1941 is also the year of *Citizen Kane*. It must be the case, therefore, that there is some secret harmony in the coincidence of these events: the end of the pre-war period, the arrival of a certain novelistic style in cinematographic ecriture, and through Bogart, the triumph of interiorization and of ambiguity. One can in any case easily see in what respect Bogart differs from those pre-war heroes for whom Gary Cooper might be the prototype: handsome, strong, noble, expressing much more the optimism and efficiency of a civilization than its anxiety.[15]

There we have it from the master himself: a new period, a shift in Hollywood's evolution, a new style, and the ambiguous noir hero who forms the center of the new, more somber genre.

Naremore cites a portion of this passage (26) in his discussion of Bazin and existentialism. But instead of disputing the "essentialist" implications of what Bazin is saying, he instead comments on "ambiguity" and "interiorization," concluding that "the themes of isolation, uncertainty, and ambiguity must have exerted a strong appeal to anyone who was wary of collective politics and inclined to treat social issues in terms of personal ethics" (26). In other words, Naremore turns Bazin's objective description of something that happened in Hollywood in 1941 into a subjective expression of Bazin's state of mind or world view. He then goes on to say that "During this period the younger critics at *Cahiers du cinema* began to project Bazin's ideas onto Hollywood" (26).

Such a misreading of Bazin stems from Naremore's thesis that the French "invented" film noir (13, 15, 216). To be sure they gave the phenomenon the name that stuck, but as we shall argue in Chapter 3, Hollywood and the most perceptive of the critics of the era were well aware of this new breed of film. So rather than the French critics projecting their own notions onto Hollywood, Naremore, and those who take up this view, are in fact projecting their own ideas about film noir, in borrowed French terminology, back onto the French.

Despite Naremore's initial statement that film noir "has less to do with a group of artifacts than with a discourse" (11), by the end of his book he's admitting that "If we abandoned the word noir, we would have to find another, no less problematic, means of organizing what we see." And the final paragraph begins, "But I would also argue that even if noir is only a discursive construct, it has remarkable flexibility, range, and mythic force, maintaining our relation to something like an international genre" (276–77).[16] He then concludes by suggesting that film noir has proven more lasting than Westerns:

> All the while, the old thrillers—one way streets and dead ends, mad love and bad love, double crosses and paranoid conspiracies, discontents in the nuclear family and perverse violence in every corner of the society—are as topical as ever and still productive of good films. (277)

Given these statements, I cannot help thinking that Naremore has a very clear idea of the genre of film noir, but the tiresomeness (276) of the debate and prevailing ideology have caused him to take another approach to the subject.

So where do I come into the picture? Near the end of his book Naremore says, "We can never know exactly how audiences in the 1940s and 1950s viewed the dark movies of their day" (261). "Exactly," maybe, but we have a pretty good idea from their own statements of what everyone from Joe Breen at the Production Code office to Barbara Deming at the Library of Congress was thinking at the time. And I, now an octogenarian, have my own memories. I was, after all, part of the audience for which these pictures were made.

In contrast, then, to Naremore's explicit thesis, I believe that the "group of artifacts" constitutes a genre, which though an idea, is an idea that can be looked at and described in its own right as well as in its contexts. Furthermore, I believe that although the French dubbed these artifacts film noir, the "idea" of noir was not a French back projection or "invention," and that Hollywood itself was very much aware of what it was doing and what was happening. In the chapters which follow, I will attempt to define film noir as a genre, discuss the relationship between the genre and the style it adopted, and illustrate how the two played a major role in creating the period. As a genre, film noir continues on as "neo-noir," but as a period style it remains forever fixed in the 1940s and 1950s. I suspect that if critics could free themselves from anxieties about genre as being rigid or essentialist, and if they had a better understanding of period style, an art historical concept that has gone out of favor if not usage, a great deal of light would shine into the dark corners of noir.

NOTES

1. Rick Altman, *Film/Genre* (London: British Film Institute, 1999), 70. [Hereafter Altman's book will be cited parenthetically in the text.]
2. The date of a film is given only the first time it appears in the text.
3. Nathaniel Rich, *San Francisco Noir* (New York: Little Bookroom, 2005), 8.
4. The default position also taken by Jans B. Wager, *Dames in the Driver's Seat* (Austin: University of Texas Press, 2005), 16.
5. Robin Wood, "*Rancho Notorious* (1952): A Noir Western in Color," in *Film Noir Reader 4*, eds. Alain Silver and James Ursini (Pompton Plains, NJ: Limelight Editions, 2004), 264.
6. Michael Walker, "Film Noir: An Introduction," in *The Book of Film Noir*, ed. Ian Cameron (New York: Continuum, 1992), 8, 38.
7. R. Barton Palmer, *Hollywood's Dark Cinema: The American Film Noir* (New York: Twayne Publisher, 1994), 30.
8. Thomas Elsaesser, *Weimar Cinema and After: Germany's Historical Imaginary* (London: Routledge, 2000), 424.
9. Steve Neale, *Genre and Hollywood* (London: Routledge, 2000), 151–77.
10. James Naremore, *More than Night: Film Noir in Its Contexts* (Berkeley: University of California Press, 1998). [Hereafter this will be cited parenthetically in the text.]
11. In his updated and expanded second edition (Berkeley: University of California Press, 2008), 282–83, he says that "in recognition of the inherent instability of generic classifications, I've tried to avoid excessively neat definitions of *film noir*."
12. In *The Hanging Figure: On Suspense and the Films of Alfred Hitchcock* (Westport, CT: Praeger, 2002), 1–3, Christopher S. Morris provides a succinct account of the impact of these new approaches and the dilemmas they brought about.
13. I suspect *Clash by Night* has been cited as a film noir because Robert Porfiro wrote about it in *Film Noir: An Encyclopedic Reference to the American Style*, 3rd ed., eds. Alain Silver and Elizabeth Ward (Woodstock, NY: Overlook Press, 1992), 61–62. Porfiro typically characterizes films as noir which have anguished characters with gloomy fates, even though as in this case there is no crime or investigation. See his "No Way Out: Existential Motifs in the *Film Noir*," in *Film Noir Reader*, 6th ed., eds. Alain Silver and James Ursini (New York: Limelight Editions, 1996 [1976]), 77–93.
14. André Bazin, *Qu'est-ce Que Le Cinema?* vol. I, *Ontologie et Langage* (Paris: Les Editions Du Cerf, 1958), 136.
15. André Bazin, "Mort d'Humphrey Bogart," in *Cahiers du Cinema: The 1950s, Neo-Realism, Hollywood, New Wave*, ed. Jim Hillier (Cambridge, MA: Harvard University Press, 1985 [1957]), 99–100.

16. In the expanded and updated 2008 edition, he concludes by saying, "It is perhaps unimportant whether we give *Mulholland Dr.* [2001] a generic or stylistic label, but if we call it noir, and if film noir in its self-conscious, postmodern manifestations is occasionally capable of this kind of wrenching dramatic effect, then it remains capable of almost anything" (310).

Chapter One

Theory of Genre

Genre means a type, a kind, a species, or a category. As such it is a concept or an idea. You can hold a movie in your hand, as a reel or a CD, and you can project it and make notes and comments on its content. It does not change; it is a thing. Not so with genres. Because they exist in the minds of observers, they can be invented, changed, joined with others, redefined, and also denied. They have always engaged philosophers, for they enable us to think about things. Without them we would be reduced to pointing and grunting. As Socrates explained, there is no such thing in nature as "equal," by which he illustrated that concepts are realities and that we learn by recollection (*Phaedo,* 74a–75c). Theories, whether of genre or evolution, are also concepts, abstractions, not perceivable entities.

Thus all seekers after knowledge have attempted to create objective categories or sciences through which they could organize their subjective perceptions, or as David Hume, the skeptical philosopher of the eighteenth century called them, "customary connections." Following the Greeks, we call them "ologies," meaning "knowledge of something," as in geology, the knowledge of the earth; biology, the knowledge of living things; anthropology, the knowledge of man; psychology, the knowledge of the mind; sociology, the knowledge of society. Though from a skeptical perspective all of them are suspect and can by rigorous analysis be deconstructed, none of these branches of science or social science can exist without a common sense recognition of patterns of evidence and behavior. And so it is in with art.

We needn't be philosophers to recognize the various arts: the visual—painting, sculpture, architecture; the performing—music, dance, and drama; and the literary—poetry and prose. Right away, we notice that the categories have porous borders and cross over into one another. Architecture employs decoration, so sculpture and painting enter the picture. Paintings can contain sculptural elements, and sculptures have been painted or otherwise colored. Dance, drama, and certain forms of music, are also visual. Drama in turn is a form of literature, and poetry and prose often depend on how a work is printed. In art, it would seem, transgression is the rule, but then no work can transgress without recognizable boundaries to begin with. Thus, genre and innovation depend on one another. Not infrequently two genres hybridize and create a new genre, as when oratorio and drama joined to form opera. Such was the creation of cinema, which combined visual, performing, and literary arts with the new technology of "motion pictures."

If we consider for a moment a large category such as painting, we quickly see into how many categories it can be subdivided. For instance, mediums such as oil, watercolor, tempera, and acrylic can be applied to canvas, wood, metal, clay, or mixed with plaster. Art historians divide paintings into periods and styles, and then argue over their decisions. When it comes to painting, the term genre can refer to a Dutch tavern scene or to any gathering of ordinary people, but it also refers to types of subject matter such as history, landscape, portrait, and still life. To these categories modern studies have added ones of patronage and usage, and we think of religious art, courtly art, and public art.

Film, as a newcomer to the arts, presents some special problems, the first being "Qu' est-ce que le cinema?" as Bazin phrased it, or "what is it?" Adding to Bazin's own answers which centered on film's relation to reality, Gilberto Perez, through his discussion of major directors has placed film in its various contexts, such as its relationship to landscape and theater.[1] Christian Metz, another major theorist, has demonstrated that film does not have a unique language of its own, but consists of some eight autonomous segments, ranging from shot to sequence.[2] In an article entitled "Pure Cinema,"[3] I attempted to describe what to me seemed the three main types of film, namely, documentary, avant-garde, and fictional narrative, the proponents of each type imagining that they alone made the pure thing. As with other categories, these also cross over into one another, though for the most part one can distinguish among them. The third type, fictional narrative, commonly known as the movies, has proven by far the most popular and has spawned the most sub-species. It is here that we find not only Bazin's "grands genres" but also film noir. And it is on this level that most discussions of film genre take place.

The most challenging of the many studies is Rick Altman's *Film/Genre*. As something of an iconoclast, Altman wishes to overthrow the notion that genres are permanent, transcendent entities. Instead he favors "problematizing" genres, that is, challenging received opinions about them. He notes, for instance that even as fixed a genre as the musical was not at first perceived by that name, but rather as "musical romances," "musical dramas," or "back stage comedy" (32). Typically, he argues, a genre begins as an adjective and only later becomes a noun (50). This process was also true of the Western, another fixed genre that proves on closer analysis anything but fixed (34–38). He also favors "discursivity," that is, looking at genres from different angles and perspectives. For instance, he points out that critics see a family of films having similar qualities or conventions, but producers are looking at what succeeds and how to repeat that formula while adding new elements that will give their product a competitive edge over their rivals (38). Advertisements for films consistently appeal to what the critics would see as several genres, usually combining thrills with romance (54–62), as in the poster that provided the title for Pauline Kael's book, *Kiss, Kiss, Bang, Bang*.[4] Through this discursive method, any film can be seen as fitting into a multitude of genres, while the genres themselves constantly shift and hybridize. Genres then should be seen not only in their own right but, as Naremore illustrates, in other contexts.

As much as one admires the freshness and depth of Altman's theorizing and his genuine contribution to genre studies, one cannot overlook some overreaching and flaws in his presentation. For instance, I have trouble with his notion that following Aristotle, "Horace sets up a simple generic model for the ages: poets produce by imitating a predefined original sanctioned by the literary-critical oligarchy" (4). One of the myopic neoclassic critics mentioned by Altman is Alexander Pope. In 1711 he published an imitation of Horace's *Ars Poetica* entitled *An Essay on Criticism*.[5] To be sure he asserts that "Those RULES of old *discover'd* not *devis'd,* Are *Nature* still, but *Nature Methodiz'd"* (88–89) and that *"Nature* and *Homer* were . . . the same" (135). Yet, alongside such neoclassicism, we also discover a great deal of "discursivity":

> *You* then whose Judgment the right Course wou'd steer,
> Know well each ANCIENT'S proper *Character,*
> His *Fable, Subject, Scope* in ev'ry Page,
> *Religion, Country, Genius* of his Age:
> Without all these at once before your Eyes,
> *Cavil* you may, but never *Criticize.* (118–23)

Each of these represents a discourse and introduces relativity not transcendence into the discussion. As to the rules, here is perhaps Pope's most famous dictum:

> If, where the *Rules* not far enough extend,
> (Since Rules were made but to promote their end)
> Some Lucky LICENSE answers to the full
> Th' Intent propos'd, *that License* is a rule.

> Thus *Pegasus,* a nearer way to take,
> May boldly deviate from the common Track.
> Great Wits sometimes may *gloriously offend,*
> And rise to *Faults* true Critics dare not mend;
> From *vulgar Bounds* with *brave Disorder* part,
> And *snatch* a Grace beyond the reach of Art. (146–55)

It would seem that Pope too is aware of the hybridization, the crossing of boundaries, the instability of genres, and the critics need to be aware of them.

Since Altman acknowledges postmodernism's "distaste for totalizing discourse" (7), we are not surprised to see him dispute with Northrop Frye. He lumps Frye with others who lift generic texts "out of time" and place them "in a timeless holding area as if they were all contemporaries. . . . [T]his synchronic approach strips away historical differences" (19). Later he remarks that "the myth oriented rediscovery of genre criticism . . . jeopardized our ability to think of genres as anything other than the stable manifestations of more or less fundamental and permanent human concerns" (49). "Once filled by prayer, the role of mediating between man and the eternal has now fallen to genre" (50).

By genre here, Altman means archetypes and basic myths, not the Western, the musical, or the biopic. And he hits upon the implication of all such structural studies, namely that humans possess some kind of imaginative DNA, common to all cultures. We are not blank tablets as Locke would have it, but pre-coded with innate ideas, or more frightening, made in the image of God. Altman, like other post modernists, does not need to argue with these structuralists or attempt to refute them. Rather such notions are too heinous, too antithetical to contemplate and just stating them or revealing them serves to refute them. But why? Why can't we have archetypes *and* discursivity? Why make an either/or argument, along the lines of heredity vs. environment? Why insist on one at the expense of the other? Altman here displays some of his own rigidity. He's absolutely right in drawing attention to what Frye calls "the stubborn structure" of the archetypes. But he completely ignores what Frye calls "the Theory of Modes," namely the variations of those structures in different periods of history. Rather than acknowledge Frye's "problematizing" of these structures, he prefers to set up a straw man.

Strictly speaking, Frye's four archetypal plots are genres or types of plot. But as archetypes they do not preclude the instability of what we commonly call genres, their rise or fall, their hybridization and mutations, their historic and institutional causes, the subjectivity of their definitions, or our ability to find the hidden agendas which give them support. Genres such as the epic, the novel, the Western, and film noir are not archetypal. On this level of genre, there is no such thing as essential or timeless, but rather historic phenomena which the genres themselves do much to interpret and explain. Every era creates genres; all artists make use of them, but their only constant is mutability. What Frye would insist upon, and illustrate for that matter, is that any genre which tells stories, any narrative, will, upon analysis, reveal its stubborn structure. As outrageous as that may sound, it is true. Or rather I should say that for more than fifty years now I have yet to find any narrative work from any time or culture that does not build upon or utilize his archetypal plots. From comic books to grand opera, from Hollywood to Bollywood, one can, if so inclined, discover them, and the best a post modernist with a distaste for totalizing discourse can do is categorically reject them as irrelevant or not worth considering because of their hateful essentialist implications.

At one point in his argument Altman examines a statement by Wittgenstein about "family resemblances" (83). Needless to say he is skeptical about the permanent implications of such an idea, so following Wittgenstein's own advice to look rather than think about such things, he goes to the supermarket to examine what are labeled as nuts (86–89). Immediately he sees that the word refers to all kinds of nuts which come in a variety of packages and are associated with mixes and cooking oils. At home, he discovers that the nuts he has bought are shelved according to differing ideas than the ones in the store, and on an additional trip to the warehouse he sees that nuts and oils, placed together at the market, are stored in completely opposite locations. To top it all off, he reads an encyclopedia and finds out that cashews are fruits and peanuts legumes. From all this looking, he reaches some general hypotheses, the concluding one stating that "The perceived nature and purpose of genres depend directly and heavily on the identity of purpose of those using and evaluating them" (98). From here, after a short consideration of a commonly accepted genre such as the Western, he states:

> When we look more closely at generic communication, however, it is not sharing and understanding that appear, but competing meanings, engineered misunderstandings and desire for domination rather than communication. . . . [G]enres must be seen as a site of struggle among users. Our challenge is to discover the ways in which the authors and consumers of generic terminology disguise their interests and activity (99).

Two observations: First, Altman unintentionally engages in what William Empson called "double irony."[6] Empson used the term to describe how Fielding made fun of Richardson's conventional morality, but through the unfolding of the plot, especially having to do with incest, he comes around to supporting Richardson's views. In Altman's case, irony one results from the deconstruction of the commonly used category of nuts, but irony two results from the fact that despite all the problematizing and discursivity about nuts, the category stands and neither the supermarket nor the consumer will have any difficulty in using it. Second, Altman, a true man of the 1960s, leaps from nuts, an innocent grouping relatively free of disguised interests, to the cultural anxiety of conspiracy theory.

Let us then look at the Western from Altman's and Frye's points of view. Rather than one large permanent category, Altman points out how the alleged first Western, *The Great Train Robbery* (1903) was not perceived as a Western at all, but rather as a railway or crime film (34). A few years later they became known as "cowboy films" as opposed to "noble Indian" films (36–37). And once critics had consolidated these types into the Western, one cannot help noticing the many trail mix variations: musical Westerns such as *The Harvey Girls* (1946), *The Beautiful Blonde from Bashful Bend* (1949), and *Seven Brides for Seven Brothers* (1954); burlesques such as Laurel and Hardy's *Way Out West* (1937), the Marx Brothers' *Go West* (1940), and *Cat Ballou* (1965); and contemporary and rodeo Westerns such as *Lonely Are the Brave* (1962), *The Lusty Men* (1952), and *Junior Bonner* (1972). When considering dominant views and ideology one must consider films such as *The Virginian* (1929) in which Eugene Pallette remarks that we "must turn this prairie into the United States of America," and other nationalistic epics ranging from *The Iron Horse* (1924) to *Union Pacific* (1939) and *Western Union* (1941), the latter two appearing after a drought of A Westerns at a time when the United States was coming under threats from abroad. One can still distinguish between gunfighter Westerns, the kind Robert Warshow, at the outset of the Cold War, saw as central to the genre,[7] and the multitude of Indian Westerns from *Broken Arrow* (1950) on that appeared in the 1950s, films dealing with race relations in what must be considered as a displaced and allegoric treatments of black and white tensions at the outset of the Civil Rights Movement. What politics lie behind wilderness vs. civilization Westerns, law and order Westerns, cattlemen vs. sheep herder Westerns, land and water right Westerns? Why did Westerns prosper during the Roaring '20s, making Tom Mix one of the most popular box office stars of the time, and then during the Depression decline into B movies and serials whose audiences tended to be juvenile, rural, and southern? How were Monogram and Republic, the two minor studios who made most of these films, financed? What arrangements did they make with the major studios for distribution, the use of studio ranches, and the hiring of wranglers, stunt men, and equipment? What economic or personal factors influenced changing locations from the San Fernando Valley to Old Tucson, Lone Pine, or the Monument Valley? Then as to the stability of the established genre, who is not aware of how the 1960s transformed the seeming pride in the national epic of the winning of the west into the shame of greed, corruption and genocide? In an early article I called this "The Losing of the West,"[8] resulting in films such as *Little Big Man* (1970), *McCabe and Mrs. Miller* (1971), and *Dances with Wolves* (1990), in which the cavalry turns villainous and the town remains corrupt, the protagonist but adding to the mess, his girlfriend not a virgin but a prostitute. At present, the Western has altogether disappeared from view. Its last great star, Clint Eastwood, has turned to urban problems. The most famous, most written about of all the genres, is anything but impermeable and transcendent.

Yet all this mutability cannot do away with Frye's stubborn structures. On the whole, Westerns favor, or used to favor, the plot of romance. Here a group of primarily good people—there's always an innocent heroine and domestic animals—led by a hero, set out on a quest—the wagon train west. En route they meet and overcome obstacles, wicked men, swollen rivers, deserts, and hostile Indians spurred on and misled by the wicked white men, but in the end they reach their goal, the green world of some happy valley in the Promised Land. Such is *The Covered Wagon* (1923) and all its successors. Or another group led by a scout or some such Natty Bumpo type of heroic frontiersman sets out to build a railroad or string the telegraph. They too meet all sorts of obstacles, including those wicked whites and deluded Indians, but in the end complete their task and drive the golden spike uniting a now harmonious community or country, as in John Ford's *The Iron Horse*. Another favorite version of the plot of romance consists of some kind of Captain Virility, a Hopalong Cassidy, Lone Ranger, or Singin' Sammy who, fully formed as a hero, rides into a town and rids it of a nest of vipers or defends the innocent but plucky virgin from the sexual and land-encroaching villain. With a slight twist, this story turns into a plot of comedy. Here the protagonist, as in *Destry Rides Again* (1940), begins as an *eiron,* an anti-hero, who enters a corrupt town run by some male blocking figure, a corrupt land owner or political boss, and after suffering numerous humiliations, rises to cleanse the town and in most instances wins the love of a threatened young woman. Tragic plots, though more rare, also occur. Gary Cooper portraying Wild Bill Hickok in *The Plainsman* (1936) meets a tragic end as does Tyrone Power in *Jesse James* (1939), Gregory Peck in *The Gunfighter* (1950), Burt Lancaster in *Apache* (1954), Paul Newman in *Left Handed Gun* (1958), and John Wayne, in his last film, *The Shootist* (1976). As to plots of irony, seemingly antithetical to American optimism and the myth of the west, these too abound. Here psychologically troubled protagonists never escape from a fallen or "mad" world where "blocking figures" and oppressive laws win out in the end. Not surprisingly, such films became common during the period of film noir, starting with *The Oxbow Incident* (1943) and are now commonly referred to as "noir Westerns," films such as *Pursued* (1947) and *The Naked Spur* (1953).

Altman and Frye, discursivity and structuralism, rather than contradicting one another can both be useful in the analysis not only of individual works but also of genres. Armed with this hypothesis, let us turn to a consideration of film noir as a genre.

NOTES

1. Gilberto Perez, *The Material Ghost* (Baltimore: Johns Hopkins University Press, 1998).
2. Christian Metz, *Film Language: A Semiotics of the Cinema* (New York: Oxford University Press, 1974). See pages 123–33.
3. William Park, *Pure Cinema*. Essays by Sarah Lawrence Faculty, no. 1 (Bronxville, NY: Sarah Lawrence College, 1972).
4. Pauline Kael, *Kiss Kiss Bang Bang* (New York: Bantam Books, 1969).
5. Alexander Pope, *Pastoral Poetry and an Essay on Criticism*, ed. E. Audry and Aubrey Williams (New Haven, CT: Yale University Press, 1961). [Hereafter lines will be cited parenthetically in the text].
6. William Empson, "*Tom* Jones," *Kenyon Review* 20 (1958): 217–49.
7. Robert Warshow, "Movie Chronicle: The Westerner" (1954), in *The Immediate Experience* (New York: Atheneum, 1972), 135–54.
8. William Park, "The Losing of the West," *The Velvet Light Trap* 12 (Spring, 1974): 2–5.

Chapter Two

Film Noir: The Genre Defined

Crime is everywhere. It plays a prominent role in all genres, and is almost as common to drama as conflict itself. When it comes to the movies however, crime commonly refers to a family of films, all of them in contemporary settings. So many examples offer numerous discursive possibilities. Arthur Lyons, for instance, lumps all B movie crime films into the noir category.[1] One thinks of caper or heist films, newspaper crime fighters, prison films, spies and secret agents, to name but a few other possibilities. Bazin designated police and gangster films as one of his "grands genres." I would break that down into two subordinate genres, gangsters and police, depending on the main characters who typically meet different fates, death or triumph. The gangster film, despite numerous precedents, became a full-fledged genre early in the Depression, primarily through the example and success of three classics, *Little Caesar* (1931), *The Public Enemy* (1931), and *Scarface*. In his famous essay, "The Gangster as Tragic Hero," (1948) Robert Warshow endowed them with critical respectability,[2] unlike the Hayes Office which in the early 1930s attempted to suppress them or change their nature.

The New Deal, with its optimism and faith in progressive government, gave rise to a counter genre, the G-Man or gangbuster film. People now tend to praise the New Deal and look down on the Production Code Administration, which did to gangster films what the newly formed FBI attempted to do to public enemies. Yet the Roosevelt Administration and the Roosevelts themselves, particularly Mrs. Roosevelt, fully and directly supported the Code and its aims.[3] In Hollywood the New Deal meant a shift from fallen women to child stars, from Mae West to Shirley Temple. Despite the cleanup, however, the gangster film and the gangsters survived, but so then did the gangbusters, especially in the multitude of police and law enforcement procedural films which filled post-war screens.

In the late 1960s and early 1970s, with films such as *Bullitt* (1968), *The French Connection* (1971), and *Dirty Harry* (1971) the police procedural took a new turn. Now instead of departmental know how and collective derring-do, a lone cop finds himself caught between the crooks outside the department and the crooks and corrupt city officials within, a trap from which there seems no escape. I called this "the Police State."[4] This development may well be a trend or series and not an enduring genre, for lately such films have disappeared from view, one of the last being *L.A. Confidential* (1997). Commonly referred to as a "neo-noir," in large part because of its setting in the classic noir period, in my discourse it is more a "police state" type since almost all the conflict occurs within the L.A. department.

A third genre or type, very popular in the 1930s, was the mystery or "Whodunit." These featured a super sleuth: Philo Vance, Sherlock Holmes, Ellery Queen, Perry Mason, Charlie Chan, Mr. Moto, the Saint, the Falcon. Rather than being somber or threatening, many of them were lighthearted and comical. *The Thin Man* (1934), starring William Powell and Myrna Loy as Nick and Nora Charles, was typical of this type. Focused more on the romantic relationship between the stars and their post Prohibition drinking habits than on the crimes, it can just as easily be considered a screwball comedy. Five sequels followed. These were all based on Dashiell Hammett's last novel.

With Hammett we turn to the question of whether film noir spreads itself all over the family of crime films or is a genre in its own right. By widespread consensus, film noir begins to come into focus in October, 1941 when Warner Brothers' released the third version of his novel *The Maltese Falcon* (1930). That the two earlier versions did not establish a genre illustrates the importance of period in the creation of film noir and how intermingled are period and genre in its history. The first version of 1931 starred Ricardo Cortez. But instead of being cynical and hard boiled or world weary, he plays Sam Spade as a leering womanizer who lives in an elegant apartment, more suitable to Philo Vance or Sherlock Holmes than Spade. Bebe Daniels, in playing the femme fatale Miss Wonderly, appears repeatedly in lingerie, in a bathtub, and never loses an opportunity to display her cleavage. In short, this *Falcon* displays many of the conventions of pre-Code Hollywood. Not so the 1936 version, *Satan Met a Lady*, starring Warren William and Bette Davis. This interprets the *Falcon* as a screwball comedy, in the then very popular manner of Frank Capra. The woefully miscast William cavorts about in an oversize hat and at one point comically (except it is not funny) pulls a beret over the head of the Wilmer Cook substitute. The names of the characters have all been changed, but the British comedian and comic butler Arthur Treacher plays the Joel Cairo part and Alison Skipworth, one of Hollywood's grande dames, plays the fat man. It's a catastrophe which even Bette Davis cannot salvage.

No wonder then that on the eve of America's entry into World War II a more somber Hollywood could be persuaded by John Huston to attempt a faithful version of the classic novel, this time with a cast, fortunately headed by Humphrey Bogart (George Raft turned down the part), who embodied perfectly Sam Spade and the type of the hard-boiled protagonist. It made him a star.

This tough, wise cracking private eye, dwelling in a grungy no man's land between the criminals and the incompetent and corrupt authorities, represents something new in crime films. Borde and Chaumenton saw its hero, unlike previous crime fighters, as "barely distinguishable from the classic gangster."[5] What makes Sam Spade and his offspring different is not just the down and out milieu of the dark city, the femme fatale, and the double cross, but the fact that the hard-boiled protagonist becomes enmeshed in the treachery and falsehood of the other characters, most often through his sexual involvement with a female client or prime suspect. This never happens to the super sleuths, though some like Holmes and his precursor, Poe's Dupin, can identify with the mind of the criminal. This involvement in the lives of the criminals ensures that this new kind of detective remains in the foggy, nightmare world between the criminals and the law. As Louis Markos aptly puts it, he solves the crime "by physically and emotionally entering into the morally ambiguous realm of the criminal, a sort of Dantean descent into the underworld. . . . Indeed the detective at times seems as corrupt as the criminals he is tracking down."[6]

Following this lead, Karimi, Schatz, and Luhr[7] all look to the hard-boiled detective film or what Krutnik calls the "tough crime thriller"[8] as central to any generic framework for film noir. Such a definition makes more sense than other efforts, such as equating film noir with "realism"[9] or, as is often the case, with any 1940s crime film. Schatz believes that the detective film is the genre and that film noir is the style, a style derived from *Citizen Kane*.[10] Here we encounter the two meanings of film noir—a genre or a style. The majority of those attempting to define the genre, as well as those who deny that noir can be a genre, look at the main characters and the subjects, what Altman would call the syntactic qualities of the film. Schatz and also Luhr look at the visual style as definitive. We shall have more to say about these distinctions later.

One can construe hard-boiled detective films as a genre—why not? Its wisecracking tough guy protagonist makes them easy to identify. But neither such films nor the visual style and narrative structures of *Citizen Kane* fit all the films commonly alleged to be film noirs. Thus numerous critics balk at seeing noir as a genre, claiming it is too amorphous to qualify. Krutnik and Neale make the case very well. A claim that film noir centers on the hard-boiled detective excludes *Double Indemnity* and such noir stalwarts as

Detour, *The Killers* (1946), *Criss Cross* (1949), *D.O.A.* (1950), and *Sunset Boulevard* (1950), to name but a few. A claim that noir centers on a femme fatale omits *Laura*. A claim that it centers on a visual style leaves out *The Postman Always Rings Twice* (1946). If it centers in a dark city, there's no place for *They Live by Night* (1949) and *Gun Crazy* (1950). If noir depicts a fallen world and employs tragic and ironic plots, so do gangster films and many melodramas. So-called noir films exhibit great differences in their treatment of sexuality and gender. Male anxiety exists in other genres and many other types of film use flashbacks and the other narrative and visual devices claimed for film noir. No group of films, not even a single film encompasses *all* the characteristics of film noir.[11] *Double Indemnity* lacks a nightclub and dark city corruption; there's no psychiatrist in *Out of the Past*. And so it goes, whatever defining characteristic one sets up serves only to marginalize some noir films that other critics find essential. Unlike the gangster film, the Western, and the war film, film noir, so the argument goes, cannot be defined by a character, a locale, or a subject.[12]

Understandably then, English speaking scholars have been debating noir's identity ever since the 1970s when the French term came into popular usage, thanks largely to Paul Schrader's "Notes on Film Noir,"[13] and have fallen back on "movement," "cycle," "series," "hybrid," among other such nomenclatures, to describe this "transgeneric phenomenon." The discussions then have resulted not in consensus but rather in a kind of exhaustion which has favored either the solution offered by James Naremore or the dismissal of the problem from those who don't want to listen to scholarly quibbles and say "Let's just enjoy the films; we know which ones they are."

Undaunted by these problems, a number of critics still consider it a genre. Robert Porfiro favors film noir as either a hybrid genre created out of preexisting categories and as a response to the Production Code or as a genre "in the broadest sense as a 'sort' or species of film not strictly defined."[14] Mark T. Conard believes that an existential "mood and sensibility" characterize film noir, but that the same Nietzschean philosophy which created such a mood also makes noir impossible to define.[15] James Damico makes the best effort. He takes a Stanley Cavell–like approach, that is, one that limits a genre to a few perfect examples, and offers a more restricted definition: briefly, a world-weary man meets a femme fatale who leads him and herself into crime and destruction.[16]

That Damico's list omits Sam Spade and Philip Marlowe is not the strange oversight one might at first believe. Although Hammett and Chandler cannot be overestimated as major sources of film noir, the films based on their novels are *not essential to the genre*. To be sure Hammett gave us the cynical hard-boiled investigator who himself is morally flawed amidst a cast of scoundrels and a fallen world. The third version of *The Maltese Falcon* justly shares credit for initiating the disputed category. But had it never been remade, *Citizen Kane*, which was released five months earlier, by itself popularized the visual style and narrative conventions associated with film noir. And *I Wake Up Screaming* (1941) released but thirteen days after *The Maltese Falcon*, joined by *Double Indemnity*, *Laura*, and *Phantom Lady* (1944) would have raised considerations about a new wave of crime films. Of these, *Double Indemnity* is by far the most important, for, as Sheri Chinen Biesen has shown, it was this film more than any other that brought the new genre into contemporary consciousness.[17]

Raymond Chandler gave us the seedy, corrupt dark city and a wise cracking hero, but in his novels and the screenplays based on them during the classic period of noir, the hero never falls. Strange though it may seem, Chandler's screenplays, *Double Indemnity*, *The Blue Dahlia*, and *Strangers on a Train* (1951) are much more central to the notion of film noir than the films based on his novels. As Chandler wrote in *The Simple Art of Murder*, "But down these mean streets a man must go who is not mean, who is neither tarnished nor afraid."[18] Chandler's statement provides the clue we have been looking for—"tarnished." It helps us define the noir protagonist, a man *or woman* who is "tarnished, that is to say "fallen," not an innocent hero like Philip Marlowe but someone like Sam Spade who crosses a moral boundary and becomes—if not the criminal himself—enmeshed and tainted by criminality. Remember that Spade had been sleeping with the wife of Miles Archer, his murdered partner, and then commences an affair with the murderer, Bridgid O'Shaughnessy. If one goes over the list of films proposed for the "canon," one finds again and again a protagonist who has taken a false step, attempted a cover up, become an accomplice, or in some way fallen into crime. Either he or she commits the crime or in some way, through chance, a mistake, a moral lapse, or bad decision, becomes implicated in it, most often as the chief suspect. Admittedly some of the most interesting protagonists—Sam Spade or Jeff Markham in *Out of the Past* or Scotty Ferguson in *Vertigo* (1958)—are detectives. But other professions, types of work, or stations in life fit just as well. To illustrate the point, I list below but one single example of the range of occupations we find in classic film noir.

Actor	Ronald Coleman	*A Double Life* (1947)
Artist	Edward G. Robinson	*Scarlet Street* (1945)
Author	Chester Morris	*Blind Spot* (1947)
Boxer	Burt Lancaster	*The Killers* (1946)
Business Man	Edmond O'Brien	*D.O.A.* (1950)
Business Woman	Joan Crawford	*Mildred Pierce* (1945)

Circus Performer	John Dall	*Gun Crazy* (1950)
Cop	Gig Young	*City That Never Sleeps* (1953)
Doctor	Kent Smith	*Nora Prentiss* (1947)
Drifter	Dana Andrews	*Fallen Angel* (1945)
Ex-Con	Dick Powell	*Cry Danger* (1951)
G.I.	Robert Ryan	*Crossfire* (1947)
Housewife	Joan Bennett	*The Reckless Moment* (1949)
Ice Skater	Belita	*Suspense* (1946)
Insurance Agent	Fred MacMurray	*Double Indemnity* (1944)
Lawyer	Edward G. Robinson	*Illegal* (1955)
Magazine Editor	Ray Milland	*The Big Clock* (1948)
Mechanic	Mickey Rooney	*Quicksand* (1950)
Museum Curator	Pat O'Brien	*Crack-Up* (1946)
Newsman	Broderick Crawford	*Scandal Sheet* (1952)
Pharmacist	Richard Basehart	*Tension* (1949)
Pianist	Tom Neal	*Detour* (1945)
Priest	Montgomery Clift	*I Confess* (1953)
Professor	Loretta Young	*The Accused* (1949)
Scientist	Ray Milland	*The Thief* (1952)
Screenwriter	Humphrey Bogart	*In a Lonely Place* (1950)
Secretary	Ella Raines	*Phantom Lady* (1944)
Telephone Operator	Anne Baxter	*The Blue Gardenia* (1953)
Tennis Star	Farley Granger	*Strangers on a Train* (1951)
Truck Driver	Steve Brodie	*Desperate* (1947)
Tycoon	Brian Donlevy	*Impact* (1949)

In other words, no job or profession or skill makes one immune to corruption. Film noir can happen to anyone. It is a situation. As Eddie Muller points out, "what characterizes genuine noir is not the depth of depravity a writer is willing to depict, but rather the depth of empathy he or she brings to characters who, through a twist of fate or their own destructive nature, face dire, life and death situations."[19] Roger Ebert put it this way: film noir "is a movie where an ordinary guy indulges the weak side of his character and hell opens up beneath his feet."[20] Foster Hirsch in his *Film Noir: The Dark Side of the Screen* (1981),[21] one of the first American books on film noir and still the best introduction to the subject, did not strain to define the genre but took a common sense approach, discussing its sources, conventions, and the films that best exemplified them. Lately, however, in the third edition of his book (2008), fully aware of the years of debate, he writes, "Despite some qualms, my own sense is to anoint noir as a genre." For him "a film with a crime scene, a neurotic protagonist, and a menacing atmosphere is on its way to grabbing the prize."[22] He or she is not necessarily neurotic as Hirsch suggests, but the fall does serve to bring out the darker side of his or her psyche. And lately, Naremore remarks that "Noir tends to be about losers and has never been accused of promoting moral uplift or the American dream. It certainly isn't a proletarian art, but its protagonists are very often social outsiders or criminals."[23]

Film noir then *can* be defined by a subject, a locale and a character. It consists of all three. Its subject is crime, almost always a murder but sometimes a theft. Its locale is the contemporary world, usually a city at night. Its character is a fallible or tarnished man or woman. From these givens, from this *situation*, an investigation almost always ensues which further involves the protagonist as it unravels the web of misadventures. Not all investigators are private eyes or cops. He might be a supporting character, an insurance investigator such as Edward G. Robinson in *Double Indemnity* or Edmond O'Brien in *The Killers*. He might be a reporter, such as John Derek in *Scandal Sheet* or a returning veteran, keen on discovering what happened to a friend or relative, as in *Cornered* (1945), *Act of Violence*, and *Dead Reckoning*, both of 1947. Not a few noir heroes are amnesiacs carrying out an investigation leading to themselves, such as John Hodiak in *Somewhere in the Night* (1946) and John Payne in *The Crooked Way* (1949). Most ironic of all, of course is

Figure 2.1. The Investigator: Edmond O'Brien in *The Killers*

Edmond O'Brien in *D.O.A.*, a business man who sets out to investigate his own murder. Whether it leads to punishment and doom or redemption is not as important to the genre as there being an investigation. Such then are the components which make up the genre of film noir: a crime, a fallible protagonist, a contemporary setting, and, usually, an investigation by someone or some agency, not necessarily the protagonist.

In the classic period, this situation gives rise to a typical cast, no one type of character being absolutely essential to the genre. In addition to the fallible protagonist and the investigator, one is likely to find a femme fatale, a conventional girlfriend or wife, a psychopath, numerous police (good and bad) corrupt politicians, gangsters or criminals, not as protagonists but as villains or obstacles, returning G.I.s, and a psychiatrist.

There is nothing new in this combination. It occurs in *Oedipus Rex*,[24] *Hamlet*, and *Crime and Punishment*, three of the most outstanding examples. Two of course are plays, tragedies in fact, and the other is a novel. But film noir applies to the movies, quite a different means of presentation. It also applies to a *group* of films, a large and distinguished group. And it also applies to the milieu of the crime, the fallen world of the dark city which like the social environment of the naturalist novel envelopes the protagonist and contributes to his fate. It is at this point that the genre of film noir and the style of film noir merge.

So, Nino Frank and the other French observers didn't get it wrong. They were just the first to give the name that stuck to those films of the early 1940s which embodied conventions that set them apart from previous crime films. Of course there were predecessors. Aren't there always? One thinks of Fritz Lang's *M* (1931) and *You Only Live Once* (1937), among others, but as with the early novels, these were not a group but isolated examples that fit into other categories such as social anatomy or gangster films, whereas the noirs came as a barrage, an explosion on the screen, of crime and betrayal, not unlike the gangster and fallen women films of the early 1930s.

Thus, when these characteristics—crime, faulty and morally confused protagonist living in the contemporary world, and an investigation—are complemented by chiaroscuro, expressionistic camera work, dark city and night settings, and narrative devices such as the voice over and flashback, all elements of the noir style, we know that, unlike the characters, we are safe within this *NEW* genre. If no single element of noir is new, what is new is the concentration of such elements in crime films and the shift in Hollywood conventions which they represent. In the 1930s, Hollywood gave us heroes and heroines who were resourceful, energetic and interesting, but, on the whole, innocent. If they fell, as in the gangster films, one could usually blame society and the class system. The protagonists of the 1940s are not only confused but culpable, and if they fall, it's their own fault, or it's because the mistakes of a former time catch up with them. Rather than being the opposite of the villain, as in the 1930s, the hero or heroine becomes his mirror image, secret sharers of the same dilemma, usually some sexual obsession or disorientation. Femme fatales abound in 1930s films—think of Claire Dodd—but she is always less glamorous or appealing than the heroine—think of Joan Blondell or Irene Dunne. That film noir arrived without the benefit of a new theory or new techniques of film making reminds one of the seventeenth century artists who changed the look of painting and created the Baroque style without altering the theory of art, the means of production, or the technique of painting as developed in the Renaissance. Like the Baroque, film noir also followed a classic period and has been called by both admirers and critics decadent.

But to me the most compelling proof that film noir is a bona fide genre is its reemergence in the 1970s in what the critics have dubbed "neo-noir."[25] Film noir was not just a period phenomenon but a genre that can be reinterpreted for a later era. In the history of art we see similar phenomena. Whereas some genres, such as the masque, have a relatively short life span, arising and dying within a specific period, others live on. Thus opera, a creation of the Baroque and a quintessential Baroque form, survived the seventeenth century and adapted itself to other periods. Likewise, the novel, a Rococo creation, lived on long after the period which established it became synonymous with frivolity and decadence. It too adapted.[26] So film noir soon reappeared, changed somewhat but remaining noir nevertheless. Though born out of the anxiety, despair, gloom and tragedy of the 1940s, it adapted to the paranoia and Weltschmerz of our times. Todd Erickson presents a variation on this idea, contending that the original "movement" (by which he means period style) of noir later became a genre.[27] But it was a genre to begin with, the sure sign of which is that artists from a later era continued to use it.

In neo-noir we immediately recognize the favorite noir subjects: the private eye, somewhere in between the police and the criminals as in *Kill Me Again* (1989); the cop who becomes enmeshed with the femme fatale, as in *Klute* (1971) and *Basic Instinct* (1992); the so-called normal guy who goes over the edge as in *Body Heat* (1981) or makes a bad decision as in *No Country for Old Men* (2007); the sympathetic couples who have become involved in crime and are on the run, as in *Badlands* (1973) and *Thelma & Louise* (1991); the psychopathic protagonist only slightly more deranged than the world he inhabits, as in *Taxi Driver* (1976) and *Falling Down* (1993); the anatomy of the conventional town, as in *Blue Velvet* (1986); the private lives of petty criminals and losers as in *The Grifters* (1990), *One False Move* (1992), and *Pulp Fiction* (1995); and finally the seemingly dead man who through flashbacks seeks comprehension and revenge as in *Point Blank* (1967), a film considered by many the first neo-noir. In addition, old film noirs, such as *Out of the Past* have been remade,[28] and several new ones, such as *Chinatown*

(1974) are set in the classic noir period. One of these, *Devil in a Blue Dress* (1995), for the first time features a black private investigator who discovers racism at the heart of the crime.

So the genre persists, but not the style. Visually, neo-noirs differ because they are filmed in color and favor brightness over chiaroscuro. Rather than the city at night, the favorite image of a dangerous wasteland has switched to the desert. The Great Basin of Nevada, the Salt Flats of Utah, and particularly the Coachella Valley between Palm Springs and Indio and northward to Las Vegas have all served well, as has semi-arid Los Angeles itself. That locale just east of the San Bernadino Pass which contains all the windmills has proven almost irresistible. When the desert isn't appropriate, the tropics will do, the humid, sweat-soaked, stultifying tropics of the bayous and South Florida. *Fargo* (1995) introduced the frozen north, which continues in such recent films as *Transsiberian* (2008).

But the main difference between the classic and neo versions lies in the depths of evil they portray. In retrospect, film noir, which seemed somewhat shocking at the time, seems relatively tame today or even camp. Then sex could lead to murder. But now it takes the form of rape, abuse of women, and incest. Greed has become drug trafficking and maniacal sadism, which flourishes in a totally corrupt, racist, non-system of criminal justice. Whereas classic film noir always provided a saving framework of law (crime did not pay, and if the mayor was corrupt, the governor was not), neo-noir presents a paranoid, nightmare world where everyone is victimized and no one can leave Las Vegas. So the genre persists, but the style and some of its conventions have changed as a new period has emerged.

Whether the genre will survive the twenty-first century, no one can tell. One wonders why a form so interesting lingered so long in the swamps of pulp fiction. But it took more than a depression; it took a World War to blast America out of its traditional optimism and imagined innocence. At the moment, the prospects for noir are bright. Noir thrives on pessimism, cynicism, and paranoia. It depends on ambiguous sexual identities, instabilities, and the crossing of traditional boundaries. It feeds on political corruption and moral decadence. Given these conditions, the twenty-first century seems well on the way to providing a suitable habitat.

NOTES

1. Arthur Lyons, *Death on the Cheap: The Lost B Movies of Film Noir* (New York: Da Capo Press, 2000).

2. Warshow, *The Immediate Experience* (Cambridge, MA: Harvard University Press, 2001), 127–34.

3. See Giuliana Muscio, *Hollywood's New Deal* (Philadelphia: Temple University Press, 1996).
4. William Park, "The Police State," *Journal of Popular Film* 3 (1978): 229–37.
5. Raymond Borde and Etienne Chaumenton, *A Panorama of American Film Noir, 1941–1953* (San Francisco: City Lights Books, 2002 [1955]), 34.
6. Louis Markos, "In the Mind of a Madman: How Film Noir Got Its Look," *American Arts Quarterly* (Winter, 2007): 32.
7. A. M. Karimi, *Toward a Definition of the American Film Noir (1941–1949)* (New York: Arno Press, 1976); Thomas Schatz, *Hollywood Genres: Formulas, Filmmaking, and the Studio System* (Boston: McGraw Hill, 1981), 111–49; William Luhr, "*The Maltese Falcon*, the Detective Genre, and Film Noir," in *The Maltese Falcon* (New Brunswick, NJ: Rutgers University Press, 1996), 3–16.
8. Frank Krutnik, *In a Lonely Street: Film Noir, Genre, Masculinity* (London: Routledge, 1991), 24.
9. Carl Richardson, *Autopsy: An Element of Realism in Film Noir* (Metuchen, NJ: Scarecrow Press, 1992).
10. Schatz, *Hollywood Genres*, vii.
11. Neale, *Genre and Hollywood*, 174.
12. Krutnik, *In a Lonely Street*, 17–23.
13. Paul Schrader, "Notes on *Film Noir*" [1972], in *Film Noir Reader*, 54.
14. Robert Porfiro, "*The Killers*: Expressionism of Sound and Image in Film Noir," in *Film Noir Reader*, 187, n. 2.
15. Mark T. Conard "Nietzsche and the Meaning and Definition of Noir," *The Philosophy of Film Noir* (Lexington: University Press of Kentucky, 2006), 17–20.
16. James Damico, "Film Noir: A Modest Proposal" [1978], in Film *Noir Reader*, 95–106.
17. Sheri Chinen Biesen, *Blackout: World War II and the Origins of Film Noir* (Baltimore: Johns Hopkins University Press, 2005).
18. Raymond Chandler, *The Simple Art of Murder* (New York: Vintage Books, 1988 [1944]), 18.
19. Eddie Muller, "Noir for a New Century," *Noir City Sentinel* 4, no. 2 (May/June 2009): 2. In his comments on the DVD of *Where the Sidewalk Ends* (1950), he refers to the moment when the noir protagonist, usually knowingly, makes his or her immoral move as "the break."
20. Quoted in Jake Hinkson, "The Lord of Godless Town," in *Noir City Sentinel, Annual #2: The Best of the Film Noir Sentinel* (San Francisco: Film Noir Foundation, 2020), 22.
21. Foster Hirsch, *Film Noir: The Dark Side of the Screen* (New York: Da Capo Press, 1981).
22. Hirsch, "Afterword," *Film Noir*, 3rd ed. (Cambridge, MA: Da Capo Press, 2008), 211–12.
23. Naremore, *More than Night*, expanded and updated edition (2008), 298.
24. An association noticed by Raymond Durgnat, "Paint it Black: The Family Tree of the *Film Noir*" [1970], in *Film Noir Reader*, 37.

25. See for instance, Foster Hirsch, *Detours and Lost Highways: A Map of Neo-Noir* (New York: Limelight Editions, 1999).

26. William Park, *The Idea of Rococo* (Newark: University of Delaware Press, 1992), 96–106.

27. Todd Erickson, "Kill Me Again: Movement Becomes Genre," in *Film Noir Reader*, 307–29.

28. Hirsch, *Detours and Lost Highway*, 23–65.

Chapter Three

Objections

NOIR WAS AN AFTERTHOUGHT

As we have seen, Naremore and others see film noir not only as having been named by the French but as a projection back onto American culture of post-war and even pre-war French concerns. Bolstering this idea, critics cite numerous post noir interviews with directors and actors who, when asked if they knew they were making film noirs, answered No, though of course the question itself implies the existence of some sort of entity. My favorite response is that of femme-fatale stalwart Marie Windsor who, when asked by co-stalwart Audrey Totter what she called film noir, replied, "B movies."[1] Steve Neale even goes so far as to say film noir cannot be "verified by contemporary sources."[2]

But the argument that film noir was an afterthought, that film noir as a category only came into existence *ex post facto*[3] cannot be sustained. The evidence to the contrary is overwhelming, some of it supplied by Neale himself. To begin with, the fact that a genre does not acquire a name until later does not mean the genre did not exist prior to its naming. All genres are *ex post facto*, as a group of films must exist before anyone can see family resemblances. As Altman points out, even musicals and Westerns were not instantly recognized as such. Movies still do not have a commonly acknowledged name, and this after more than a century: photoplay, pictures, motion pictures, flicks, movies, film, cinema—take your choice. Nor is there any term in English, such as the Greek word *poem*, which designates what we clumsily refer to as "a work of literature," and this after more than ten centuries. All the styles of art history: Romanesque, Gothic, Renaissance, Mannerist, Baroque, Rococo, and Neo-Classic were named *after* the contemporary event, many of them originally having pejorative connotations.

Figure 3.1. Marie Windsor in *The Narrow Margin*, with Don Beddoe and Charles McGraw

In literature, the novel serves as a perfect example of a phenomenon named after the fact. Prose fiction existed from ancient times onward, but the novel, associated with the term realism, was a much later development. Many think that the modern genre first appeared in 1554 with the publication of the picaresque *Lazarillo de Tormes* or in 1605 when Cervantes published the first part of *Don Quixote*. The first French novel, *The Princess of Cleves*, appeared in 1678, and what are now considered the first English novels, *Robinson Crusoe* and *Moll Flanders* in 1719 and 1720. Yet none of these were considered novels or a type of fiction by their contemporaries. Rather they were seen as criminal biographies, historic romances, or in the case of *Don Quixote*, as a work in a category all its own. It was not till Marivaux published *Marianne* (1731) and *Le Paysan Parvenu* (1735), Richardson published *Pamela* (1740), and Fielding *Joseph Andrews* (1742), works that were rapidly imitated by other writers, that the public became conscious of another genre. Even at that time in English the word "novel" indicated a short story, as in Cervantes' *Exemplary Novels* (1613). Longer works of prose fiction were called "romances" or "comic romances." Dr. Johnson called the novels of his day "modern romances." Fielding facetiously referred to his *Joseph Andrews* as a "comic epic poem in prose," and Richardson and his admirers thought that he had created "a New Species of Writing." From the 1740s until the 1770s—a full generation after the novel had blossomed with its two masterpieces, *Clarissa* (1747) and *Tom Jones* (1749)—readers and critics were conscious of the genre but the word "novel" did not become attached to it, and then only in English. Because *Don Quixote* was not recognized as a novel until more than a century after it was written, does that mean it is not a novel?

The naming of film noir came much earlier in its history. That happened not a generation later, not in the 1970s, but in 1946,[4] only four and a half years from the outset of the phenomenon, and well before noir peaked in the early 1950s. Borde and Chaumenton's *Panorama du film noir americain* appeared in 1955, three years before the "movement" had ended. That at least

Figure 3.2. Robert Aldrich showing his awareness of noir.

someone in Hollywood knew of this concept is shown in a photo of Robert Aldrich, director of *Kiss Me Deadly* (1955) on the set of *Attack* (1956) holding a copy of the book.

There's hardly an astute observer of the 1940s that did not notice the changes in Hollywood films of the time. Neale himself cites two superb examples, an article in *Variety* (March 3, 1947) that speaks of the "murderous ladies cycle," and another in *The Spectator* (December 2, 1947) that notices the new Hollywood Freudianism. In 1945 Lloyd Shearer wrote an article for the *New York Times Magazine* that begins:

> Of late there has been a trend in Hollywood toward the wholesale production of a lusty, hardboiled, gut and gore crime stories, all fashioned on a theme with a combination of plausibly motivated murder and studded with high-powered Freudian implication. Of the quantity of such films now in vogue, "Double Indemnity," "Murder My Sweet" [1944], "Conflict" [1945], and "Laura" are a quartet of the most popular which quickly come to mind. Shortly to be followed by Twentieth Century-Fox's "The Dark Corner" [1946] and "The High Window,"[5] MGM's "the Postman Always Rings Twice' and "The Lady in the Lake" [1946], Paramount's "Blue Dahlia" and Warners' "Serenade" [1956] and "The Big Sleep"[1946]. . . . [This] quartet constitutes a mere vanguard of the cinematic homicide to come. Every studio in town has at least two or three similar blood freezers before the camera right now, which means that within the next year or so movie murder particularly with a psychological twist will become almost as common as the weekly newsreel or musical.[6]

D. Marshan wrote another like it for *Life* (August 25, 1947) noting the villains and heroines with "deeply rooted diseases of the mind" flashing across the screen in a "display of psychoneurosis, unsublimated sex, and murder most foul."[7] In an article written in 1946, no less a critic than Siegfried Kracauer noted the change and described the attributes of noir, especially its pessimism.[8] Manny Farber praised noir in his early essay "Underground Film,"[9] but the most acute observer of all was Barbara Deming, who, working for the Library of Congress in the late 1940s, perceived the shifts in conventions that constituted film noir, particularly the characterization of men and women, and by 1950 had written a book about them, some of its chapters being published in *City Lights* in the early 1950s, and the book as a whole appearing in 1969 as *Running Away from Myself: a dream portrait of America drawn from the films of the forties*.[10]

But the book that demolishes the afterthought and non-existent theories is Sheri Chinen Biesen's *Blackout: World War II and the Origins of Film Noir*. Through her painstaking exploration of studio records, press books, publicity, contemporary reviews, and media gossip, she establishes without further discussion that by 1944, two years before Nino Frank in France dubbed the phenomenon "film noir," Hollywood's producers, directors, and reporters were fully conscious of a "new kind of Red-Blooded Mystery."[11] "Red meat crime" was an even more popular term, as we see in this 1944 article by Fred Stanley, the *New York Times'* Hollywood reporter of the era.

> Last week's high mark in the "red meat" trend was the disclosure that Metro-Goldwyn-Mayer is to co-star John Garfield and Lana Turner in Mr. Cain's "The Postman Always Rings Twice." The property, bought several years ago, was kept in the studio's archives until now because (to use a favored Hollywood expression) of Metro's inability to clean it up. . . . Closer to the cameras is another of Mr. Cain's novels, "Mildred Pierce" . . . scheduled to go into production this week at Warner Brothers . . . reported to be negotiating for the author's "Serenade." The screen version of Raymond Chandler's "The Big Sleep," in production at Warners, is said to be another example of ingenuity in treating of psychopathic and physiological matters.[12]

While such comments come from critics and observers, the best evidence of noir consciousness comes from Hollywood's own productions. What is imitation if not a form of consciousness? The creators of *The Maltese Falcon* and the even more influential *Double Indemnity* could not possibly have been aware that their efforts would result in a new type of crime film, but that cannot be said of the creators of the multitudes of films spawned in the 1940s and 1950s by these two originals. I am not speaking of noir elements in other genres but of crime films that belong to this genre. In his *Film Noir Guide*, Keaney discusses over 700 candidates.[13]

Were the sheer numbers of imitators not enough to convince us of an awareness that goes beyond the fuzzy notions of trend or *zeitgeist*, we can see such consciousness in contemporary parodies. As Borde and Chaumenton put it in 1955, "Film noir wouldn't be a series worthy of the name if it hadn't given rise, in Hollywood itself, to various parodies."[14] The 1953 film *The Band Wagon*, directed by Vincente Minnelli, who also directed the noirish *Undercurrent* (1946), includes a dance, "The Girl Hunt Ballet," performed by Fred Astaire as a hard-boiled detective and Cyd Charisse as a femme fatale, which mimics the conventions of hard-boiled detective films. How could such a dance be created if Hollywood were not aware of the phenomenon? To anyone who might claim this dance has more to do with the novels of Mickey Spillane than film noir, there is an even better example. This is the Bob Hope film *My Favorite Brunette* (1947), which though mentioned by Borde and Chaumenton, has been ignored by those disclaiming the contemporary evidence for noir consciousness. The film opens with Hope in prison, on death row, but a flashback takes us to Hope as a children's photographer whose seedy office is next door to that of a hard-boiled private eye, played in a cameo by Paramount's number one noir hero, Alan Ladd. Ladd, who is

Figure 3.3. Parody as awareness. Alan Ladd and Bob Hope in *My Favorite Brunette*

taking some time off, asks Hope, who is in awe of him, to take in the mail and watch his office. While Hope busies himself there, a beautiful seeming femme fatale (Dorothy Lamour) enters and asks him to help her. When Hope foolishly impersonates Ladd, he falls into all sorts of comic difficulties with a den of criminals that includes Peter Lorre. How could contemporary Hollywood make a parody of a genre if it were unaware of its existence?

Lest there be any doubt about Hollywood's consciousness of film noir, one need only look at its effect on the office of Joe Breen, head of the Production Code Administration. Thomas Doherty's book, *Hollywood's Censor*, documents numerous complaints about this "genre without a name," as Doherty calls it.[15] For instance, in December 1947, Abram F. Meyers, general counsel of the Allied States Association of Motion Picture Exhibitors wrote:

> Those of us who lived through the outburst against moral laxity on the screen in the early 1930s, and witnessed the skillful job done by Will Hayes in putting out that fire, cannot help wondering why the situation was again allowed to get out of hand.[16]

Things got so out of hand that "On June 28, 1949, Breen called a full-dress meeting that brought together the PCA staff, representatives from all the major studios, and prominent independent producers" to discuss the problems caused by film noir and the changes it represented in Hollywood conventions.[17] Unfortunately for Breen, the Production Code focused on moral details, not tragic and ironic plots. It could ban nudity, foul language, and getting away with murder, but it had no provisions for banning a fallen world characterized by crime, betrayals, and double crosses as long as justice prevailed in the end, even a justice wrought by Fate and an inescapable dark past. The Code had long winked at the violence in Westerns, particularly saloon brawls, but now it had to deal with savage individual violence. It could tone down the brutality, but it could not do away with film noir. As Doherty puts it, "No soothing Voice of Morality or lawful end reel wrap up could wash away the grime of a netherworld that from studio logo to final frame smeared the entire running time."[18] Like the menace in a horror film, it might not yet be named, but Hollywood knew it was there.

Alain Silver sums up the argument against those who believe noir was invented by later observers by saying they "continue to confuse lack of term for lack of intent." The proof of contemporary consciousness of film noir lies in the works themselves.

Whether they had a name for it or not, whether they called their pictures thrillers or mysteries, actioners or mellers, the pictures themselves affirm that the filmmakers of the noir cycle were well aware of what type of movie they were making.[19]

NO CANON

Neale claims that "noir, in my view, never existed,"[20] and that it has no fixed canon. Absolutely fixed, of course not, but as fixed as the readings in any course in the Victorian novel. Not even the books of the Bible are fixed. To this day Catholics and Protestants cannot agree on which are the Ten Commandments. Canons, like genres, are never fixed, but at the first critical mention of film noir, we see the formation of a canon of its works. Nino Frank cited *The Maltese Falcon* and *Double Indemnity*, and to these Borde and Chaumenton include and discuss the following: *This Gun for Hire* (1942), *The Killers*, *The Lady in the Lake*, *Gilda*, *The Big Sleep*, *Shanghai Gesture* (1941), *The Set-Up* (1949), *Rope* (1948), *The Asphalt Jungle* (1950), *Fallen Angel*, *Where the Sidewalk Ends* (1950), *The File on Thelma Jordan* (1950), *Night and the City* (1950), *Gun Crazy*, *He Walked by Night* (1948), *White Heat* (1949), *The Lady from Shanghai* (1947), *Ride the Pink Horse* (1947), *The High Wall* (1947), *Red Light* (1949), *Kiss of Death* (1947), *T-Men* (1947), *Border Incident* (1949), *Chicago Deadline* (1949), *The Crooked Way*, and *Somewhere in the Night* (1946).

If film noir had no canon, it would not lend itself to one semester courses in the history of film. Phillip Gaines published his own version of such a course where again we find agreement about the essentials. His basic list includes *Double Indemnity, The Maltese Falcon, Nobody Lives Forever* (1946), *The Naked City* (1948), as 'Docu-noir, *Gun Crazy, The Woman in the Window* (1944), *Detour, D.O.A., Kiss Me Deadly, The Killing* (1956), and *Touch of Evil*. For further viewing he recommends *The Postman Always Rings Twice, Laura, This Gun for Hire, Murder, My Sweet, Phantom Lady, The Blue Dahlia, The Dark Mirror* (1946), *The Dark Past* (1948), *Brute Force* (1947), *The Two Mrs. Carrolls* (1947), *The Killers, Border Incident, T-Men, Beyond a Reasonable Doubt* (1956), *The Big Heat* (1953), *Fallen Angel, Angel Face* (1952), and *Scarlet Street*.[21]

My own course on film noir usually included the following: *Shadow of a Doubt* (1943), *Double Indemnity, Scarlet Street, Detour, Mildred Pierce, The Killers, The Big Sleep, Out of the Past, In a Lonely Place, Sunset Boulevard, Strangers on a Train, The Killing, and Vertigo*. As you can see, I placed Hitchcock in the genre, whereas most film courses treat him as a genre in himself. More about that later. Similarly, Alain Silver's top ten are *Kiss Me Deadly, Gun Crazy, Double Indemnity, Criss Cross, The Woman in the Window, Ride the Pink Horse, Out of the Past, Night and the City, Caught* (1949), *White Heat*, and *The Big Sleep*.[22] Silver and his coeditor James Ursini devote their *Film Noir Reader 4* to what they call "The Crucial Films," which consist of *Double Indemnity, Detour, The Big Sleep, Out of the Past, The Unsuspected* (1947), *Gun Crazy, D.O.A., The Big Night* (1951), *Kiss Me Deadly, The Big Heat, The Big Combo* (1955), and *Touch of Evil*. And in his newest anthology Nicolas Saada discusses five films he considers prototypes of variations on noir style: *Murder My Sweet, Panic in the Streets* (1950), *The Big Heat, Kiss Me Deadly,* and *Touch of Evil*.[23] And James Damico names nine essential films: *Double Indemnity, The Woman in the Window, Scarlet Street, The Postman Always Rings Twice, The Killers, The Lady from Shanghai, Out of the Past, Pitfall* (1948), and *Criss Cross*.[24]

Again and again, critics and scholars, whether pro or con genre, choose to discuss the same films. I doubt that courses in Greek Drama or Shakespeare show as much consistency. No one will agree on the top ten or the ten most typical. Such a listing depends on personal tastes and favorites, but all involved will choose from the same group of films from the same time frame. A few of them belong more to the period than the genre, but whether they comprise a cycle, a movement, or a genre, unquestionably they make up a canon.

TOO AMORPHOUS

Genres and literary categories are not mathematical concepts. As Altman has demonstrated, all genres are amorphous, so why discredit film noir for its own fogginess? There's hardly a film made that does not fit several genres. Is *The Benny Goodman Story* (1956) a musical or a biopic? Is *Sweet Dreams* (1985) a musical, a biopic, or a women's film? Even *Double Indemnity* and *Out of the Past* can be classified as love stories. But I maintain that a crime story set in the contemporary world and featuring a fallible protagonist, especially if it also features an investigation, will aid one in discriminating noir from non-noirs, such as *Clash by Night* which depicts a somber and complicated love triangle but lacks any crime. That Fritz Lang directed it and Clifford Odets wrote it does not make it a noir, nor does its gloomy philosophizing.

All genres and styles have works that are central to them, perfect examples so to speak—in the case of film noir, *Double Indemnity* and *Out of the Past*. From these central works, others radiate outward toward a periphery where they can just as easily be construed as other genres. For instance, there are dozens of crime films with murders and the noir style that to me do not qualify as generic film noirs. Take for instance *The Window* (1949), based on a story by Cornell Woolrich. In this film a young boy, Bobby Driscoll, witnesses a murder. Because of his propensity to fantasize and tell stories, neither his parents nor the police believe his account of the crime. His mother even takes him upstairs to the killers' apartment to make him apologize to them for his lie, of course tipping them off about the threat the kid poses. Then follows a cat and mouse suspense drama, filmed almost entirely at night on dark stairways and prison-bar-like fire escapes. It's a wonderful and effective example of noir style. By a stretch, one could say that the boy's making up stories, such as his father having a ranch in Texas, and telling it to the other kids as the truth marks him as a noir-like fallible protagonist. But to me, he is just too innocent. Silver and Ward, however, include *The Window* in their encyclopedia of noir, where Robert Porfiro describes the setting of the film as "an American urban landscape that seems almost infernal. . . . Such a world represents the inverse of the American dream of freedom."[25]

Because of its depressed urban setting and its noir style, Porfiro can place *The Window* in the context of film noir, but surely he would not claim it as central to the idea of the genre as, let us say, some of the other films he describes, such as *Decoy* (1946), in which a crazed femme fatale kills no less than three men duped into carrying out her mad schemes.[26] Likewise many critics for good reasons see *White Heat* as a film noir. It departs from classic gangster films such as *Scarface* and through its psychological themes moves away from that center. To me, however, it remains a gangster film, influenced by film noir, belonging to the noir period, but a gangster film nevertheless.

By the same token, almost all boxing films might be seen as film noirs. The nighttime settings, the involvement of the mob in controlling the boxer and the odds, the femme fatale who tempts the hero, his moral weaknesses contrasted to his physical strength, the violence within the ring and without, all bring them into noir territory. But except for a boxing-caused death, the result of a fight which never should have taken place, they lack both murders and investigations. To be sure, a film such as *The Set-Up*, being of the period, will be noir than an earlier classic such as *Golden Boy* (1939), which is much more concerned with class issues. More central to noir is *99 River Street* (1953) about a *former* boxer, haunted by his previous career and down on his luck, who becomes a chief suspect in the murder of his unfaithful wife. This stands in relation to boxing films much as *Kiss of Death* does to gangster films, the one about an ex-boxer, the other about an ex-gangster trying to go straight. [27]

Michael Keaney places *Love Letters* (1945) in his *Film Noir Guide*.[28] Fair enough. In it, a wounded veteran, Joseph Cotten, suffers from guilt over the love letters he wrote for a buddy during the war. To his despair, he discovers that the friend married the girl, but that she soon after killed him and has since reportedly died. As fate would have it, he meets Jennifer Jones, an amnesiac, who it turns out was the recipient of the letters, very much alive, but without any memory of who she is or what she has done. Accompanied by the haunting "Love Letters" score, which was turned into a popular ballad, they fall in love, and he begins an investigation of her past, fearful however that if she does recover she will not forgive his deception. So here we have the key elements of the genre: a murder, an investigation, and two protagonists, one guilt ridden, the other an amnesiac mental case convicted of murder. Yet, even more than *The Window* it has moved far from the noir center into the realm of the love story. It lacks the noir style. What matters is not the alleged crime but the romance between the two, who rather than being star-crossed, as it first seems, providentially recover their innocence and each other. Rather than being an example of the amorphousness of noir, *Love Letters* illustrates how noir's conventions permeated the other genres of the time. Genre and amorphousness go together, and in this case it is not the proponents of film noir as a genre that are too rigid but the opponents who are demanding of film noir standards of clarity and unity that no genre can meet.

NOTHING NEW

Bordwell, Staiger, and Thompson object to noir as a genre because they find nothing new in it.[29] On the whole they are speaking about noir as a visual style whose components have often appeared before, notably, but not exclusively, in the German films of the 1920s from which noir descended. And they are also referring to the principles of editing and camera placement which remained constant throughout the entire studio period. All the high contrast, key lighting and chiaroscuro, the night scenes, the wet pavements, slats of light, and dark stairways at best contribute to an atmosphere. The same may be said for the convoluted narrative devices, flashbacks, and voiceovers as well as the gloomy perspective on life.

All this is true. But Bordwell, Staiger, and Thompson do not take into consideration the quantitative aspect of film noir. Classic Hollywood, the heyday of the Production Code (1934–1940), made films that were bright looking and sunny. To be sure they might have a scene or two that appeared ominous; all the techniques were there and available to make them. But such scenes do not characterize the films as a whole. On the whole, the same cameramen created both the classic period and film noir. Not to see the shift, the refusal to recognize it, contests all contemporary evidence. As we have seen, everyone—observers, critics, censors, all Hollywood expressed its awareness of a paradigmatic shift in genre from roughly 1944 on, when *Double Indemnity* brought the as yet unnamed film noir into consciousness and inspired untold hundreds of successors. After the war when the films became available for the first time Hollywood-deprived France noticed the change immediately—and gave the films a name. And as we have seen, André Bazin perceived a new stage in Hollywood's evolution. If *Double Indemnity* wrought a new perception of genre, then *Citizen Kane* initiated a change in style and narrative structure. Yes, one can find such effects as chiaroscuro, low ceilings, and depth of focus shots in previous films, notably in *Stagecoach* (1939), a film Welles is reputed to have watched forty times. But prior to *Citizen Kane* such techniques were the exception; after *Citizen Kane* they became conventions.

For ten years, Joe Breen had blocked the filming of *Double Indemnity*. Then even he changed and allowed an only slightly cleaned up version to go into production. As its author, James M. Cain remarked at the time: Producers "have got hep to the fact that plenty of real crime takes place every day and that it makes a good movie. . . . The public is fed up with the old-fashioned melodramatic type of hokum."[30]

THE IDEA OF FILM NOIR CONFUSES GENRES

As usual Neale states the problem most clearly. According to him, no distinction exists between alleged film noir and the gothic women's film. In fact, he concludes, the idea of noir confuses no less than four genres: the hard-boiled detective film (*The Maltese Falcon*), the psychological melodrama

(*Possessed*, 1947), the post-war social problem film (*Crossfire*), and the rogue cop (*Touch of Evil*).[31] Most of such confusion results from believing that a film belongs to but one genre, but let us examine these complaints.

The Gothic Women's Film and Psychological Melodramas

To be sure most of the "gothic" women's films made during the 1940s and early 1950s have the noir look. What else? But they remain within their genre or sub-genre of gothic. Gothic refers to the gothic novels of the late eighteenth and early nineteenth century, the ones in which an innocent woman is tricked or kidnapped into confinement in some castle or monastery and threatened with all sorts of physical and sexual evils. In the modern versions, the villain is often the husband. Thus in *Gaslight* (1944) Charles Boyer attempts to drive Ingrid Bergman into suicide or an insane asylum. There is a detective (Joseph Cotten) and an investigation, but the creaky old house, the period setting, and the psychic distress of the heroine keep the film centered in the gothic tradition. The same applies to *Shock* (1946)). Here the heroine (Anabel Shaw), who has witnessed a murder, is placed in a psychiatric institution run, unknown to her, by no less than the murderer, psychoanalyst Vincent Price. Most of the film consists of her efforts to escape and to the increasing tortures and threats that she undergoes. Her war vet husband, ineffectual of course, and Price's pseudo Freudianism give the film its noir flavor. The psychiatric institute is the perfect setting for the female gothic, as we see in *The Snake Pit*. Olivia de Havilland plays a mentally ill woman suffering a long drawn out cure in a state mental hospital. Though the film partakes of noir conventions, especially the pop Freudianism of the period and the investigation into her past, it lacks the crime, duplicity, and culpability needed to qualify for the genre. In *The House on Telegraph Hill* (1951), Valentina Cortese becomes imprisoned in a mansion where her no-good husband, Richard Basehart, decides he must kill her in order to gain an inheritance. This is almost pure gothic, as a seemingly wicked and domineering housekeeper, in the manner of *Rebecca*'s (1940) Mrs. Danvers, aids Basehart in his nefarious plot. The only truly noir element in the film consists of the fact that Cortese herself is an imposter, having taken the identity of a friend who died while the two were in a Polish concentration camp.

Hitchcock's *Rebecca* and *Suspicion* (1941) are two other examples of the female gothic, both starring Joan Fontaine and both centering on the "sleeping with the enemy" plot, that is, the murderous husband version of this genre. There is, however, a genuine film noir example of the gothic. I refer to *Sunset Boulevard* which neatly reverses the conventions. Here there's a spooky old mansion, but instead of entrapping an innocent virgin, it lures a down and out male screen writer (William Holden). And instead of a sadistic male tormentor, an authority figure turned satanic, it features a psychotic female one (Gloria Swanson), a monstrous mother figure given to fits and hallucinations. Rather than resisting her perverse seduction, he submits, and rather than escaping in the end, as do all the women, when he tries to walk out he's murdered. At the opening we see him dead, floating in the swimming pool, so that the entire film is a flashback and an investigation, starting with the voice over of the dead man. Comparing *Sunset Boulevard* to *Gaslight* and the other female-centered films should make it easier to see the distinction between film noir and what Neale calls "psychological melodrama," a less chauvinistic appellation for "women's film," of which the gothic constitute a subdivision.

Typically, women's films feature a mega-star female protagonist such as Bette Davis, Joan Crawford, or Barbara Stanwyck. She finds herself surrounded not by male stars but by talented supporting players, such as George Brent, Paul Henreid, or Herbert Marshall. Invariably the men in her life just don't get it; they misunderstand her and whether willingly or not let her down. One admirer will prove too lusty and domineering; another too weak and ineffectual, much like Rochester and St. John in *Jane Eyre*. The greatest of all these films, in epic scope at least, is *Gone with the Wind* (1939),

Figure 3.4. Gloria Swanson and William Holden in *Sunset Boulevard*

in which Scarlett O'Hara must deal with the too passionate Rhett Butler and the too pallid Ashley Wilkes, both of whom fail her. A husband may become crippled or go away for years at a time, his place taken by a gangster, as in *Blonde Venus* (1932), the gangster in this case being Cary Grant before he became a star. Because such heroines rise to Emersonian heights of self reliance, Stanley Cavell has written an entire book about his favorites among the genre.[32]

Possessed rather than being a typical women's film or psychological melodrama, as Neale claims, demonstrates how film noir makes a recognizable genre its own. It stars Joan Crawford who has two men in her life, Van Heflin and Raymond Massey, hardly Jimmy Stewart and Cary Grant. She loves Heflin, who will not commit himself to her, whereas the less attractive Massey loves her. Thus, we have the set-up for the psychological melodrama through which the heroine will demonstrate her moral superiority to the inferior and unworthy males. But not here. In this film, we first see Crawford wandering the dark streets of the noir world.

Like so many of her male counterparts, she has lost her memory. Gifted psychiatrists help her recover it, and in a series of flashbacks we discover that

Figure 3.5. Joan Crawford wanders in *Possessed*

having been rejected by Heflin, she became a nurse to Massey's mentally ill wife. The wife, imagining an affair between Massey and Crawford drowns herself, whereupon Crawford, who up to this point has been innocent and noble, marries Massey. But when Heflin returns and begins to court Massey's daughter, she herself begins to suffer a mental breakdown, imagining that she has killed the first wife. Though a psychiatrist warns her of her precarious state, she confronts Heflin, who again rejects her. Instead of rising above it all, she murders Heflin and wanders off into the streets. The noir setting, the amnesia, the flashbacks, the murder, the psychiatric investigation, and the culpability of the female protagonist cumulatively all mark *Possessed* as a film noir. There's nothing confused about the designation.

In contrast, consider another Crawford vehicle, *A Woman's Face* (1941), in which she also kills a man. This film was a remake of one of Ingrid Bergman's early Swedish films, brought up to date by Donald Ogden Stewart, who turns the crook of the Swedish version into a Nazi, played by Conrad Veidt. Crawford, whose face is horribly disfigured, works for con man Veidt. When plastic surgeon Melvyn Douglas catches her in the act of blackmailing Osa Massen, his unfaithful wife, he takes pity on her and restores her classic Crawford beauty. As her face is transformed so is she. She breaks with the Svengali like Veidt, foils his plot to kill a young heir, and like Crawford in *Possessed*, she kills him. But he is an out and out villain; she committed this act to prevent the murder of a child and in self-defense. In effect, there's no crime, no investigation, no flashbacks, no dark city, no psychiatrists, and no amnesia, just a pathetic woman who rises to heroism and chooses the mild doctor, who has been freed from his wife's tyranny, over the fierce criminal.

Mildred Pierce is an even better example of how noir transforms melodrama. It shares the conventions of a noble, sacrificing woman, again Joan Crawford, surrounded by inadequate, unworthy men: in this case a wimpy, adulterous first husband (Bruce Bennett), who leaves her, a masher partner (Jack Carson), who is too hot and vulgar, and a thorough cad (Zachary Scott), who marries her and then makes love to her obnoxious daughter (Ann Blyth). All this is the stuff of women's films, but notice the twists. It begins with a murder. There follows an investigation, punctuated by flashbacks, in which Mildred, the chief suspect, tries to frame her business partner. This is not Mary Noble, backstage wife, but a flawed woman trying to protect the real perpetrator, her daughter, the little monster she herself has created. None of this is in James M. Cain's novel. So rather than telling the story of Mildred as a kind of middle class Stella Dallas or Sister Carrie who raises a spoiled daughter who turns on her, the film transforms its source into a murder mystery centering on the pathology of a mother/daughter relationship and a fallible female protagonist.

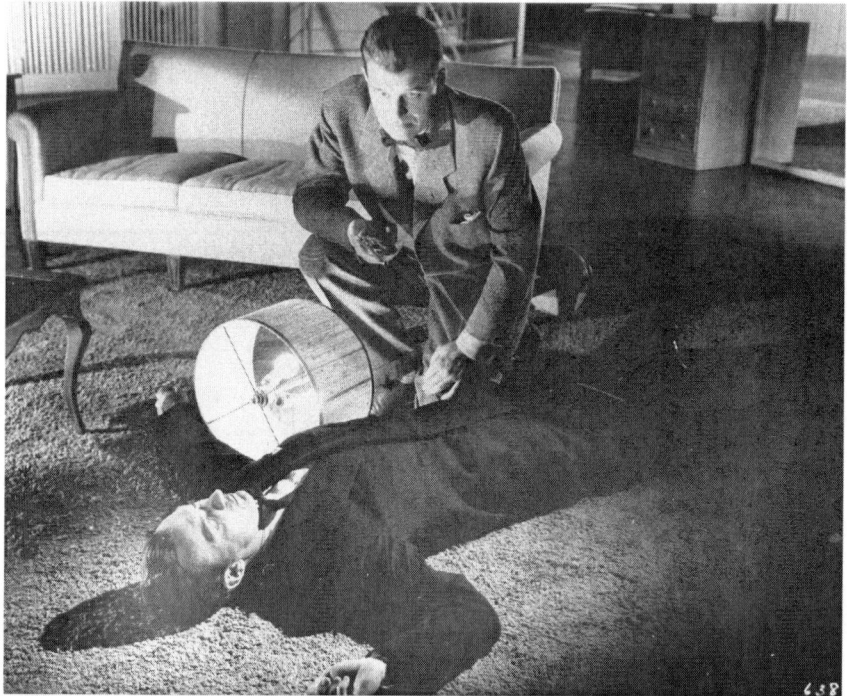

Figure 3.6. More than a women's film. The scene of the crime in *Mildred Pierce*

Film noir does not confine itself to femme fatales and good girls. When a woman serves as the protagonist in a film noir, she behaves just like the males.[33] Two excellent examples, no doubt inspired by the success of *Mildred Pierce*, are *The Accused* and *The Reckless Moment*. In both we see a woman covering up a crime or what could be perceived as a crime. In *The Accused*, psychology professor Loretta Young, fighting off an attempted rape by one of her students, kills him and then tries to make the death look like an accidental drowning. The cop investigating the death (Wendell Corey) and the victim's lawyer (Robert Cummings) both become attracted to the sexually repressed and lying Young, who in the end breaks down and confesses her all too human behavior. Likewise Joan Bennett, in *The Reckless Moment*, to protect her daughter from the charge of murdering her blackmailing lover (Shepperd Strudwick), covers up his death. This move leads to her further involvement with another blackmailer, James Mason, who becomes romantically attracted to her and actually dies not only defending her but also providing her with an alibi so that she can return to her "normal" life. When the female "distress" of the psychological melodrama takes the form of murder and its cover-up, when the protagonist enters into the dark underworld of noir or suffers hallucinations and mental breakdowns as a criminal investigation succeeds in implicating her, all this accompanied by narrative and visual motifs characteristic of film noir, we are not confused but certain about the genre of the film. Other examples include Ann Sheridan in *Unfaithful* (1947), Barbara Stanwyck in *The Lady Gambles* (1949) and *Crime of Passion* (1957), and Loretta Young in *Cause for Alarm* (1951).

Figure 3.7. More than a femme fatale. Douglas Dick and Loretta Young in *The Accused*

A number of film noirs center on a female investigator, the most famous one being *Phantom Lady*. Like her male counterparts, the heroine, Ella Raines must descend into the underworld of sleazy bars and nightclubs. There, in order to get information about the phantom lady who could free her boss from death row, she pretends to be a prostitute and uses her sex to seduce mad drummer Elisha Cook Jr. In *Spellbound* (1945), Ingrid Bergman's skills at analysis not only cure Gregory Peck's amnesia but solve the murder of which he was falsely accused. A superb example of the female investigator and her complicity in the fallen world of noir may now be seen on DVD. It is the genuinely B-movie *Destination Murder* (1947). In it Joyce Mackenzie, fed up with the police's pursuit of her father's killer, starts an investigation of her own. She first becomes the "girlfriend" of the hired killer, Stanley Clements, who had a perfect alibi. Then taking a job as a cigarette girl in Albert Dekker's nightclub—he who had arranged the killing—she discovers that the real boss of the mob who wanted her father killed is Hurd Hatfield, who only poses as Dekker's underling. She becomes his fiancée. Of course, there are no sexual scenes, but anyone familiar with the workings of the Code and its signifying omissions, realizes that she has probably slept with all three men in order to bring them to justice.

Figure 3.8.   The indispensable Elisha Cook, Jr. in *Phantom Lady*

Still a third type of women's film, a negative variation of the other two, features a virago heroine who trods roughshod over unsuspecting and deluded males to achieve her selfish ends. *Harriet Craig* (1950) and *Born To Be Bad* (1950) belong to this category, as do *Guest in the House* (1944) and *All About Eve* (1950), both of which star Anne Baxter as the scheming and destructive female. All of them make use of noir devices but do not belong to the genre primarily because the heroine does not kill. Quite different is *Leave Her to Heaven* (1945) in which Gene Tierney rejects her weak fiancé, Vincent Price, in favor of the gullible Cornel Wilde, and in her deranged desire to control him murders his brother and ultimately kills herself, though pregnant with his child. In this Technicolor film, Leon Shamroy, the cinematographer, recreates in color the black and white chiaroscuro typical of film noir. For all these reasons, it has crossed into noir territory, though it lacks an investigator.

As a final example of how film noir differs from psychological melodramas, we can compare two films dealing with female twins, one good, the other bad, both from 1946, and directed by two brothers. In the first, *A Stolen Life*, directed by Curtis Bernhardt, the good Bette Davis loses the imperceptive Glenn Ford to her unscrupulous bad sister. Having been rejected by the safe or mild man, she undergoes a relationship with a wild man, the artist Dane Clark. This too proves devastating to her, so when bad sister dies by drowning, good sister takes her place. But further complications arise when she discovers her evil twin was having an affair with the married Bruce Bennett. What a mess! But in the end a kindly older man (Charles Ruggles) enlightens the not too bright Ford and all ends well. This is a psychological melodrama.

How different is *The Dark Mirror*, directed by Robert Siodmak! Here Olivia De Havilland plays the dual role. Instead of frustrating love affairs, we have a murder, an investigating cop (Thomas Mitchell), an investigating psychiatrist (Lew Ayres), and a plan by bad sister to murder her loving and good natured twin and take her place. This is a film noir. Whereas *A Stolen Life* has a bright look to it, *The Dark Mirror*, as the title implies, employs the visual motifs of noir, of which Siodmak was a master. That *A Stolen Life* has a different look does not result from Bernhardt's personal vision, but from the difference in the two stories, for Bernhardt could also make film noirs. As well as being Siodmak's brother, he was the director of *Conflict*, *Possessed*, and *High Wall*.

Were there no *Double Indemnities* or *Out of the Pasts*, films such as *Possessed* and *The Dark Mirror* would rightly be regarded as women's films. But like a black hole, the power of noir has drawn them toward its dark center.

The Hard-boiled Detective and the Rogue Cop

Of course film noir and hard-boiled detective films overlap. On the one hand, detective films can be perceived as an easy to spot genre in their own right, but on the other hand, a significant number of them form an important sub-species of film noir, perhaps the most important. After all, hard-boiled detective fiction, more than any other literary genre, created the world of film noir, and if one had to pick the most characteristic film noir protagonist, one would probably choose the hard-boiled detective, embodied perfectly on the screen by Humphrey Bogart. But that does not prevent us from making distinctions. As I argued in Chapter 2, hard-boiled detectives are not essential to film noir. What matters is whether or not they are "tarnished," so soiled that they become almost indistinguishable from the sordid, fallen world they inhabit. Many of these tough guys are as innocent as super sleuths—think of Philo Vance and Perry Mason. One also thinks of Boston Blackie, played by Chester Morris in no less than fourteen films during the noir period. Such films do not belong in the genre of film noir but rather to lower on the social register whodunits.

Any confusion that exists between film noir and the hardboiled detective genre results primarily from Raymond Chandler. As I pointed out in Chapter 2, his screenplays are more central to noir than his novels. Remember that his hero Philip Marlowe, unlike Sam Spade, walks down those mean streets, which Chandler better than anyone else imagined, unafraid and untarnished. *Farewell My Lovely* was the first of his novels to be filmed. This happened in 1942, two years before Hollywood became conscious of film noir. So instead of featuring Philip Marlowe, Hollywood in its all too familiar efforts to give literature a bad name,[34] transformed him into the Falcon, played by George Sanders, in the third of that series, entitled *The Falcon Takes Over*. Then in 1944, RKO made a somewhat more accurate version of the novel, now calling it *Murder, My Sweet* in which a stubble faced and grubby Dick Powell played Marlowe, supported by Nicholas Musuraca's fully realized noir cinematography. As is well known, the studio changed the title of the book over fears that a film entitled *Farewell My Lovely* starring Dick Powell would be construed as a musical. Though an outstanding example of noir style, *Murder, My Sweet* is unusual among canonized film noirs in its romantic happy ending.

The High Window, another Chandler novel, met a similar fate, when, again in 1942, it was made into *Time to Kill*. This time Marlowe is changed into Michael Shayne, another tough guy private eye, here played by Lloyd Nolan. Although Shayne is more low down and seedy than the Falcon, this film too is a whodunit, as is the 1947 remake, *The Brasher Doubloon*, starring George Montgomery as Marlowe. Robert Montgomery played Marlowe in

The Lady in the Lake, an unhappy experiment with the camera acting as the first person which limits Marlowe's relationship with both the cast and the audience. Undoubtedly the most famous of all the Chandler renditions is *The Big Sleep*, made in 1945 but not released until 1946. Its convoluted plot has become something of a joke; neither Howard Hawks the director nor William Faulkner, one of the screenwriters, admits to understanding what went on in the film. Despite the presence of Humphrey Bogart as Marlowe, the makers of the film shifted Chandler's focus on the fallen world onto the romantic chemistry between Bogart and his new bride in real life, Lauren Bacall. If one assumes that the novels of Raymond Chandler are central to any understanding of film noir, and if one also assumes that films can belong only to one genre, then when one looks at the films based on Chandler's novels, one can indeed become confused.

This is not the case with the rogue cop. He too can be conceived as a genre in his own right. But he also falls neatly into film noir and joins company with other film noir investigators. In fact, almost all the private eyes began as cops, usually leaving the force because of their assumed violations of proper police behavior. So the rogue cops of *Where the Sidewalk Ends*, *The Prowler* (1951), *On Dangerous Ground* (1952), *Rogue Cop* (1954), and *Shield for Murder* (1954) may well be regarded as belonging to a genre of their own, but they also make up a sub-species of film noir. It's their being "rogue" that places them in the genre, all of them descending in varying degrees into the nether world of crime, none of them innocent, even though their guilt, like that of other noir protagonists, often grows from mitigating circumstances.

3) The Social Problem Film

As with other genres, film noir takes the social problem film and transforms it. The social problem film, a branch of one of Bazin's grand genres, was not just a post World War II genre, as Neale asserts. It goes back at least to D. W. Griffith, as in *Broken Blossoms* (1919) and was alive and well in numerous 1930s melodramas, such as *Imitation of Life* (1934). By citing *Crossfire*, Neale means to link it with other postwar films dealing with race and anti-Semitism, films such as *Gentleman's Agreement* (1947), *Lost Boundaries* (1949), and *Pinky* (also 1949). To be sure, *Crossfire* deals with anti-Semitism. But look at the differences between it and *Gentleman's Agreement*. *Gentleman's Agreement* is a story about social discrimination and hypocrisy; *Crossfire* is about murder. Its bigot is not a country club snob, but a psychopath. It features a detective and an investigation, disoriented returning veterans, a potential femme fatale (no less a noir icon than Gloria Grahame), and a man running away from himself (Paul Kelly), not to mention the casting

Figure 3.9. Noir icons Robert Ryan and Robert Mitchum in *Crossfire* with Robert Young

of two other noir icons, Robert Mitchum, here an innocent, juxtaposed to Robert Ryan, the murderer, whose very appearance in a film almost assures it will be a film noir. So yes, *Crossfire* hybridizes the social problem film with the crime film, but the result is film noir. Call it a hybrid or a transgeneric phenomenon if you will, the result is still film noir. Genres are born of hybridization, and once established cultivate them. Fielding, we recall, defined the novel as "a comic epic poem in prose."

What then can we say? Admitting that a film is a thing and genre an idea, acknowledging the fluidity of genre, its instability and hybridization, not to mention the agendas of its creators, and recognizing the special difficulties presented by film noir and the reasonable arguments against it, despite all this, we conclude that film noir is a genre, a very grand one. It can be defined, and it has endured beyond any notion of movement, cycle, or series.

NOTES

1. As reported by Barbara Ward in the commentary on the DVD of *Tension* (1949).
2. Neale, *Genre and Hollywood*, 153.

3. The view taken by Naremore, Neale, and Elsaesser, as well as by David Bordwell, Janet Staiger, and Kristin Thompson, *The Classical Hollywood Cinema: Film Style and Mode of Production to 1960* (New York: Columbia University Press, 1985), 75.

4. Nino Frank, "A New Kind of Police Drama: The Criminal Adventure" (August 1946), in *Film Noir Reader 2*, ed. Alain Silver and James Ursini (New York: Limelight Editions, 1999). 15–20.

5. Made in 1947 as *The Brasher Doubloon*.

6. Lloyd Shearer, "Crime Certainly Pays on the Screen," *New York Times* (August 8, 1945), quoted in Biesen, *Blackout*, 193.

7. Quoted in Schatz, *Hollywood Genres*, 111.

8. Siegfried Kracauer, "Hollywood's Terror Films: Do They Reflect an American State of Mind?" *Commentary*, 2 (August 1946): 132–36.

9. Manny Farber, "Underground Films," in *Negative Space* (New York: Praeger, 1971 [1957]), 12–24.

10. Barbara Deming, *Running Away from Myself* (New York: Grossman Publishers, 1969).

11. Biesen, 116.

12. Fred Stanley, "Hollywood Crime and Romance," *New York Times* (November 19, 1944), quoted in Biesen, 117.

13. Michael F. Keaney, *Film Noir Guide: 745 Films of the Classic Era, 1940–1959* (Jefferson, NC: McFarland & Company Publishers), 2003.

14. Borde and Chaumenton, 122–23. They list as other parodies *It's in the Bag* (1945), *The Fuller Brush Girl* (1950), *The Lemon Drop Kid* (1951), the beginning of *Murder He Says* (1945), and *Behave Yourself* (1951).

15. Thomas Doherty, *Hollywood's Censor* (New York: Columbia University Press, 2007), 243–51.

16. "Meyers Scores Breen Defense of Studio Code," *Motion Picture Herald* (December 6, 1947): 16, cited in Doherty, 250.

17. Doherty, 251.

18. Doherty, 244.

19. Alain Silver, *Film Noir: The Encyclopedia*, edited by Alain Silver, Elizabeth Ward, James Ursini, Robert Porfirio, and coeditor Carl Macek. 4th ed. (New York: Overlook Duckworth, 2010), 349.

20. Neale, *Genre and Hollywood*, p. 173.

21. Philip Gaines, "Noir 101," in *Film Noir Reader 2*, 329–41.

22. Alain Silver, Introduction," in Film *Noir Reader 4*, ed. Alain Silver and James Ursini (New Jersey: Limelight Editions, 2004), 3.

23. Nicolas Saada, "The Noir Style," in *Film Noir Reader 4*, 186–88.

24. Damico, F*ilm Noir Reader*, 95–105.

25. Silver and Ward, *Film Noir*, 313.

26. Silver and Ward, *Film Noir*, 87.

27. Robert Warshow criticized *Kiss of Death* for not conforming to the tragic conclusion of the classic gangster film, an example of a categorical judgment preceding a value judgment. Unlike Deming and others, he had not recognized the new genre,

which shifted the emphasis away from the gangster, in this case a psychotic Richard Widmark in his first role, onto the hapless Victor Mature, a family man trying to extricate himself from the mistakes of the past. Warshow, *The Immediate Experience*, 129.

28. Keaney, 261.

29. Bordwell, Staiger, and Thompson, 75–77.

30. Quoted by Lloyd Shearer "Crime Certainly Pays on the Screen," *New York Times* (August 8, 1945), and cited by Leonard J. Leff and Jerold L. Simmons, *The Dame in the Kimono: Hollywood, Censorship, and the Production Code from the 1920s to the 1960s* (New York: Grove Weidenfeld, 1990), 127.

31. Neale, *Genre and Hollywood*, 153–74.

32. Stanley Cavell, *Contesting Tears* (Chicago: University of Chicago Press, 1996).

33. Vincent Brook in *Driven to Darkness: Jewish Émigré Directors and the Rise of Film Noir* (New Brunswick: Rutgers University Press, 2009) argues that the Jewish experience of the German/Austrian directors of noir led them to favor female protagonists, more likely to be victims than the hardboiled detective types.

34. A phrase borrowed from A. O. Scott in his review of *The Last Station* in the *New York Times* (December 4, 2009), C19.

Chapter Four

Style

Nothing is simple when it comes to film noir. The term has at least two meanings, genre and style. Most observers think of it as a genre, even those who oppose it as such. Here genre refers to a particular subject or content. But we have also noted that Schatz and Luhr, among others, think of film noir primarily as a visual style. In the most outstanding examples of noir, in films such as *Out of the Past*, genre and style go together, but in a significant number of film noirs, including *The Maltese Falcon* and *The Postman Always Rings Twice*, they do not. Although we have argued that the genre was new, Bordwell, Staiger, and Thompson have demonstrated that the style was not. Most of its techniques go back not only to German Expressionism but can even be found in D. W. Griffith's and Billy Bitzer's early days at New York's Biograph before they took their methods to Hollywood. To further complicate matters, the style, which proved to be detachable, was in the 1940s and 1950s applied across the entire spectrum to Hollywood genres, a fact which has created the chief stumbling block in defining film noir.

Nevertheless, the nature of the style has proven much less controversial than the genre. In one of the essential articles on film noir, Janey Place and Lowell Peterson describe its components.[1] Let us list them.

High contrast or chiaroscuro, that is, shadows and areas of darkness juxtaposed to more lighted areas.
Key lighting, that is, a point of light on one object or face.
Slats of light: the Venetian blind effect. Or bars of light, like prison bars.
Night scenes.
Wide angle photography.
Depth of focus.
Hallucinatory dissolves.

Dream montages.
Strange camera angles.

But the noir look can also result from more conventional techniques. In his discussion of John Alton, "the prototypical noir cameraman," and his book *Painting with Light*,[2] Naremore points out how Alton achieved his noir effect by means other than the ones described by Place and Peterson (172). Among them he mentions:

The filament of a lamp as the only bright space.
"Jimmy Valentine lighting," that is, a key light directly beneath the faces of the villains, giving them a grotesque look.
Wet pavements to reflect the light sources.
The effect of a passing auto headlight on the ceiling of a dark interior.
Fluctuating neon signs.
A hanging light on the ceiling.
Flashes of guns in absolute darkness.
The opening and closing of a refrigerator that has a light inside.
The well known street lamp.[3]

Naremore then continues with a brilliant illustrated discussion of Nicholas Musuraca's camera work in *Out of the Past* (175–85). In this he demonstrates that:

> Musuraca's work involves no night-for-night scenes, no distorting lenses, no extreme deep-focus compositions, no "choker" close-ups, and very few radical angles—in other words it manifests almost none of the traits that Place and Peterson claim are essential to the visual atmosphere of film noir. The photography of *Out of the Past* nevertheless seems definitively noir like, chiefly by virtue of its low-key, deeply romantic "painting with light." (175)

I think Place and Peterson were concentrating on the more unusual techniques of film noir, not the full range of methods by which gifted cameramen created the noir look. What we notice in almost all of them, what unites them, is some form of chiaroscuro. It is the dominant motif that takes full advantage of the aesthetic possibilities of black and white film. Of course all these techniques were used in the 1930s. I think of *Blonde Venus*, *Scarface*, and *The Informer*, but I also think of Fred and Ginger, he in black, she in white, the dance floor black, the set itself bright and shadowed, as in "Let's Face the Music and Dance" from *Follow the Fleet* (1936). But whereas the films of the post-Code 1930s might punctuate their glossy look with a dark sequence, the film noirs of the 1940s reversed that practice. In addition to these light effects, other visual motifs, such as typical locales, also characterize film noir:

Figure 4.1. The Nightclub. Dan Duryea and June Vincent in *Black Angel*

Nightclubs and bars.
Dark stairways.
Dark city streets.
A car racing along these streets, a favorite opening shot.
An ambulance pulling away from a crime scene, a favorite concluding shot.
Amusement parks or piers at night.
Run down store fronts.
Run down apartment buildings.
Run down apartments.
Tunnels, basements, sewers, anything underground.
Interrogations under bright lights.
Wharfs and waterfronts at night.
Fog.

Various narrative devices accompanied the visual style. Again, they may not have been new, but joined to the visual element listed above, they too became conventions of film noir.

The voiceover.
The flashback, or multiple flashbacks.

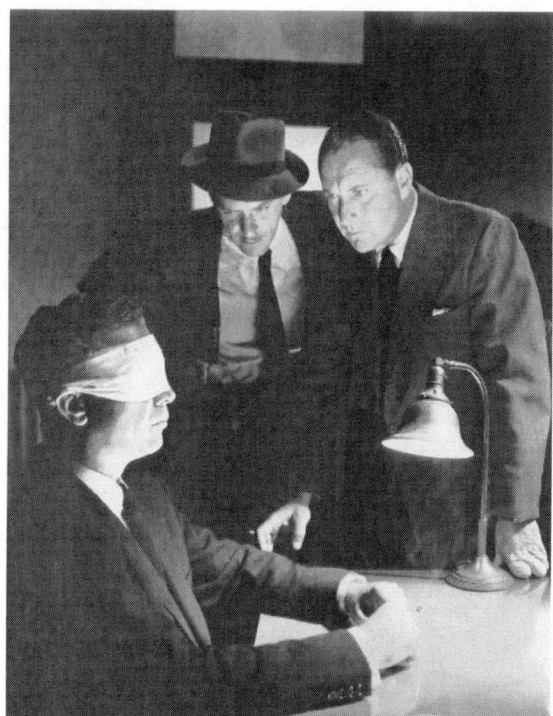

Figure 4.2. Dick Powell under the light in *Murder, My Sweet*

Multiple narrators or perspectives.
Unreliable narrators.
Dreams and hallucinations mixed up with reality.

 Žižek excludes Hitchcock from film noir on the basis that his films lack the integration provided by voiceovers and flashbacks.[4] But neither of these devices is essential to the noir style or genre. Too many canonized and beloved noirs, apart from those by Hitchcock, lack them altogether, among them, *The Maltese Falcon* and *Touch of Evil*, the two films commonly thought to begin and end the "cycle," as well as *The Asphalt Jungle*, *The Big Combo*, *The Big Heat*, *The Big Sleep*, *The Dark Corner*, *Fallen Angel*, *In a Lonely Place*, *Kiss Me Deadly*, *Scarlet Street*, *This Gun for Hire*, and *Woman in the Window*.
 One associates voiceovers with film noir because they are indeed common and are used with great effect in early, formative noirs such as *Murder, My Sweet*, which carries over into film the tough guy, hard-boiled, first person narration of Chandler's novel, and helps to cement the convention, already at work in *Citizen Kane* and *I Wake Up Screaming*. In *Double Indemnity*, the

wounded and dying Walter Neff (Fred MacMurray) explains to his colleague Keyes (Edward G. Robinson), via Dictaphone, how he came to this tragic end. In *Out of the Past*, Jeff Bailey (Robert Mitchum) explains to his new girlfriend (Virginia Huston) that he is really Jeff Markham, a former private eye who is unable to escape from his past. In both films, the voiceovers provide a double perspective, a kind of moral overlay, something like the chorus in a Greek tragedy, which plays against the self destructive visualized behavior of the protagonist. *Sunset Boulevard* carries the device to its ultimate end by opening the film with the death of the narrator and having him tell the story from his watery grave in a Hollywood swimming pool.

At their best, such voiceover narrations deepen and complicate the characterization of the protagonists, helping them, in Henry James's phrase, to become "vessels of consciousness." In B movies they also serve as economic and effective means to hasten along any needed exposition. In a recent article in *Noir City Sentinel*, Jake Hinkson takes a dim view of yet another form of voiceover which he calls "First Person Authoritarian." This occurs when a tangential character, a cop or a psychiatrist comments on the action, as in *Side Street* (1950) or *The Dark Past*.

If cops were most often presented as moral authorities who preached the film's message, the shrink was there to operate as a disinterested amoral authority—the man of science teaching his classroom of doltish theatergoers to let go of their simpleminded notions of character and embrace his diagnosis of the problem.[5] Even more annoying to Hinkson is the "Third Person Authoritarian" voiceover, a standard component of the "docu-noirs." It arrives with bombast at the beginning of the film and makes sure you understand that the story you are about to see is good for you."[6] Yet however much this convention has dated, its celebration of government agencies, everything from the FBI to postal inspectors, had to result from deep anxieties about the government and its post war effectiveness, its image assaulted on the one hand by the extravagant claims of Senator McCarthy and on the other by the perjury of Alger Hiss. The voiceovers assure an edgy, not a complacent audience that the much admired G-Men of the New Deal were still on the job and ever more effective.

Although all these elements of style preexisted film noir, they merge together and are given a new life in *Citizen Kane*. From Bazin onwards, almost all commentators have remarked on this relationship between *Citizen Kane* and noir style. As Eddie Muller put it, "*Citizen Kane* forever changed the grammar of motion picture storytelling and set the cinematic syntax for film noir: the shadowy quest for the truth in morally ambiguous terrain, the cynical take on the corrupting influence of power, the daring, off-kilter visual style."[7] Yet despite its standing at the head of the "cycle," despite its being the chief model for all that followed, no one classifies, categorizes, or lists *Citizen Kane* as a film noir. On the whole *Citizen Kane*, like *Don Quixote* for so long, would seem to have transcended concepts of genre and become an entity unto itself. If one had to classify it, one would probably call it a biopic, a fictional one, based unmistakably, however inaccurately, on the life of media mogul William Randolph Hearst. So much has the film fixed Hearst in the popular imagination that it comes as something as a shock to visit Hearst's Castle, called in the film Xanadu, and discover that it is not a gloomy swamp-like place but a cheerful, sunny, tasteful Mediterranean palace, designed by an outstanding woman architect, Julia Morgan, which overlooks the picturesque central coast of California.

That along the way the style which *Citizen Kane* assembled, integrated, and popularized acquired the name film noir suggests how suited it was to that particular genre. But it was not unique to it; Hollywood used it everywhere. Thus, from its outset, the style could exist apart from the genre. The two were wed, but it was an open marriage, which suffered a serious separation in the 1950s.

Following the end of the war, Hollywood studios engaged in more location work. This resulted in a group of films often referred to as "docu-noirs," the model and most famous of the type being *The Naked City*. The majority of these films abandoned the style of film noir, which on the whole was a studio technique. To be sure, they dealt with crime, big time crime, big city crime: the mob, the syndicate, counterfeiters, smugglers, spies, and traitors. But this branch of the crime film family I do not consider as generic film noirs. First, the police or government officers opposed to the criminals are Dudley-Do-Right characters, old fashioned G-Men, upright and flawless, professional crime fighters who, for the most part, do not suffer from emotional and domestic problems. And second, many of the films, rather than having the noir style, look just the opposite: crisp black and white cinematography, shot for the most part in daylight, and looking, as their name indicates, like documentaries. The title "Naked City" came from Weegee's famous photos of sensational nighttime crime in New York City, but the look of these films owes much more to Italian Neo-Realism than to Weegee.[8]

Only some spirit of inclusiveness would admit them into the noir fold. As early as 1955 Borde and Chaumenton pointed out that film noir does not have a monopoly on crime films and went on to describe what they called "police documentaries," which we now call "police procedurals."[9] Despite similarities, they say, the two series differ in important ways. And first and foremost a different angle of vision. The documentary considers the murder from without, from the official police viewpoint; the film noir from within, from the criminals'. In movies of the *Naked City* type, the action begins after the crime, and the murderers, heavies, and their accomplices traverse the screen solely in order to be tailed, spied on, interrogated, hunted down, or killed. If a flashback evokes a scene between gangsters, it's to illustrate a confession or a testimony, the transcript of which figures in the report. The police are omnipresent, so as to intervene or lend an ear. There's none of this in film noir, which is set in the criminal milieu itself. The second difference is of a moral, and maybe even more essential kind. It's part of the tradition of the police documentary to present the investigators as upright, incorruptible, and courageous men. None of this exists in the noir series. If there are policemen, they're of a dubious character—like the inspector in *The Asphalt Jungle* or that evil-looking corrupt brute played by Lloyd Nolan in *The Lady in the Lake*—even murderers at times (Otto Preminger's *Fallen Angel* and *Where the Sidewalk Ends*). Or at least they allow themselves to get caught up in the machinery of crime, like the attorney in *The File on Thelma Jordan*.[10]

Police procedurals can, however, mutate into generic film noirs. For instance, *He Walked by Night* presents a typical gangbusters structure. It begins with a magisterial voiceover by Reed Hadley, the dean of such voices, assuring us that the authorities can deal with any contingency. But then it shifts

Figure 4.3. Just as good as Vienna. The L.A. sewer in *He Walked by Night*

to a psychologically disturbed serial killer (Richard Basehart) and in much of the film we see from his perspective, which of course causes us to sympathize with him. Added to this angle of vision, rather than being filmed in the documentary style, the film provides John Alton the opportunity to give it a stunning noir look, culminating in a chase through the Los Angeles sewers that rivals in its effectiveness and beauty the better known Viennese sewer chase of the same year in *The Third Man*. Still another example is *T-Men*. Here again John Alton creates his "mystery lighting" noir, while the chief law man, Dennis O'Keefe so submerges himself into the criminal element that he virtually becomes a part of it. In *Appointment with Danger* (1951) John Seitz, using similar devices, gives the noir look to the Gary, Indiana locations, though on the whole the film is a standard police procedural. Alan Ladd begins the film as a cold, cynical crime fighter, but the good example of a nun, played by Phyllis Calvert, has by the end warmed his heart.

The Turning Point (1952) perfectly illustrates the difference between film noir and a police procedural. It opens with the appointment of Edmond O'Brien to lead the fight against a syndicate, led by Ed Begley. But though shot on locations (supposedly Midwestern, but including the Flight of Angels) in a documentary style, it focuses not on the step by step victory of the forces of law and order, but on the inner drama and psychology of its three principles: O'Brien, an academic law professor, Alexis Smith, his society girl coworker and fiancée, and William Holden, playing a cynical (typical for him) reporter, who suspects the crusade will come to naught and the idealists will be defeated by reality. Yet in an undercover manner, withholding key information from O'Brien, he discovers that O'Brien's father, Tom Tully, a revered cop, is actually a mob informant. The bribes Tully took put O'Brien through college. Holden confronts Tully and urges him to double cross the syndicate, but when another informant squeals on Tully, the syndicate arranges to have him shot in a fake holdup and then kills the gunman so as to leave no traces. Meanwhile Holden and Smith fall in love, and via a Production Code fade out, consummate it. O'Brien, stunned by the truth about his father, hurt by the betrayal of Smith, wants to resign. Holden now urges him to fight on, and helps in locating the widow of the hired gunman, the key witness, who can bring down the gang. But in the film this never happens. Instead Holden is lured to a boxing arena and killed by hired assassin Neville Brand, so that the film ends not triumphantly, as is usual in police procedurals, but tragically, as so often in film noir.

In the Appendix called "Period Pieces," I have listed many crime films of the noir period, which though sometimes called noir, to my mind have radiated from the center into other genres, chief among them the police procedurals and gangster films. Many of these films, such as *Love Letters* dwell on the cusp, and Porfiro, Silver, Ward, and Keaney have every right to place them within the noir category. Others, such as *Call Northside 777* (1948) and other investigative reporter films, make use of the style of noir, and for this reason may also be included as noir, as are the films like *The Window* in which innocents are threatened by gang and criminal activities. One of the advantages of Altman's problematizing of genre consists in the fact that in breaking down ironclad notions of genre, he legitimizes anyone's reasonable "discourse" or subjective groupings. So I trust the reader will be patient with my own subdivision of the grand families of crime and melodrama.

What is not subjective and a matter of opinion is the fact that, as Schrader noted, "most every dramatic Hollywood film from 1941 to 1953 contains some noir elements."[11] The noir look and the conventions associated with it so infiltrated every single Hollywood genre or type that, as we hope to show in the next chapter, the style became the period style of the era.

NOTES

1. Janey Place and Lowell Peterson, "Some Visual Motifs of *Film Noir*" (1974), in *Film Noir Reader*, 65–76.

2. John Alton, *Painting with Light* (Berkeley: University of California Press, 1995 [1949]).

3. Alton, 47–48, a list which Naremore compares to a haiku or imagist poem (173).

4. Slavoj Žižek, "In His Bold Gaze My Ruin Is Write Large," in *Everything You Wanted to Know about Lacan (But Were Afraid to Ask Hitchcock)*, ed. Slavoj Žižek (London: Verso, 1992), 258. Nevertheless, both *I Confess* and *Vertigo* use these devices.

5. Jake Hinkson, "Hearing Voices: The Varieties of Film Noir Narration," *Noir City Sentinel* 5 (Summer 2010): 43.

6. Hinkson, 43.

7. Eddie Muller, *Dark City: The Lost World of Film Noir* (New York: St. Martin's Press, 1998), 51.

8. Naremore (*More Than Night*, expanded edition, 280–81) believes that the style of noir was influenced by such urban street photography.

9. Borde and Chaumenton, 5–6.

10. Borde and Chaumenton, 6–7.

11. Paul Schrader, "Notes on Film Noir," 54.

Chapter Five

Period Style

THEORY OF PERIOD STYLE

Discussions of period style run into the same problems as those of genre. We need categories in order to have a discussion, but none of them can withstand rigorous analysis.[1] Take for instance the concept "Baroque." It did not appear until centuries after the phenomenon to which it refers. No one quite agrees on its time span, though most would allow a good part of the seventeenth century. Wolfflin,[2] who did more than anyone else to create the concept, does an excellent job of describing its features, particularly in painting, so that we may characterize the work of Caravaggio as Baroque, but what about that of Vermeer or Poussin? Was Baroque a period style, a national style, a school, or just a style used by a few distinguished contemporaries?

Just to add to the confusion, the whole concept of period style itself is an afterthought. It resulted from a huge shift in the way Westerners thought about history. Until the end of the eighteenth century, both ancients and moderns saw history as a static drama, its characters serving "to point a moral or adorn a tale" as Johnson put it in one of his earlier poems, "The Vanity of Human Wishes" (1748). Only with the rise of a totally secular or scientific perspective, as in Gibbon's *Decline and Fall of the Roman Empire* (1776), did historians begin to see their subject in terms of essential changes, more often in terms of social progress and development than of decline. Darwin and his theory of biological evolution itself was an offshoot of this fundamental change in perspective. Newman even adapted it to the history of Christianity.

At the outset of its own conscious history then, *art* history dedicated itself to delineating the various stages in the development of Western art, the world's most restless culture. Antiquity became Archaic, Classical, Hellenistic, Roman and Late Roman, and the rise of Europe became Carolingian,

Romanesque, Gothic, Renaissance, Mannerism (a later addition), Baroque, Rococo (or Late Baroque), and Neo-classical. Lacking the hindsight of several centuries, art historians have not settled on the terms to describe the nineteenth and twentieth centuries, though most discussions recognize Romantic, Realist (or Victorian), Modern, and Post Modern. But since the 1960s, such discussions have fallen out of favor. Metonymy became more fashionable than metaphor. Categories of any kind, even biological ones such as male and female, became suspect and the whole Linnaean project of classification in the arts was dropped as hopelessly passé or merely forgotten. No wonder then that film historians, beginning to speculate about film noir in the 1970s, on the whole, ignored the concept of a period style.

Yet unaware of the concept, in their deliberations about whether or not noir is a genre, a movement, or a phenomenon, a significant number of writers edge into *period* style territory. For instance, Paul Schrader in his famous article, from which all subsequent articles have descended, remarks that film noir "is an extremely unwieldy period" not only because it harkens back to earlier periods but also because it "can stretch at its outer limits from *The Maltese Falcon* (1941) to *Touch of Evil* (1958), and most every dramatic Hollywood film from 1941 to 1953 contains some noir elements."[3] Raymond Durgnat denies film noir is a genre but claims it is a "motif and tone" which he finds everywhere in Hollywood.[4] Jane Root asks, "How did it become so dominant in Hollywood for more than 20 years, touching (one might say consuming) almost every genre whilst retaining a specific visual and narrative structure?"[5] Todd Erickson calls film noir "a movement that darkened the mood, or tone, in virtually all of the cinematic products of Hollywood from that era."[6] Robert Sklar says "the term describes the psychology and the look not simply of a genre, but a surprisingly pervasive tone in Hollywood films of the 1940s."[7] Elizabeth Cowie claims that film noir was not a genre but "a set of possibilities for making existing genres 'different.'"[8] Similarly Walker's "generic field" and Palmer's "transgeneric phenomenon" indicate what I believe characterizes a period style, as does Krutnik's "noir phenomenon," which includes generic, stylistic, and cyclic "manifestations."[9] And Neale, by denying film noir as a genre or consistent category, illustrates how wide-ranging its components were across the entire spectrum of Hollywood's productions. Either it did not exist, or it was everywhere.[10] Among historians of the studio system, only Thomas Schatz makes use of the term *period style*. In *Hollywood Genres*, he described film noir as a system of visual and thematic conventions not associated with story formula but with style and period,[11] and in *Boom and Bust* he states "The development of *film noir* into a distinctive period style was evident not only in the dark crime thrillers and hard-boiled detective films of the era but in many other genres and cycles as well."[12]

Mike Chopra-Gant takes issue with all of these proponents of what he calls "zeitgeist theories of film noir."[13] From his study of postwar American culture, not only its movies but its magazines, books, and stated concerns, he came to the conclusion that film noir represented but a minority view, primarily made in retrospect by elite intellectuals who have overlooked the middlebrow, upbeat, patriotic, traditional, and official view expressed in the most popular films from 1946 to 1950, many of them comedies and musicals. In so doing, he misconstrues the idea of period style, imagining that it must be absolute, that any list of most popular films must contain a majority of film noirs and that Hollywood's production should be numerically dominated by this most questionable of genres. That is not how period style manifests itself, as I hope to demonstrate.

Period style does not mean that every single work within the period must contain all the elements of the style. As Hauser explained, "The assumption that a style finds expression in the entire artistic production of an epoch or a region, in great works and in slight, in the monumental and in the minutest detail of decoration, everywhere with the same intensity and completeness, is untenable."[14] By such an assumption, Baroque does not exist, only the works of Bernini. Rather period style indicates a dominant style that influences or can be found in most of the art of the period. *To qualify as a period style, a style must meet at least two requirements: one, it must be the style most often used by the best artists in the best works of the period; and two, it must be dominant enough to make its influence felt and seen in works not otherwise partaking of the style.* It works indeed like a black hole, a great gravitational force exerting its magnetic power in all directions. Clearly, unlike the concept of genre, an awareness of period and period style necessarily occurs only after the fact. And it is precisely this notion of period style that is expressed by the writers struggling with the problems of film noir as a genre.

Period style as used by cultural historians from Burckhardt to Sypher always includes the typical content and subject matter associated with the dominant visual style. It is hard to imagine the Renaissance, for instance, without Madonnas, the Baroque without supernatural epiphanies and enormous churches and palaces, or the Rococo without salons, love stories, and the pursuit of happiness. In art style and content are bound up with one another. And so it is with film noir, in which a set of visual motifs accompany conventions of plot, character, and world view.

CITIZEN KANE AND THE BIRTH OF NOIR

When then did the genre and the period begin? Even though Bordwell and company can point to earlier examples of the visual motifs, singly and sometimes in combination that typically characterize film noir, no such style became dominant until the 1940s. One of the first examples was the 1940 B film *Stranger on the Third Floor*, which indeed contains almost all the noir ingredients, including Elisha Cook, Jr. We have also made numerous references to the 1941 *The Maltese Falcon*, which is usually cited as the beginning of the "cycle," though, for the most part, filmed in the classical 1930s style. In *Blackout*, Sheri Chinen Biesen presents a slightly different but plausible dating. These films and other "dark" films made from 1940 through 1943 she sees as "proto noir." For her, noir proper begins with *Double Indemnity* in 1944.

Biesen bases this notion on three facts. First, *Double Indemnity* represents the most notable wartime breakdown of Production Code Administration standards. When James M. Cain published the popular novel in 1934, Joseph Breen was quick to write all the major studios saying that under no conditions would the PCA approve of any film based on it, consisting as it does of adultery, a perfect crime, and murderers who escape justice. But during the war, due to the Office of War Information's ability to override the PCA and allow and even encourage the depiction of brutality and atrocities—when committed by the Axis enemies—and due to the example of war scene newsreels, the PCA relented and considered a somewhat "sanitized" version of this novel. Second, the studio records and the publicity attending the film as well as comments by critics such as Lloyd Shearer, fully reveal a *consciousness* that this film broke down a barrier and represented a new trend of the "red meat" variety. And third, the popularity of the film immediately brought about numerous imitations.[15] In this regard, *Double Indemnity* was like Richardson's novel *Pamela* (1740) which though not the first English novel—was there ever a first anything?—brought this new species into consciousness, of which imitation is the surest sign. What better corroboration of her theory than the remark made by Raymond Chandler on September 4, 1948 in his letter to Cleve F. Adams:

> I did not invent the hard boiled murder story and I have never made any secret that Hammett deserves most or all of the credit. Everybody imitates in the beginning. . . . Since Hammett has not written for publication since 1932 I have been picked out by some people as a leading representative of the school [the hard boiled murder story]. This is very likely due to the fact that *The Maltese Falcon* did not start the high budget mystery picture trend, although it ought to have. *Double Indemnity* and *Murder My Sweet* did, and I was associated with both of them.[16]

As to the commencement of the period, 1941 represents a surer starting point. I say this not because the October 18, 1941 release of *The Maltese*

Falcon was followed two weeks later by *I Wake Up Screaming*, a film overlooked by Biesen yet containing all the noir ingredients: plot, characters, narrative structure, world view, and visual style. Nor because between these two and the release of *Double Indemnity* in August 1944, more than half a dozen other noirs had been produced and released, not the least of them *This Gun for Hire, Shadow of a Doubt, The Phantom Lady*, and *Christmas Holiday* (1944). I say it because the period of film noir, like the birth of Athena from the head of Zeus, came out of the head of Orson Welles on the first of May, 1941 in the form of *Citizen Kane*. It was, as Schatz remarks, "a much more significant work in the evolution of the *noir* tendencies" than *The Maltese Falcon*.[17]

As it was produced at RKO, the studio of *Stranger on the Third Floor*, one cannot help wondering if Welles saw that film before or while he was shooting *Citizen Kane*. But it matters not, for his film, justly admired as one of the greatest films ever made, changed not only the look of subsequent Hollywood films but also their narrative structures and visions of life. In it for the first time we find assembled the low ceilings, the dark stairway, the chiaroscuro, the key lighting, and the expressive camera work that characterize noir.

With them we find the disjointed narrative structure, the main body of the story as a series of flashbacks, multiple narrators and points of view,

Figure 5.1. In search of Kane in *Citizen Kane*

including old newsreels, the whole film being an investigation. And add to this an ambivalent protagonist who invents a femme fatale to destroy his marriage. She, of course, kills no one, but like the real femme fatales ends up as a victim of the male she helped to bring down. There's no doubt that the film exposes the flaws of a "great" man and by extension the capitalist system, but emotionally it works like a gangster film, in that the audience sympathizes with Kane and all his riches while warned that it's best not to reach that high. Thus *Citizen Kane* at one bold stroke creates the style of film noir and links it with most of the conventions of the genre. It lacks only a murder. As Robert B. Ray wrote, "*film noir* borrowed *Kane's* tactic of using a thoroughly subjective style to call into question a purportedly conventional conclusion,"[18] a view also shared by Robert Philip Kolker.[19] Thus the gigantic figure of Welles frames the period, creating the style with *Citizen Kane* and concluding seventeen years later with *Touch of Evil*, a film so noir that it becomes, whether consciously or not, a send up of the style. For despite its serious themes of corruption, racism, and artificial boundaries, *Touch of Evil* through its more than baroque visual style, the absurdly unfulfilled honeymoon of Charlton Heston and Janet Leigh, and the grotesquerie of Welles himself also crosses a boundary, the one between noir and parody.

A truly startling example of the influence of *Kane* may be seen in *I Wake Up Screaming*, a Twentieth Century Fox film that went into production in August, just a few months after *Kane's* general release on May 1st. As we have mentioned *Kane* came out of RKO, the studio with both the best noir precedent, *Stranger on the Third Floor*, and the most distinguished subsequent history. No such film or anything like it came out of Twentieth Century Fox. Yet in this Betty Grable, Victor Mature, Carole Landis vehicle, we see not only key lighting, chiaroscuro, low ceilings, shadowy figures, odd camera angles, and the flickering lights of a projection room showing documentary footage, but also a broken narrative pattern consisting of flashbacks and multiple points of view. How could this studio, director H. Bruce Humberstone, and cinematographer Edward Cronjager ever have come up with all this had they not had the example of *Citizen Kane* before them? It's as though they said, Let's have fun and give this crime novel by pulp writer Steve Fisher (which by the way had a straight linear narrative) a *Citizen Kane* look. Of course they would not have made this decision if noir, as the spirit of the time, had not already manifested itself. Not coincidentally, Warner Brothers was shooting *The Maltese Falcon* one month earlier, and both films feature that noir stalwart, Elisha Cook, Jr.

The role of Betty Grable in this film deserves special attention. From 1930 to 1940, she appeared in no less than fifty films, as a chorus girl, a dancing co-ed, and in *The Gay Divorcee* (1934) as a featured dancer. In *Follow the*

Fleet, she accompanies Ginger Rogers as she sings "Let Yourself Go." But despite her singing and dancing talents and her good looks, she never made it to stardom. 1930s heroines—think of Bette Davis, Carole Lombard, Barbara Stanwyck, Katharine Hepburn, Irene Dunne, Claudette Colbert—were tough and smart, good looking but not gorgeous. Betty Grable, like Lana Turner, another new star, was "cute." She had a great figure but was more soft, cuddly, and reassuring than these 1930s types. Then in 1940, she got her big break as the lead in the Technicolor musical *Down Argentine Way*, and in the numerous musicals that followed its success she became not only a number one box office female star but also the number one pin up girl of World War II. Already big by 1941, in *I Wake Up Screaming* she attempted a more dramatic role. But notice the difference between this role and the familiar ones played by the great 1930s heroines. Here she is a conventional, sweet, well meaning good girl, juxtaposed to her much more interesting, devious, scheming and femme fatale younger sister, Carole Landis, whose death points the finger of guilt at every male in the film. The star here becomes less interesting and important than her opposite, and for the first time we witness that cleavage characteristic of film noir between the safe girlfriend or wife and her lethal opposite. Alice Faye met a similar fate in *Fallen Angel* when she,

Figure 5.2. Sisters: Betty Grable and Carole Landis in *I Wake Up Screaming*

the alleged star, had to play opposite to the more alluring and doomed Linda Darnell.

I Wake Up Screaming also established Victor Mature as the type of male lead appropriate to the world of noir, that is a "hunk," a big guy, not cut in the WASP mold of Gary Cooper or Randolph Scott, who despite his size and physical prowess proves vulnerable to suspicions and pitfalls. And if all this were not enough, it also introduces the sexual perversity characteristic of noir, in this case the obsession of the ominous Laird Cregar with both Carole Landis and Mature. And he's a cop too!

How quickly this style and content became normative in Hollywood may be seen by reviewing *The Keeper of the Flame* (1942), an MGM film directed by George Cukor that almost slavishly imitates the style, plot, and vision of *Citizen Kane*. Like *Kane*, it uses newsreels to announce the death of a "great" man. Like *Kane*, an investigative reporter (Spencer Tracy) attempts to tell the true story of this man's life, a man who lived in a dark, high, fenced off mansion, not unlike Xanadu. Like Charles Foster Kane, Charles Forrester corrupted whatever original ideals he had into a lust for power (fascism no less), all this shielded by his faithful seeming and suffering wife (Katharine Hepburn) who, it turns out, murdered him by not telling him the bridge over which his high speed car must travel on a dark, rainy night was washed out. There's no night club or dark city, just a gothic mansion inhabited by creepy suspects and accomplices.

THE DOMINANCE OF FILM NOIR

Of course a voiceover narration or the presence of a psychiatrist in the script do not turn a movie into a film noir. If all the techniques or motifs associated with film noir existed before, what differs is where and how the movies used them. In the 1930s, as Vivian Sobchack points out, a nightclub was a moderne, art deco site (or "chronotype") of public celebration, a place where one found Ginger dancing with Fred, but in the 1940s and 1950s it became a sinister place of intrigue and confusion.[20] Such differences have led commentators to see noir across the spectrum of 1940s and 1950s Hollywood production. What finally matters, however, is not the statistical presence of pure noir or partial noir or bits and pieces of noir but the fact that the best films, the representative films, the films that have attracted the greatest critical attention and have been canonized in film courses, are almost exclusively the ones that figure most prominently in any discussion of film noir. For instance, The American Film Institute's list of the 100 best

Hollywood films (as shown on the Internet Movie Data Base) includes ten from the period 1941–1950:

Casablanca
Citizen Kane
It's a Wonderful Life
Sunset Boulevard
All About Eve
The Maltese Falcon
The Treasure of the Sierra Madre
The Best Years of Our Lives
Double Indemnity
The Third Man [actually a co-British production]

Nine of them are either considered to be film noirs or have been associated with film noir, and a strong case can be made that the tenth, *The Treasure of the Sierra Madre* (1948), directed by John Huston, one of the creators of noir, also contains many noir elements. When one adds classics like *Out of the Past, The Killers, Vertigo, The Asphalt Jungle, The Killing, The Big Sleep, Notorious, Woman in the Window, Gilda,* and several dozen others, then considers that every major director working in Hollywood during the 1940s and 1950s—every, as Andrew Sarris calls them, "Pantheon" and "Near Side of Paradise" auteurs, including even Chaplin and Preston Sturges—made film noirs, then one must conclude that it was indeed the dominant genre.

As to the second requirement, making itself felt in other genres, all the commentators agree that noir's influence was everywhere. Obviously, it was caused by and reflected World War II, the war that Charles Foster Kane assures us will not take place. We see its influence in the gloom-drenched early war films such as *Air Force* (1943) and *Bataan* (1943), films which typically end with a speech rather than a victory. We see it in the profusion of maladjusted veterans returning after the war. And we see it in the anxieties about the atomic bomb and the commencement of a new war, which led to combat in Korea, McCarthyism, and blacklisting. These concerns characterize what may be discerned as the three overlapping phases of the period. First, a dark wartime phase, embodied in films like *Casablanca* (1942). This is followed by a second phase, from 1944 to 1952, which is marked by the high—or low—point of the genre of film noir, and then to a final phase characterized by a flood of law and order films which typically use a documentary style. In the Appendix "Period Pieces" I have listed the numerous crime films and melodramas which though not generically film noirs, have, by one critic or another or in some listing, been associated with the genre.

THE DARKNESS OF THE OTHER GENRES

But to comprehend the extent to which film noir influenced other genres, let us consider them, beginning with Hollywood's original genre, the Western. In the 1940s, audiences began to see such as *The Ox-Bow Incident*, in which law and order do not triumph, where values become twisted and outcomes tragic. Among the best of these were the films of Anthony Mann, five of them starring the archetypal good guy, James Stewart. But in these films, as in his films with Hitchcock, Stewart plays an unsympathetic, more neurotic role. In *The Naked Spur*, for instance, he appears as an unscrupulous and tormented bounty hunter, who is actually seeking revenge for a past crime. He pursues Robert Ryan, one of the chief players in the noir world, who though a villain and just as unscrupulous as Stewart, seems less obsessed and in some ways more sympathetic than the putative hero. Likewise in *Bend of the River* (1952), Ryan portrays an outlaw turned wagon master whose behavior parallels that of the villain, Arthur Kennedy, his former partner. In all of these Westerns, the world is corrupt, the hero and villain mirror images of one another, and the sexuality is strained and tormented. Mann of course came into prominence as a film noir director with such B-films as *Desperate*, *Side Street* (1948), and *Raw Deal* (1950).

In an article entitled "Noir Westerns,"[21] James Ursini discusses six Westerns he considers noir: *The Ox Bow Incident*; *Duel in the Sun* (1945); *Pursued*; *Ramrod* (1947); *Blood on the Moon* (1948); and *Devil's Doorway* (1950). All of them, as opposed to the classic pre-war Westerns, make use of typical noir conventions, such as conflicted, alienated protagonists, femme fatales, existential angst, determinism, and a noir visual style. He concludes his study by asserting that:

> Noir as a style was undoubtedly the single most important influence on American films of the forties and early fifties. And so it is little wonder that it is not confined to the detective/mystery genre or even the Western. Traces of its dark mode can be seen in period films, the gangster film, the science fiction film, even the musical. The style's ability to express the dark side was adopted again and again by filmmakers no matter the genre.[22]

Like Hitchcock, John Ford towers above other directors, and his Westerns are regarded almost as a personal genre. But by 1946 when Ford set out to make his first post-war Western, *My Darling Clementine*, he too rode into noir territory. Its setting is a desert town named "Tombstone," which consists not only of the typical raucous and fallen world of the saloon (not unlike the nightclub of noir) but initially of a craven community afraid to make a stand against the criminals who tyrannize it. "What kind of a town is this?" exclaims Wyatt Earp (Henry Fonda). The plot splits the conventional cowboy hero in two, the stiff-necked lawman Earp and the more romantic and sympathetic but lawless and mortally ill Doc Holliday (Victor Mature). Unlike the Ringo Kid (John Wayne) in *Stagecoach*, who was sent to the pen unjustly when he was seventeen, Wyatt and Doc are experienced, notorious killers. Whereas both the femme fatale, Chihuahua (Linda Darnell) the dance hall girl and Clementine (Cathy Downs) the good girl love Doc, he rejects each of them. And after he kills Chihuahua (by abandoning her and by botching the operation to save her), and then dies in the gunfight, Wyatt cannot quite bring himself to claim Clementine, to whom he is attracted. Though hopeful about Tombstone, the film is a study in ambiguity, not the least of which is the perilously fine line it draws between justice and revenge. And its title song reminds us that Clementine is "lost and gone forever."

Ford's next Western, *Fort Apache* (1948) takes us further into the universe of noir. Again we see the conventional hero split between the martinet leader of the cavalry, Colonel Thursday (Henry Fonda), and his wiser subordinate Captain York (John Wayne). Roughly based on Custer's Last Stand, this film blames the commander and depicts him not only as a fool but also as an outrageous bigot and snob. Ford's version stands in stark contrast to the traditional treatment of the story, the patriotic *They Died with Their Boots On* (1941) in which Errol Flynn played the dashing and sympathetic Custer. Even more startling than the Indians winning a battle in a Hollywood film or a U.S. leader being deranged is the epilogue. Captain York, now the unit commander, to sustain a false legend, deliberately lies about the heroism of Colonel Thursday. What an astounding Brechtian moment of alienation is this! As Gilberto Perez points out, the epilogue is intentionally contradictory and troubling because of "its undeceived recognition of the loss as well as the gain which the legend abets."[23]

This is the world of noir, an ambivalent, corrupt, and political tangle which entraps even heroes such as Kirby York. Ford affirms the worth of the community, now narrowly confined to the military, but more typical of noir is the complete failure of the community to save itself, as in a favorite of the period, *High Noon* (1952). If salvation comes at all, it comes at the hands of the Production Code, which insisted on a saving framework of law and order, despite what the plots of the films implied. From this perspective, Ford's troubling epilogue can be seen as an ironic commentary on the Production Code itself and its demands for poetic justice.

What many consider Ford's greatest work, *The Searchers* (1956), though shot in color, takes on all the other hues of noir. Its hero, war vet, rebel, and fugitive Ethan Edwards (John Wayne), harbors an incestuous love for his brother's wife, Martha (Dorothy Jordan). When the Indians kill her, he transfers his obsession to her daughter, Debbie (Natalie Wood), a white captive whom at the outset he intends to save. But as time passes and he becomes aware that she will have become a "squaw," his tormented psyche drives him to seek her death. He too is a split personality, seemingly a white man, but a wild and lawless one who knows all the ways of the "Comanche." And, as in other noir films, the putative villain, the renegade Scar (Henry Brandon), acts as an alter ego to Ethan, which is why both of them are of the same stature, have blue eyes, and speak parallel lines. Ford brilliantly turns all this dualism into a sustained commentary on race and racism, which Hollywood also began addressing for the first time during the noir period. Instead of the triumphant mode of the "winning of the west" Western, such as Ford's own *The Iron Horse* (1924) or DeMille's *Union Pacific* (1939) that treated the Indians as natural obstacles to progress or as dupes to unscrupulous whites, numerous films such as *Broken Arrow* now treated the Indians sympathetically, all of them complicating received opinions and undoing what before had seemed resolved conflicts.

Unlike Ursini, Neale, who also doubts the pervasiveness of noir, does not look carefully enough at other genres. He cites *The Bells of St. Mary's* (1945) as an example of Hollywood's optimism,[24] but what happens in that film? Sister Ingrid Bergman is not only frustrated in her love for Father Bing Crosby, she is fired by him and then dies of cancer. Not exactly the Flying Nun. Even more somber and noirish is *The Song of Bernadette* (1943), in which the heroine undergoes an investigation, suffers intensely, and as her lover watches in despair, is carried off in a cart to a nunnery where she is further persecuted and dies of a painful, incurable disease. Not even biblical epics could escape. What could be a greater subject for noir than *Samson and Delilah* (1949)? Victor Mature, by now a noir regular, plays Samson, a not too bright good guy who becomes infatuated with a femme fatale who leads him to his destruction, but not before (as the 1940s Production Code would insist) he redeems himself by bringing down those big time crooks, the Philistines.

And so it is with other genres. Horror films turn psychological in the works of Val Lewton, as in *The Cat People* (1942) directed by Jacques Tourneur, and *The Leopard Man* (1943).[25] Made at RKO, these films invariably enter into discussion of film noir as demonstrating its amorphous boundaries. Nor does science fiction escape the noir influence as we see in *Invasion of the Body Snatchers* (1956), directed by Don Siegel—like Anthony Mann, a director who came up through the ranks of the B crime film. Shot largely at night

Figure 5.3. Bernadette's departure in *The Song of Bernadette*

it explores the dangers of second marriages, the precariousness of bourgeois life, and the corruption of the all-American town.

A quick look at the most enduring and beloved films of the 1940s, none of them considered as film noir, reveals how widespread were the noir ingredients. *Casablanca* combines a love story with a war film. Yet it is set in a nightclub in a totally corrupt city whose chief of police (Claude Rains) is a cynical womanizer and whose governors are international gangsters. Its narration includes an important flashback; its hero (Humphrey Bogart) is haunted, one might say frozen by his past; and its heroine (Ingrid Bergman) turns out to be a treacherous woman, unfaithful to both her husband and her lover.[26] The most honored and popular film of the decade was *The Best Years of Our Lives* (1946). Generically a soap opera or melodrama, it relates the interlocking stories of three World War II veterans. That the mid-forties would concern itself with this subject is only natural, but typical of noir, the veterans, who are almost always heroes, come back wounded, maladjusted, and haunted by their pasts. One of them (Harold Russell) is actually an amputee; another (Fredric March), a bank officer, dislikes his old job and turns alcoholic, while the third (Dana Andrews), reduced from an officer to a soda jerk, wanders confusedly between his frivolous and potentially destructive wife (Virginia Mayo) and the innocent good girl (Teresa Wright) who wants to set him straight. Things precariously work out okay in the end, but the world of the film is a fallen one whose realism partakes of the conventions of noir. Still another favorite, *All About Eve*, consists of several flashbacks within flashbacks, the voice over of a cynical narrator (George Sanders), himself totally corrupted, multiple points of view, and a femme fatale type (Anne Baxter) who successfully displaces her mentor (Bette Davis) and manipulates herself to stardom in an all too human world.

We even see evidence of noir in the romances of Frank Capra. In *Meet John Doe* (1941), the villain, D. B. Norton (Edward Arnold), like Charles Foster Kane, is a media tycoon seeking political control, and the hero, played by the archetypal innocent Gary Cooper, really has no self. Unlike his prior role as Mr. Deeds, a Jonathan figure,[27] that is, a yokel who has more savvy than the city slickers who try to corrupt him, he is created by an ambitious woman reporter (Barbara Stanwyck) who gives him a name and an ideology not his own. Of course, he comes to his senses, as does she, and tries to save the day, but Norton's machine triumphs over them, and the ending, in which he's persuaded not to commit suicide, remains unconvincing as well as inconclusive. Borde and Chaumenton refer to *Arsenic and Old Lace* (1944) as "*humour noir*."[28] The Christmas fable, *It's a Wonderful Life* (1946) contains a complete noir world in Pottersville, the example of what would have happened to Bedford Falls if George Bailey had never lived. But even in Bedford Falls, Bailey exhibits some typical noir behavior in his crack-up and attempted suicide.

Jimmy Stewart, who played George Bailey, may well have been the most versatile movie star of his time, but he was not alone in being drawn into the world of noir. In addition to Gary Cooper, other innocents, such as Dick Powell, the juvenile singing star, and Robert Taylor, the matinee idol, became noir protagonists. In *Nightmare Alley* (1947) the swashbuckling Tyrone Power turns into a geek. They were joined by Ginger Rogers in *The Black Widow* (1954) and *Tight Spot* (1955), a Phil Karlson crime film, as well as in *Storm Warning* (1951), an anti–Ku Klux Klan social problem film with many noir overtones. Ann Sothern, the good natured working girl of the Maisie series, became murderous in *The Shadow on the Wall* (1950). Even Deanna Durbin had a go in *Christmas Holiday*, here joined with song and dance man Gene Kelly as the confused and culpable male noir protagonist. Mickey Rooney, the former Andy Hardy, turned to noir roles in *Quicksand*, *The Strip* (1951), and *Drive a Crooked Road* (1954), and his long time girlfriend Polly (Ann Rutherford) morphs into a quasi femme fatale and thief in *Inside Job* (1946). A female counterpart to Rooney's Andy Hardy, Bonita Granville, the Nancy Drew of the 1930s, turns into a cheap little tart who in *Suspense* murders her former lover, Barry Sullivan.

As the power of noir transformed the stars of the 1930s, so it created new stars, chief among them Humphrey Bogart, too dangerous, too ambivalent, too sinister in the 1930s to be more than a bad gangster as opposed to the more charismatic James Cagney. It brought into stardom Victor Mature and other he-man, hunks, who didn't seem bright enough to avoid the pitfalls noir laid in their way, men such as Robert Mitchum, Robert Ryan, Burt Lancaster, John Payne (like Dick Powell, a former song and dance man), and Sterling Hayden. It also brought to the fore average-looking guys, too small and not good looking enough to be stars in the 1930s, but everyman types, all the more vulnerable to the pitfalls of the noir world, men such as Glenn Ford, Dana Andrews, and Mark Stevens. The great female stars of the 1930s, such as Bette Davis, Joan Crawford, and Katharine Hepburn made the transition to noir, but a new set of female stars rose to accompany the hunks down the dark streets where the sidewalks ended, more experienced good/bad girls such as Gloria Grahame, Lauren Bacall, Jane Greer, Rhonda Fleming, Marie Windsor, and Lizabeth Scott.

Figure 5.4.   Sterling Hayden in *The Asphalt Jungle*

A comic view of life does not suit film noir, but here too we detect its shadows. Of Stanley Cavell's "comedies of remarriage," only *Adam's Rib* (1949) came from the noir period. Not surprisingly, it begins with a femme fatale (Judy Holliday) and an attempted murder, then moves to an investigation of the crime, and deals not with inadequate rivals and girlfriends, as in the 1930s versions, but with the dangers of adultery itself. And as in other noir films, the seemingly ideal couple (Spencer Tracy and Katharine Hepburn) fall apart and spiral downward into potential violence. Another example of period's influence on romantic comedy is *A Foreign Affair* (1948). Set in an urban wasteland (bombed out Berlin), it features a femme fatale, Marlene Dietrich, and a good girl, Jean Arthur, vying for the affections of a criminal army officer, John Lund, engaged in the black market, who frequents the local nightclub, the Lorelei. Not surprisingly, Billy Wilder, one of the masters of noir, made it. Nor was Preston Sturges immune. In *Unfaithfully Yours* (1948), he abandons the zanies of his early comedies and makes a film about a jealous husband's (Rex Harrison) efforts or fantasies about killing his wife (Linda Darnell).

Even the musical was infected by noir. *Roxie Hart* (1942), the original talkie version of *Chicago*, consists of a prolonged flashback, noir lighting, and a comic femme fatale, a miscast and misdirected Ginger Rogers. In *Cover Girl* (1944), as slight a piece of Technicolor fluff as one could ever see, despite one good song by Jerome Kern ("Long Ago and Far Away"), we discover a maladjusted war veteran (Gene Kelly) trying to control Rita Hayworth. His jealousy and possessiveness drive her away, whereupon she takes up drink. Unlike a 1930s show biz heroine who could have her man and still be a star, Hayworth, repentant, for what we know not, returns to the morose Kelly, who has been consoling himself with comic homoerotic song and dance routines with Phil Silvers. The film even features a series of flashbacks wherein Rita's life, or destiny, repeats the life of her Gay Nineties show biz grandmother. Troubled veterans, forced domestication of women, flashbacks: these are the conventions of noir slipping into a non-noir genre. This is how a period style manifests itself. And was there ever a musical, such as *The Thrill of Brazil* (1946) in which the featured number and climax to this black and white film is shot, like a film noir, through venetian-blind-like slats?

In *Romance on the High Seas* (1948), Doris Day's first film, the farcical plot involves a typical mix up of couples and mistaken identities. But instead of the potential male adulterer being a handsome young man, here, as in the best of noir, the role is taken by a seedy, third-rate private eye (Jack Carson) working out of a rundown office, who is hired by Don Defore to investigate the seemingly faulty morals of the wife (Janis Paige). Such a comic spoof of noir conventions again illustrates Hollywood's consciousness of the genre.

Neptune's Daughter (1949), an Esther Williams musical with Red Skelton, makes use of voice over narration. I do not recall any 1930s musical that uses this device, which makes it all the more startling in an Esther Williams film. *It's Always Fair Weather* (1955), demonstrated storms ahead, as again three veterans reunite to explore their post-war difficulties. Its director and star Gene Kelly, with his self-absorbed style and choreography, replaced Fred Astaire as the most popular dancer of the era. Nothing escaped. Not only Ronald Colman (*A Double Life*) but also Charlie Chaplin turned noir. First playing a split personality in *The Great Dictator* (1940), he abandoned his Tramp persona altogether and in *Monsieur Verdoux* (1947) became a serial killer.

At the farthest remove from the genre of noir, we may consider the animated cartoon. The 1930s gave us the big, bad wolf, Mickey and Minnie, Merrie Melodies and Silly Symphonies, all of them concentrating on some external threat to the innocents of the green world. But in the 1940s, Disney shifted attention to Donald Duck, the comical neurotic, and even made a feature, *The Three Caballeros* (1945) in which Donald is running away from himself on a tour of Latin America. As Barbara Deming put it in a contemporary review, "Donald Duck could be likened, in his adventures here, his confusions and translations, to most of the major characters now passing across the screen."[29] Warners came up with "Daffy" Duck and the urban wise guy Bugs (meaning psycho) Bunny and transformed Merrie Melodies into Looney Tunes.

Rather then than refuting the dominance of film noir, Chopra-Gants' list of the top box office films of 1946–1950 tends to confirm it. Here is the list:

The Best Years of Our Lives
Samson and Delilah
Duel in the Sun
The Jolson Story
Forever Amber
The Bells of St. Mary's
Unconquered
Life with Father
Welcome Stranger
Leave Her to Heaven
The Egg and I
Jolson Sings Again
The Yearling
Green Dolphin Street
The Razor's Edge

Blue Skies
Road to Utopia
Spellbound
The Green Years
The Hucksters[30]

Only two on the list are canonized film noirs, *Leave Her to Heaven* and *Spellbound*. But as argued in the discussion above, the top two box office films exhibit aspects of noir and show its influence, as does *Duel in the Sun*, which is always included in discussion of the noir Western. We have also remarked on the very downbeat and sad *The Bells of St. Mary's*. Among the other titles, *The Razor's Edge* easily falls into the "running away from myself" category, being the story of a returning war veteran, in this case World War I, who, unable to adjust to vulgar American life and his overly aggressive fiancée (a social version of the femme fatale), seeks enlightenment in eastern religion. The musicals are particularly revealing in this regard. Remember that 1930s musicals feature love and romance: Dick Powell and Ruby Keeler; Fred and Ginger; Nelson Eddy and Jeanette MacDonald; Mickey Rooney and Judy Garland. They culminate in union, marriage, and putting on the show. By contrast *Blue Skies* deals with post marital problems, separation, divorce, and the effect of an absent father on his daughter. The Jolson films, like the top box office musicals of 1946, *Till the Clouds Roll By*, based on the life of Jerome Kern, and *Night and Day*, based on the life of Cole Porter, deal not with the happy culmination of a courtship or a collective success but like other films of the noir period have shifted their focus to the personal and the psychological. They are biopics as well as musicals, and as such they delve into the difficulties, pitfalls and tragedies of the individual artists.

The Jolson Story, for instance, concludes when Jolson's wife walks out on him. Is it stretching the argument to point out that *The Ziegfeld Follies*, another top box office musical of 1946, is narrated as a flashback by a dead man, no other than Flo Ziegfeld himself? *Forever Amber*, a sanitized version of the notorious bestselling novel, treats of the rise of a prostitute, while *The Hucksters*, a contemporary version of *Mad Men*, provides a view of the not too savory machinations of the advertising industry. Like most noirs, both of them strain the sexual morality of the Production Code. As to the several family films on the list, Chopra-Gants discussion of them brings out not their opposition to the noir view of America but how much they too deal with the anxiety fraught postwar life of families who struggle to preserve some semblance of the American dream. One would imagine that *The Road to Utopia*, the fourth of the Bing Crosby/Bob Hope "Road" pictures is farthest removed from film noir, yet it consistently and self-consciously disrupts its own diegesis by self-conscious gags and includes a voice over narration by Robert Benchley.

THE CULTURE OF FILM NOIR

The popular arts, and Hollywood in particular, have always acted as a mirror of the country. What would cultural historians do without them? Though our investigation has centered on a period in the history of Hollywood, it goes without saying that the mood and subjects of film noir reflected nation-wide anxieties and concerns arising out of World War II and post-war experiences, just as classic Hollywood, in its emphasis on class and youth, reflected the optimism of the New Deal. That film noir became the period style of Hollywood in the 1940s and 1950s raises the question of whether or not it reflected the style of the other arts during the same period. Warren Sussman believed that it did.[31] He asks why did the great success of America, its realization of New Deal goals and its stupendous military victory in World War II produce an "Age of Anxiety?" Or in Hollywood terms, how did Andy Hardy turn into James Dean, a rebel without a cause?[32] Sussman does not discuss the atom bomb, the Cold War, or the threat of liberated women, all of which figure in most discussions of the causes of film noir. Instead he speaks of how the desires of the 1930s, namely a caring government, a mass culture, a home in the suburbs, and a higher standard of living had all turned into nightmares. The government became too powerful; mass culture spawned comic books and paranoia; suburbs produced juvenile delinquency; and affluence created a drug problem. The greatest plays of the period, *Death of a Salesman*, *A Streetcar Named Desire*, and *A Long Day's Journey into Night* all dealt with the collapse of the family. *The Catcher in the Rye*, *On the Road*, and the Beat Poets redefined heroism as alienated psychopathology. Painting shifted from social realism, the dominant mode of the 1930s, to abstract expressionism, to which film noir has many links. Kent Minturn cites the nearly identical titles of the films and the paintings of the period; the labyrinth, web, and vortex in Jackson Pollack's paintings; de Kooning's femme fatales; Rothko's troubled vision; Kline's noir city abstractions; and of course the numerous film noirs whose protagonists or important characters are artists or art dealers.[33]

Naremore also comments on this phenomenon:

> In *Reframing Abstract Expressionism* (1993), Michael Leja goes further arguing that Hollywood film noir belongs on the same broad cultural terrain as well-known abstract painting by Kline, Pollock, and other members of the New York group. . . . This argument may seem excessively philosophical where Hollywood is concerned, but there can be little doubt that a modernist ideology

involving male subjectivity and urban darkness or primitivism helped to condition a great deal of art in the postwar decades. (171)

With its transgressive matter, its subversion of the Production Code, its depiction of a dark underside to positive thinking, film noir was part of an extraordinary transformation of American culture. As Sussman put it: "The most important contribution of a major subgenre of detective and gangster film in the forties, film noir, similarly served to reduce the optimistic American vision to dust."[34] The result was a "dual consciousness": on the one hand Disneyland, on the other, a "degenerate utopia,"[35] represented in the movies by the split of the plucky 1930s heroines into dull good girls and alluring femme fatales. Paula Rabinowitz goes even further, asserting that film noirs "are emblematic of a cultural process, the pulp modernism of America." According to her, correcting Naremore, film noir should not be seen in its contexts, rather it *is* the context, a "leitmotif running through mid-twentieth-century American culture."[36]

The cultural historian Carl Schorske came to a similar conclusion. While acknowledging the difficulties that post Nietzschean philosophy presents to anyone attempting an overarching view of history, in writing about *fin-de-siècle* Vienna, he was encouraged by the cultural cohesion, however pessimistic, he found in post War America.

> In the decade after 1947, the historical and social optimism that had been associated with the New Deal and the struggle with the Nazis finally broke down. It is true that America had had its wave of pessimism and doubt in the past, with such eloquent statesmen as Poe, Melville, or Henry Adams. But they had not cut very deep into the culture of a nation whose intellectuals were closely integrated into its public life. Now a mood of pessimism—sometimes of impotence, sometimes of rigid defensiveness, sometimes of surrender—settled over an intelligentsia that, whether centrist, radical, liberal or Marxist, had for several decades been united in social optimism. Its shared Enlightenment premises were gravely weakened by a combination of political factors in the early postwar years: the deepening of the Cold War, the first Soviet coup in Czechoslovakia, new revelations of Stalinist iniquities, and the effects, so powerful and so astonishingly ramified throughout all social classes of McCarthyism. It was not so much that these political developments caused the intellectuals to shift political positions or abandon politics entirely, though many did so. More fundamentally the crisis seemed to force a shift in the general philosophic outlook in which liberal or radical political positions had been embedded. In short, the liberals and radicals, almost unconsciously, adapted their world-views to a revolution of falling political expectations.[37]

Whatever name mid-twentieth-century American culture ever gains, film noir will play a major role in its meaning. That film noir was named and first articulated in France points to another dimension of its period quality, that is, its relationship to an international style. Great Britain had its own film noir, its greatest example being *The Third Man*. Directed by Carol Reed with a script by Graham Greene, it starred Joseph Cotten as a disillusioned writer investigating, along with British Intelligence led by Trevor Howard, the allegedly dead Harry Lime (Orson Welles), who of course turns out to be alive. It showed a ruined city, nightclubs, and a spectacular chase through the sewers, all to the haunting tune of its "Third Man Theme" played on a zither. British noirs often made use of such American actors as Welles, Cotten, and Dana Andrews, released from their contracts by the dying Hollywood studios, as did other European countries.[38] Paul Cantor, in fact, in his essay about the relationship between film noir and the Frankfurt School, argues that the vision of America in Hollywood's film noirs, the majority of them created by European directors, is more European than American. It was recognized first in Europe because "the genre embodied a European sensibility in the first place,"[39] to which Vincent Brook's *Driven to Darkness* illustrates was not merely European but Jewish-European.

Tell that to Hammett, Chandler, Cain, Woolrich, Burnett—and Welles and Huston! Film noir was as American as a whiskey sour, and, as already noted, would have occurred, if perhaps not quite so brilliantly, even if Hitler had not provided Hollywood with the best Continental directors. Rather than proving how film noir was essentially European, Cantor illustrates how film noir was an international style. And not just a European or Western one. In Japan, Kurosawa was making contemporary crime and detective stories as well as Samurai epics. We notice that in *Rashomon* (1950), the film that drew the attention of the West to him, the plot consists of the investigation of a crime from multiple perspectives, one of them from the dead man himself, and none of them leading to a definitive solution. Eddie Muller has recently drawn attention to the Argentinean film noirs,[40] and Naremore to Brazilian, Thai, and Norwegian representatives.[41]

Robert Porfirio suggested the philosophic link to these similar developments in his 1976 *Sight and Sound* article, "No Way Out: Existential Motifs in the *Film Noir*,"[42] and his insights have been elaborated by other writers, notably Mark T. Conard, editor of *The Philosophy of Film Noir*.[43] They draw attention to the hard-boiled detective who lives in an existential abyss, a meaningless world where he, like a Hemingway hero, attempts to impose or discover some kind of worth or value, at least in his own challenged integrity. Other protagonists suffer from shifting values, moral ambivalences, confusing signs and signals, leading too often to nowhere in ironic or tragic plots. In this regard, film noir represented the reach of post Nietzschean philosophy and its resultant "normal nihilism"[44] into the world of the popular arts. Wherever one looks in the 1940s and 1950s one finds film noir as expressive of the time. From this perspective, Hitchcock and Wilder, Siodmak and Ulmer join hands with Camus and Sartre.

NOTES

1. See for instance Meyer Schapiro, "Style," in *Anthropology Today*, ed. A. L. Kroeber (Chicago: University of Chicago Press, 1953), 287–312.
2. Heinrich Wolfflin, *Principles of Art History* (New York: Dover, 1950 [1915]).
3. Paul Schrader, "Notes on Film Noir," 54.
4. Raymond Durgnat, "Paint it Black: The Family Tree of *Film Noir*" [1970] in *Film Noir Reader*, 38. Yet in his book *The Strange Case of Alfred Hitchcock: Or the Plain Man's Hitchcock* (London: Faber and Faber, 1974), 295, he calls *Vertigo* a film noir.
5. Jane Root, "Film Noir," in *The Cinema Book*, ed. Pam Cook (New York: Pantheon Books, 1985), 94.
6. Todd Erickson, *Film Noir Reader*, 308.
7. Robert Sklar, *Movie-Made America* (New York: Random House, 1975), 253.
8. Elizabeth Cowie, "Film Noir and Women," in *Shades of Noir: A Reader*, ed. Joan Copjec (London: Verso, 1993), 131.
9. Krutnik, *In a Lonely Street*, 24.
10. Neale, *Genre and Hollywood*, 153–74.
11. Schatz, *Hollywood Genres*, 112.
12. Thomas Schatz, *Boom and Bust: The American Cinema in the 1940s* (New York: Charles Scribner's Sons, 1997), 232.
13. Mike Chopra-Gant, *Hollywood Genre and Postwar America: Masculinity, Family and Nation in Popular Movies and Film Noir* (London: I. B. Tauris, Publisher, 2006), 11.
14. Arnold Hauser, "Style and Its Changes," in *The Philosophy of Art History* (Cleveland, OH: World Publishing Company, 1963), 212–13.
15. Biesen, 96–123.
16. Dorothy Gardiner and Kathrine Sorley Walker, *Raymond Chandler Speaking* (Plainview, NY: Books for Libraries Press, 1971), 52.
17. Schatz, *Hollywood Genres*, 116–17.
18. Robert B. Ray, *A Certain Tendency of the Hollywood Cinema* (Princeton: Princeton University Press, 1985), 153–54.
19. Robert Philip Kolker, *A Cinema of Loneliness: Penn, Kubrick, Scorsese, Spielberg, Altman*, 2nd edition (New York: Oxford University Press, 1988). *Kane* "attempts to grasp the personality of an enigma and to prove the impossibility of such an attempt," 22.
20. Vivian Sobchack, "Lounge Time: Postwar Crises and the Chronotype of Film Noir," in *Refiguring American Film Genres*, ed. Nick Browne (Berkeley: University of California Press, 1998), 153. She calls the 1930s nightclub an "idealized capitalist chronotype."

21. James Ursini, "Noir Westerns," in *Film Noir Reader 4*, 247–59.
22. Ursini, 258–59.
23. Perez, *The Material Ghost*, 249.
24. Neale, *Genre and Hollywood*, 158.
25. Eric Somer, "The Noir-Horror of *Cat People* [1942]," in *Film Noir Reader 4*, 191–203, provides an excellent analysis of how Lewton's films conform to noir conventions.
26. Biesen, 81–84.
27. Named after a character in the first American play, *The Contrast* (1793) by Royall Tyler.
28. Borde and Chaumenton, 203.
29. Barbara Deming, "The Artlessness of Walt Disney," *Partisan Review* XII (1945): 231.
30. Mike Chopra-Gant, *Hollywood Genres and Postwar America*, 18.
31. Warren Sussman, "Did Success Spoil the United States? Dual Representations in Postwar America," in *Recasting America: Culture and Politics in the Age of Cold War*, ed. Larry May (Chicago: University of Chicago Press, 1989), 19–37. Dana Polan also discusses this phenomenon in *Power and Paranoia: History, Narrative, and the American Cinema, 1940–1950* (New York: Columbia University Press, 1986).
32. On this transformation, see James Harvey, *Movie Love in the Fifties* (New York: Alfred A. Knopf, 2001), 123.
33. Kent Minturn discusses the relationship between abstract expressionism and film noir in "Peinture Noire," in *Film Noir Reader 2*, 270–309.
34. Sussman, 29.
35. Sussman, 28–32.
36. Paula Rabinowitz, *Black & White & Noir: America's Pulp Modernism* (New York: Columbia University Press, 2002), 4, 14.
37. Carl Schorske, *Fin-De-Siecle Vienna: Politics and Culture* (New York: Vintage Books, 1981), xxiii.
38. See for instance Andrew Spicer, ed., *European Film Noir* (Manchester: Manchester University Press, 2007).
39. Paul A. Cantor, "Film Noir and the Frankfurt School: Americas as Wasteland," in Edgar Ulmer's *Detour: The Philosophy of Film Noir*, 158.
40. Eddie Muller, "Dateline Buenos Aires," *Noir City Sentinel* 4, no. 1 (March/April 2009): 2.
41. Naremore, *More Than Night*, updated and expanded version (2008), 285–86. See also Jennifer Fay and Justus Nieland, *Film Noir: Hard-Boiled Modernity and the Cultures of Globalization* (London: Routledge, 2010).
42. Porfirio, reprinted in *Film Noir Reader*, 77–93.
43. Conard, 17–20.
44. A phrase used by James C. Edwards to describe the principal contemporary philosophical vision. *The Plain Sense of Things: The Fate of Religion in an Age of Normal Nihilism* (University Park: Pennsylvania State University Press, 1997).

Chapter Six

Alfred Hitchcock

HITCHCOCK AND FILM NOIR

Great artists best define a period, so it is appropriate to end our investigation of period with a consideration of Alfred Hitchcock. For a good part of his life, Hitchcock was considered a mere entertainer, a master of suspense. Not once did he win an Oscar as best director, though *Rebecca*, his first Hollywood film, won the award as Best Picture. In 1967, however, he was presented with the Irving Thalberg award, and in 1979, the year before he died, he was honored with an American Film Institute Life Achievement Award. In 1965 Robin Wood published *Hitchcock's Films*,[1] the first appreciative and sustained analysis of his work, and in 1968 Andrew Sarris, following the *Cahiers du Cinema* crowd, admitted him into the Pantheon of auteurs.[2] As with Shakespeare, his reputation took time to grow, until at present, like Shakespeare, he can be studied as a genre in his own right. But just as Shakespeare existed in a historic era and can be seen in terms of the "Elizabethan World Picture," so can Hitchcock be considered in terms of classic film noir, the period between 1940 and 1960 which coincides with his greatest films.

In "Hitchcock at the Margins of Noir," James Naremore undertook such a study.[3] As in *More than Night*, he implicitly treats film noir as a genre. How else could he place Hitchcock at its margins? He remarks that the discourse on film noir includes a "heterogeneous group" but:

> Even so, we can make a few generalizations about them. Considered generically, they involve what Jean Paul Sartre called "extreme situations" and are usually located in a realistic realm to one side of Gothic horror and dystopian science fiction. Stylistically, they tend to be associated with angular photography, subjective modes of narration, and an approximately Freudian or deterministic

view of character. Commercially, they blur the distinction between violent melodrama and art movies.[4]

Naremore continues by noting the many similarities between Hitchcock's work and film noir. He calls attention to: the British thrillers being a source of film nor; the arrival of Hitchcock in Hollywood coinciding with the "so called classic or historic period of Hollywood noir"; the fact that reviewers compared both *The Maltese Falcon* and *Double Indemnity* to Hitchcock's earlier work; favorite Hitchcockian themes and motifs that also characterize film noir such as the "wrong man plot" and "the rear window motif"; and certain noir character types, such as the obsessed detective and the psychopathic killer. He then concludes by comparing Hitchcock to Welles, the other cinematic giant who frames the entire period, and "who seemed equally attuned to a *noirish* repertory of situations and images."[5]

Why then has Hitchcock not been more central to discussion of film noir? Naremore refers to Hitchcock's status as a genre in his own right, but more importantly, he cites four aspects of Hitchcock that separate him from film noir. First, his Britishness—by which he means that the world of Hitchcock's films, its manners, sophistication, and whimsy—is much closer to Agatha Christie than to Dashiell Hammett and Raymond Chandler. Then there's his "Suspense and classical form." Suspense depends more on clarity than disorientation, and "Because of his desire to play games of suspense, Hitchcock is concerned with symmetrical design, straightforward narrative logic, and classical editing" as illustrated notably in *Strangers on a Train*, his "supposedly authentic *film noir*." A third un-noirish aspect concerns "Woman and mass culture." Whereas Naremore sees film noir as essentially masculine and misogynist, he points out that Hitchcock repeatedly "invited his audience to identify with the point of view of women." And the fourth is "Nostalgia." The sense of the past which haunts so many film noir protagonists "has more to do with personal than historic time." But in Hitchcock's work, the past tends to be the nineteenth century, the old world contrasted to the new.[6]

Yet at the end of his essay, after a short commentary on *Vertigo* as an example of the role of nostalgia in Hitchcock's work, Naremore somewhat reverses field.

> In the last analysis, therefore one could argue that Hitchcock is central to the larger, more broadly cultural history of *noir*, or to the long tradition of what the Victorians called "sensation fiction." He seems marginal only in a somewhat parochial context, when we consider him in relation to the American *film noir*'s Hollywood manifestation in the 1940s and 1950s.[7]

Despite all these valuable insights, let us reverse his perspective and suggest that American film noir be seen, borrowing a phrase from Naremore, in the context of Hitchcock. He is not just a source of film noir, but along with Lang and Welles one of its principal creators. From the 1920s onward he made film noirs. By my count, in Hollywood he directed no less than nine generic noirs (see below), more than any other major director except Lang, who also, by my count, made nine, and not a single film he made during the historic period from 1940 to 1960 lacks numerous noirish elements. Exceptions to Naremore's four non-noir qualities abound, and all of them have more to do with the style of film noir than the genre. No director was better at having extreme situations erupt into ordinary life, a characteristic of Hitchcock's films as prominent as the well-known transfer of guilt. And as to Hitchcock's feminine perspectives, rather than making him marginal to film noir, they make him a deeper, more profound proponent of the troubling visions and incongruities which characterize noir at its best. No wonder then that, as Naremore reports, Billy Wilder exclaimed at the outset of *Double Indemnity* that he intended to "out Hitchcock Hitchcock."[8]

Received opinion tells us that *The Lodger: A Story of the London Fog* (1927), although the third film directed by Hitchcock, is the first one that incorporates the suspenseful vision that would characterize his work thereafter. Like the German crime films that influenced it, *The Lodger* displays many

Figure 6.1.   Shades of UFA: Ivor Novello in *The Lodger*

elements of film noir and from the point of view of style *is* a film noir. So much so that it supports Bordwell's argument that the classic period of film noir had nothing new to offer, at least in terms of style. From the title onward, we see a dark city haunted by a serial killer. It abounds with chiaroscuro compositions, a prominent dark stairway, surreal shots such as the suspect seen from below through a glass ceiling, and flashbacks. Then too the characters look familiar. There's a flirty blonde model, Daisy (June), who seems headed for genuine trouble, a policeman and suitor to Daisy, Joe (Malcolm Keen), who allows jealousy to trump his professionalism, and a hysterical citizenry who turn into a lynch mob. Above all, there's the Lodger himself (Ivor Novello), a strange and disturbed upper class type whom Bettina Rosenbladt compares to the killer somnambulist in *The Cabinet of Dr. Caligari* (1920) and the vampire in *Nosferatu* (1922).[9] Hitchcock however gives a twist to the novel by Mrs. Belloc Lowndes on which he based his film. In the novel the lodger turns out to *be* Jack the Ripper. In the film, set in contemporary time, the lodger turns out to be a wrong man, unjustly suspected of the serial crimes. Although Hitchcock has teased the audience throughout with suspicions about the lodger, at the end he goes out of his way to provide a happy, romantic, even comical conclusion to the whole nightmarish story. This turn of events does not convince Rosenbladt, who believes the film so ambivalent that the ending leaves open the possibility that Daisy has married a serial murderer, contrary to Lesley Brill's reading of the film in which he claims that *The Lodger* announces Hitchcock's major concern—romance.[10] I believe Brill is right, about the ending at least, but Rosenbladt's ideas about doubles in Hitchcock's work can be rightly applied to Hitchcock himself, who, when it comes to romantic love vs. misogyny proves to be the real double agent.

From the perspective of film noir as a genre, *The Lodger* falls short. There's nothing fallible about the lodger. Though a bit eccentric, he is an admirable young man. Like the police, he too carries on a search for the Avenger, the true villain whom we never see. In a flashback we discover that the Avenger began his crime spree by murdering the lodger's sister, a fact which explains the lodger's sensitivity to the crime and associations with the murderer. Suspicion however is not enough; a genuine noir protagonist must in some way become fallible and make a false step.

This development takes place in *Blackmail* (1929), by my reckoning Hitchcock's first complete film noir, and indeed the first British one. Remember, however, that a genre cannot come into being until there are a group of such films. The protagonist in this case is Alice White (Anny Ondra), the daughter of a lower middle class shop owner (not unlike Hitchcock's own parent) who is a bit of a flirt. She has a steady boyfriend, Frank (John Longden), a police detective no less, but they behave more like a not too happily married couple than sweethearts. At a crowded tea room, while arguing about whether or not to go to the pictures, she removes from her purse a note from another man encouraging her to meet him at this same place. He (Cyril Ritchard) shows up, and she communicates to him through gestures, at first warning him off. But when Frank becomes surly at her indecision and impatiently stomps outside to the entrance, he sees her leave the establishment in the company of Ritchard.

As so often in film noir, the villain, or in this case the potential villain, is a male artist or aesthete, not quite a Waldo Lydecker type, but definitely better educated and more sophisticated than the lower class, almost tart like Alice and her former "Bobbie," up from the ranks boyfriend. Ritchard, whom we learn is Mr. Crewe, entices a somewhat willing Alice up to his studio. Guiding her hand, he helps her draw an outline of a nude woman, and then encourages her to put on a slight dancing costume, which she does. He plays the piano and sings a suggestive ballad, "Miss Up-To-Date" with lines such

Figure 6.2. Now what? Anny Ondra in *Blackmail*

as "They say you're wild," while she changes. When she is in costume, he first kisses her. Then when she resists and tries to leave, he attempts to rape her, drawing her behind a curtain onto his bed. She cries out; her hand emerges from behind the curtain, feeling at a table, and finds a knife. Next we see Crewe's hand fall out. She has stabbed and killed him. The villain has become the victim.

Rather than call the police and claim rape and self defense, she erases her name on the sketch and wanders dazed to her home. Not surprisingly, Frank is assigned to the case, and while examining the studio recognizes the body as that of his rival, and then discovers Alice's glove at the scene of the crime. Like a true noir officer of the law, he conceals the evidence and begins his descent into becoming a rogue cop.

Alice and Crewe were observed by a not too savory street person, hanging about the doorway, evidently waiting for Crewe, and asking him for money, to which Crewe condescendingly obliges. What criminal past does this suggest? This same man, Tracy (Donald Calthrope), then sees Alice leave and follows her to her father's tobacco shop on the King's Road. Later he finds Alice and Frank and devilishly confronts them with Alice's other glove and the prospect of blackmail. To this Frank responds by indicating he will pin the crime on Tracy and that his word and Alice's will trump any testimony Tracy could give. Meanwhile, the police, upon questioning the landlady, discover that a man has been hanging about the flat, and she is able to identify him in police photos as Tracy. The inspector calls Frank and gives him the news, which Frank conveys to the now somewhat jittery Tracy. As the police arrive to arrest him, Tracy bolts and races through the streets, the police in hot pursuit. He runs into the British Museum and frantically climbs to the dome above the reading room. We see the chase silhouetted in the distance, and then in a close up, Tracy stops and falls through the glass of the dome to his death.

Meanwhile Alice writes a confession of her "crime," and goes to the police station to turn herself in. But fortunate phone calls and interruptions prevent her from doing this. Frank, who keeps warning her off, finally leads her out of the station, where the two of them laugh hysterically with a sergeant who has told them a joke about her being a detective and Frank losing his job, the same sergeant who whispered a joke to Alice when she first appears in the film. Thus we have an ordinary woman who takes a series of wrong steps: two timing her undeserving boyfriend, visiting a strange man's apartment, flirting with him, undressing, and then though legally no doubt innocent of murder, walking away from the scene of the crime. By the same token, Frank is also not evil. He's conflicted between love and duty and chooses love. But his actions bring about the death of Tracy, who while guilty of blackmail and other possible minor crimes, certainly did not deserve to die. So as in subsequent noirs, the values—good girl, good cop, young love, ordinary domestic life and arrangements, the justice of the legal system, all become twisted and perverted, not by evil intentions but by chance and faulty decisions.

We notice too that the film begins with a police procedural, as "the flying squad," a high tech police unit tracks down a suspect, who looks something like Tracy, arrests and interrogates him, puts him in the "Identification Parade" (aka "line up"), where he is fingered by a young blonde, not unlike Alice, then charges him, fingerprints him and confines him in a cell. Whereas such efficiency assures the audience in the manner of gangbusters, the rest of the film completely undercuts any confidence one might have in law enforcement, as the same flying squad pursues the unfortunate Tracy to his death.

Unlike Hitchcock's American films, no trace of "Britishness" appears: the setting is seedy and lower middle class; the White's live in the back of their store; the police procedural takes place in a slum; even the artist's studio looks tacky (he after all lives on an upper floor and has no separate bedroom).

Figure 6.3. Alice (Anny Ondra) wanders in *Blackmail*

Hitchcock also makes effective use of the characteristic noir visual style. Slanted shadows appear on the faces of the police and abound on the walls. When Alice emerges from Crewe's flat, the camera cuts to a dark vertical stair well, very much like the one in the tower in *Vertigo*. When Alice leaves her bedroom to go down to breakfast, the shadows on the wall form a kind of web surrounding her.

Even more noirish is Alice's return to her home, a long sequence which employs subjective camera work typical of later noirs. She walks like a somnambulist or amnesiac, as if in a dream. People like ghosts pass her on either side. She sees an electric sign of a cocktail shaker as a knife; she sees extended arms everywhere, on vagrants, on a policeman, but also flashbacks to the arm of the murdered man. On one such image, the film cuts to the landlady screaming as she too sees the extended arm. Big Ben indicates 11:45 PM, but after an aerial shot of London, the film cuts to an empty Trafalgar Square at dawn. Though she lived nearby Mr. Crewe, Alice has completely lost track of time and has been wandering all night long. Then at breakfast, as a gossipy neighbor talks about methods of murder, the sound track becomes subjective as all Alice hears is the word "knife" repeated ever more loudly, until when asked to cut the morning bread, Alice throws the bread knife in the air, hysterically attempting to separate herself from her deed. All such distortions depart from classical form and in the 1940s became part of film noirs visual and narrative vocabulary. In every respect, from every angle, *Blackmail* is an accomplished and complete film noir, as we have since come to understand it.

Credit for being the creator of noir must also go to Fritz Lang, who older than Hitchcock and more established had been directing crime films from the early 1920s on. Brook calls him "The Father of Film Noir" and believes that *M* (1931) was the original of the genre.

> What *M* managed to accomplish, similar to what Griffith's *The Birth of a Nation* (1915) had done for the classical Hollywood style and what Welles's *Citizen Kane* (1941) would do to counter that style, was to refine, expand on, and consolidate previous cinematic developments into a coherent, if loosely defined, *system* that would come to be known (largely after the fact) as film noir.[11]

When considering *M*, made two years after *Blackmail* and to my mind the second complete noir ever made, I find it hard to believe that Lang had not seen *The Lodger*. Both films deal with a contemporary city at night, a serial killer, a distraught populace, and documentary, like police procedures, including similar maps plotting the movements of the killer. Undoubtedly, Hitchcock was directly influenced by Weimar films, but the fact that he was

English and Catholic, not Austrian and Jewish, points to the period aspect of film noir and its multiple origins.

Critics of the time of course saw *M* and the early Hitchcocks in other contexts, film noir not yet existing in enough examples to come into consciousness as a genre. Strange as it may seem, Hitchcock and Lang never met, either at UFA or in Hollywood, at least there is no record of any such meeting. Yet, the two were clearly aware of each other's work and may well have influenced each other. Thomas Elsaesser, the vehement denier of film noir, has recently written an excellent essay comparing Hitchcock and Lang.[12] He notes their common interest in wrong-man plots, women's films, anti-Nazi and Cold War films, and surprisingly, given his earlier remarks, states, "What the thriller was for Hitchcock, *film noir* became for Lang: a genre he could give his own distinctive stamp."[13]

Before Robin Wood and the auteur theory taught us to see the coherence of Hitchcock's work, it used to be the fashion to deride his Hollywood efforts, as well as Hollywood in general, in contrast to his British works of the 1930s. What gave them their own distinctive stamp, the visual stamp of the Hitchcock thriller, was of course what we now term film noir. Among these crime films and spy melodramas two stand out as generic film noirs. *The 39 Steps* (1935) is the most fully realized and accomplished film of his British period. Despite its comic plot—Stanley Cavell might even consider it a comedy of remarriage[14]—it also belongs to film noir. When Richard Hannay (Robert Donat), the protagonist, risks a sexual liaison with a mysterious femme fatale type who asks shelter in his flat, he blunders into a life-threatening adventure that pits him against both a ring of spies and the law. "Well," he says, to her, "it's your funeral," as it literally turns out to be. After she dies in his arms, stabbed in the back, he neglects to call the police. Rather he engineers the first of his five escapes with the help of a milkman, to whom he pretends to have been carrying on an adulterous affair. In Scotland, where he has gone to investigate the crime of which he naturally has become the chief suspect, he appears to be propositioning the unhappily married Peggy Ashcroft who, despite the rage of her jealous husband, helps him flee the police. Later he forces Madeleine Carroll, a woman who knows too much, to spend the night with him at an inn, threatening her and engaging in some comical and seemingly innocent sexual abuse. Throughout the film he flirts with sexual transgression and continually makes decisions and takes actions which further implicate him as a killer. Once again, all the basic elements of noir, including its visual style, are present. As the concept of film noir was still a decade away, critics and public alike perceived this film and its predecessors in the two intertwined categories of "Hitchcock" and "thriller."

The other spy melodrama is *Sabotage* (1936). As in *Blackmail*, the main protagonist is a woman, Mrs. Sylvia Verloc (Sylvia Sidney), who is married to an older man (Oscar Homolka), the two of them operating a neighborhood movie house, The Bijou. Unbeknownst to her, Mr. Verloc is a secret agent, a rather weak man who does not mind sabotaging a power plant and putting London in darkness, but has some qualms about mass killings. In a scene at the Aquarium of the London Zoo, his superior overcomes them. Another conspirator delivers a bomb to him in a bird cage which is to be exploded at the Piccadilly Circus underground at 1:45 on the Lord Mayor's Day. Because detective Ted Spencer (John Loder) is watching him, he cannot deliver the bomb himself, so he enlists Sylvia's younger brother Stevie (Desmond Tester) to take the bomb instead. By means of accidental delays, and suspenseful cross cuttings between his journey and clocks, Stevie cannot arrive on time. Shockingly, because popular movies, especially in the 1930s did not kill children, he and the bus on which he rides are blown up. On discovering what has happened and why, Sylvia in shock contemplates stabbing her obnoxious husband, who wants her to get on with their life and possibly have a kid to replace Stevie. He seems to discern what she is thinking, as she repeatedly picks up and drops a carving knife, and when he approaches her, ostensibly to take it away, she stabs and kills him.

Figure 6.4.   Guilty? Sylvia Sidney in *Sabotage*

So we have a grungy noir world, a weak and unlikeable saboteur, and now his formerly innocent wife who has turned, like Alice White, into a somewhat justified murderer. At this point the film, admittedly a bit late in the proceedings, becomes completely noir. Ted, who had earlier posed as a greengrocer in the shop next to the theater and had flirted with Sylvia in order to get information about Verloc, upon discovering the corpse, professes his love for her and quickly concocts a plan for their escape together. Like Frank in *Blackmail*, he turns rogue cop and chooses love over duty. She however, resists, but before she can confess, the other conspirator, the odd little bomb maker (William Dewhurst) has returned to pick up the birdcage and incriminating evidence. Trapped behind the movie screen, he detonates another bomb, blowing up himself and the corpse of Verloc. Ted and Sylvia—another ironic triumph of romance?—are freed from their crimes, contemplated and actual.

From 1940 to 1958, Hitchcock worked in several genres besides women's films: spy thrillers—*Foreign Correspondent* (1940), *Saboteur* (1942), and *The Man Who Knew Too Much* (1956); a screwball comedy of remarriage—*Mr. & Mrs. Smith* (1941); war movies—*Lifeboat* (1944); period melodrama—*Under Capricorn* (1949); mysteries or whodunits—*Stage Fright* (1950) and *To Catch a Thief* (1955), which is also something of a romantic comedy; and black comedy—*The Trouble with Harry* (1955). His greatest

Figure 6.5. The street where Uncle Charlie lived in *Shadow of a Doubt*

films of the time, however, belong to the genre he helped to create, a genre marked by personal guilt, ordinary life, and familiar scenes fraught with danger and death. He didn't need to see *The Maltese Falcon* or *Citizen Kane*; he simply continued making his own kind of film. With *Shadow of a Doubt* (1943), the period caught up with him.

Shadow of a Doubt begins when Uncle Charlie (Joseph Cotten), a suspected serial killer, escapes from a bleak urban environment to visit his family in the small, "green world" town of Santa Rosa, California. There in a humdrum household whose henpecked patriarch (Henry Travers) invents murder stories with his nerdy pal (Hume Cronyn), he meets his nemesis, his niece, Little Charlie (Teresa Wright).[15] At first enamored of her glamorous and mysterious uncle, she becomes suspicious of his past and undertakes her investigation, in which she is soon joined by two detectives (Macdonald Carey and Wallace Ford) posing as journalists. Once she finds proof of his guilt, after he more or less confesses it to her in a memorable speech in which he describes the world as a sty (Thornton Wilder, author of the prize winning play *Our Town*, was the screenwriter), rather than turning him in, she becomes a kind of accomplice telling him to get out of town or she will kill him herself. He in turn makes several attempts to kill her. Suddenly, the detectives announce that the real killer has been apprehended and Uncle Charlie (the right man not the wrong one) prepares to depart. But he lures Little Charlie onto the train, prevents her from disembarking, and as the train picks up speed takes her between two cars and attempts to throw her onto the tracks in the path of a locomotive approaching from the other direction. Instead, in the ensuing struggle, Uncle Charlie falls to the tracks, pushed not only by his own momentum, but as a close look as the sequence reveals, by Little Charlie. So here we have the whole noir package: a psychologically deranged serial killer who cannot escape from his past; a seemingly innocent female protagonist who shields the killer and is instrumental in killing him; the sunny small town America turned into a dark nightmare; two interlocking investigations, even a smoky dive and a dark stairway. That no one perceived it at the time as anything new illustrates how Hitchcock had made film noir his own domain over a decade before it became public property. Wilder commenced *Double Indemnity* a year later.

In *Spellbound*, one cannot help wondering if Ben Hecht, the screenwriter, and Hitchcock too, were not having fun with Freud, despite the deadpan approach to the subject. For the Oedipus complex, central to Freud's theories, is never mentioned despite the fact that Gregory Peck has an Oedipal crush on the motherly Ingrid Bergman and must displace Leo G. Carroll as the head of the sanatorium where she works. Instead his malady results from guilt over a childhood accident whereby he caused the death of his brother.

Spellbound, in the person of Ingrid Bergman, transformed the 1930s convention of the looney psychiatrist into a figure of sympathy and wisdom. Who would not wish to be cured by her? It is also a good example of how film noir alters the conventions of the whodunit. Instead of an investigation of a murder by some kind of super sleuth, the film begins with the mental ailments of Gregory Peck, who turns out to be a returning G.I. suffering from amnesia. Only after his collapse do we find out that a murder has occurred and that he is charged with it. Bergman, however, the chief investigator, does not attempt to solve the crime; instead she tries to unravel Peck's tortured psyche. Peck, of course, is not entirely innocent. We discover he has assumed the identity of the murder victim and attempted to take his place as the head of the mental hospital. He, not the murder, becomes the center of the mystery, and the solution of the crime occurs, almost accidentally, after he has been cured.

Notorious would seem to belong in Hitchcock's spy thriller category, but it too twists the conventions of that genre into a film noir. Alicia (Ingrid Bergman) is the notorious one of the title. Guilt over her father's Nazi past has driven her to drink and promiscuity, turning her into, as a campy song of the time put it, "a dypso-nympho maniac, a bundle of good clean fun." Devlin, a Dudley-Do-Right CIA agent (Cary Grant) recruits her to work for the agency, and then the two fall in love. Instead of rescuing her from a sordid sexual past however, as a genuine romantic hero might attempt to do, Devlin, unlike Frank in *Blackmail*, chooses duty over love, becoming a kind of pimp and thrusting her into the arms of Alex (Claude Rains), one of her former lovers who now heads a Nazi cell in Brazil. At the race track in Rio, where Alicia has arranged to meet Devlin in order to pass on information, she delivers one of the most shocking Production Code era lines: "You can add Alex to my list of playmates." Imagine! Ingrid Bergman, the ideal woman, not long since a nun, has slept with an older man and then married him at the behest of the younger man she truly loves. Then to add to the complexity, and to give the film a further Freudian touch, Alex, who shares a name with Alicia—and at first a more appreciative and sympathetic admirer of her than Devlin—is himself dominated by an austere and suspicious mother. As Alicia and Devlin investigate Alex, so he begins his own investigation of her, and, discovering that she's an agent, begins slowly to poison her. Devlin discovers this counter plot, recovers his manhood, and goes to the rescue leaving Alex at the mercy of his murderous colleagues, the victim in fact of his treacherous wife. Because Bergman and Grant are such appealing stars, only on second thought does one realize how the conventions of World War II spy thrillers have been turned upside down and how the name Hitchcock and the decorous look of the movie have subverted the Production Code.[16]

The Paradine Case (1947) illustrates two truisms. First, all the talent in the world folded into one film does not make a good movie. Here, one of the greatest directors of all time joins Lee Garmes, the cinematographer, Franz Waxman the composer, Travis Banton the dress designer, and then a dozen or more superb actors including Gregory Peck, Charles Laughton, Ethel Barrymore, Charles Coburn, Ann Todd, Leo G. Carroll, and Louis Jourdan, but all to no avail. Did David Selznick, who took credit for screenwriter, push aside the two better writers assigned to the case, Ben Hecht and Alma Reville (Mrs. Hitchcock)? Was Valli, the female star and femme fatale, too cold and unsympathetic, the opposite of Bergman who also betrayed her husbands in both *Casablanca* and *Notorious*? One wonders how Peck, never notable for passionate excess, could have fallen for her. Did Hitchcock's head, like Homer's, nod, or did his dislike for Selznick freeze his genius? The film died at the box office, and time has done nothing to resurrect it. And second, just being a film noir does not make a film a good movie. A murder, a prolonged investigation, a femme fatale, and an upright lawyer who falls for her: the ingredients are here, but they remain lifeless. Remember that Ed Wood also made a film noir, *Jail Bait* (1954).

Rope suffers from being a gimmick, an interesting experiment, namely a film presented as though made with one long shot that really contributes little to the film except novelty. It is also one of the very few noirs filmed in color, which in this case makes it duller to watch. Essentially, it is a filmed play (written by Patrick Hamilton) nothing more. John Dall and Farley Granger, two seemingly homosexual lovers, strangle a straight friend. They want to commit a perfect crime in order to prove themselves Nietzschean super men, beyond good and evil, and then invite their friends to a party in order to celebrate their superiority over normal emotions such as guilt. One of the guests is James Stewart, their former prep school teacher, whose proto-Nazi philosophy inspired them to commit the crime. In the original play, he too was homosexual. The investigation here consists of Stewart getting wise to them, whereupon they lose their nerve and make mistakes which help him to expose the crime and, as a result his own complicity in it. At one point, Cedric Hardwicke, the victim's father, delivers a rebuke to Stewart's philosophy, and this serves as the moral center of the film. It's a minimalist noir but a noir nevertheless, and unlike *The Paradine Case*, it improves on repeated viewings.

Strangers on a Train appears on most noir lists, and for good reasons, among them Raymond Chandler as screenwriter. It unites the psychotic killer Bruno (Robert Walker) with the not so innocent husband Guy (Farley Granger). Just as Bruno wishes his father were dead, so Guy wishes his shrewish, unfaithful wife Miriam (Kasey Rogers, credited as Laura Elliot).

At least he wishes she would give him a divorce so that he could marry Anne (Ruth Roman), daughter of a prominent Washington senator. But as she is pregnant (by someone else?) and as Guy is becoming a successful tennis star, she refuses his offer. When Bruno suggests that they exchange killings, two strangers who could never be connected with the murders, Guy humors Bruno, recognizing him as a nut case. But Bruno thinks Guy has accepted his proposition. He proceeds to Guy's home town and follows the flirtatious wife to an amusement park where he strangles her. She thus joins Gene Tierney in *Leave Her to Heaven* as one of the few pregnant women ever killed in a Hollywood movie,[17] in this, the most misogynist of all Hitchcock's films. At one point Bruno even frightens Hitchcock's daughter Pat, a guest at a cocktail party given by Bruno's father and attended by his airhead mother. Hitchcock would say, "It's only a movie," but tell that to feminist critics Laura Mulvey and Tania Modleski. Needless to say, Guy becomes the chief suspect in the murder. His only alibi, that he was on another train at the time of the death, proves futile as the stranger with whom he conversed was too drunk to remember his being there. Only a single clue and Bruno's return to the scene of the crime, the ominous amusement park at night, a favorite noir locale, absolve Guy of the crime. The Production Code also helped clean up the plot, as in the novel on which the film is based, written by Patricia Highsmith, Guy also becomes a murderer. Hitchcock likes to link good guy protagonists to the villains, making them secret sharers of guilt and murderous intentions. It's a device which gives his thrillers psychological depth and interest. It is also typical of film noir. *Strangers on a Train* carries the association to the limit. So notwithstanding its straightforward narrative logic, a logic it shares with *The Maltese Falcon* and *The Asphalt Jungle*, this film belongs not on the margins of noir but near its center.

Throughout the 1950s, Hitchcock continued to make film noirs, or to the less aware, simply Hitchcock films. In *I Confess*, a Catholic priest (Montgomery Clift) becomes the chief suspect in a murder case. He is of course innocent, but having heard the confession of the actual murderer, he is prevented by the sacredness of the confessional from revealing the truth. Yet, in the course of the investigation carried out by Karl Malden, the audience discovers that this wrong man, this priest upon whom guilt has been transferred, is in fact guilty of spending the night with his old girlfriend, Anne Baxter, who married another man while he was away at war. Despite the efforts of the Production Code to convince us that the two were only caught in the rain and that no adulterous liaison occurred, the film makes no sense at all, unless like Dido and Aeneas, the two had committed some transgression worthy of blackmail. Thus Hitchcock adds a new dimension to the noir convention of the false step and allows his hero's virtue to entrap him and lead to an implicitly guilty past.

Dial M for Murder (1954) would seem to be a women's film, except for two twists. One, the wife (Grace Kelly) is not an innocent—she has a lover; and two, she, the intended victim, becomes the killer. In contrast *Rear Window* (1954) would only seem to be a noir. It has a story by noir source Cornell Woolrich, a murder, a prolonged investigation, and a fallible, symbolically castrated protagonist, L. B. Jeffries (James Stewart) a voyeur who like the villain, Lars Thorwald (Raymond Burr) wants to get rid of his woman, Lisa Fremont (Grace Kelly). L. B.'s a man afraid to make a commitment, and in a clever reversal becomes the woman of the film. Passively, he watches Lisa get the evidence of Thorwald's crime, and he almost becomes Thorwald's second victim, until the police and Lisa come to the rescue, though not before he suffers a second symbolic castration. We should also note that in all four of the films starring Stewart, Hitchcock brings out the dark side of Mr. Smith. In *Rope* he's guilty of a proto-Nazi philosophy; in *Rear Window* he suffers from a passive misogyny; in *The Man Who Knew Too Much*, he's a chauvinistic, domineering husband; and in *Vertigo* he begins like L. B. Jeffries but ends as a madman.

Structurally, however, *Rear Window* conforms more closely to a romantic comedy than to a film noir. In it an emotionally crippled male *eiron* comes to his senses, and a ditzy society dame who loves him proves she has the right stuff. The crime solved, the murderer caught, the happy now united couple commence their future life of blissful domesticity. But then *Rear Window* could also be seen as a women's film, for there can be no doubt that Hitchcock sympathizes much more with Lisa, backed up as she is by the common sense and plain-speaking nurse (Thelma Ritter) than he does with the inert Jeffries. As in other women's films, Lisa is caught between two inadequate men, the one she prefers, an Ashley Wilkes type, not sexually aggressive enough, the other a sadistic murderer. And as in other women's films and fiction, the male must be tamed or rendered safe, in this case by having *both* legs broken. To further complicate matters, most viewers, then as now, would regard *Rear Window* as a thriller, or as a film by Hitchcock. As such the film illustrates the fluidity of genres and what to the skeptic of categories looks to be the arbitrariness of attempting to define them.

Rear Window is also a perfect example of the ambiguity or tight rope walk Hitchcock performs when it comes to the battle of the sexes. On the one hand he advocates romantic love, monogamy, and a deep sympathy for his heroines, such as Ingrid Bergman, Grace Kelly, and Doris Day. But on the other hand, he mocks marriage—as with the film's honeymooners and Miss Torso's choice of mate—and he has a long record of injuring and killing women who know too much. L. B., in a sense, sends Lisa into harm's way, where she is pushed around and almost killed by the murderous Thorwald. In the end Lisa Fremont triumphs, but then does that mark the end of the exciting career as an action photographer of L.B. Jeffries?

The Wrong Man (1957), though noir-like, and having many cinematic and philosophic virtues, has never proven popular, though that judgment may change. James Naremore is reported to have said it is the most depressing commercial film in American cinema.[18] Whatever its merits, it fails as an example of the genre not the style of film noir because the wrong man (Henry Fonda) is completely innocent, and the pathos of pure victimization does not prove as engaging as the drama of fallibility, as in the film that succeeded it.

VERTIGO

Vertigo is not only Hitchcock's most profound work, it is also the consummate film noir, the one that concludes the classic period and according to Rich commences neo-noir.[19] Like almost all films in the noir genre, or in any genre for that matter, it lacks an ingredient, namely black and white photography. But even that was not an essential, as shown as early as 1945 by *Leave Her To Heaven* and Hitchcock's own *Rope* and *Dial M for Murder*. In every other aspect of genre and style it is super-abundant.

According to Foster Hirsch, "The investigator, the victim, and the psychopath are the central figures in noir's basic story patterns."[20] *D.O.A.* combines the investigator with the victim, and numerous psychopaths could be considered victims of society, but only in *Vertigo* does the principal character John "Scotty" Ferguson (James Stewart), a man of several names, unite all three basic roles. Like his hard-boiled antecedents, he used to be a detective on the San Francisco police force, but now he has retired, not for insubordination but for medical reasons. He suffers from vertigo, a dizziness that overcomes him when looking down from heights. Whether this condition was caused by the trauma of his near death during a roof top chase that serves as the prologue to the film, or whether in fact it caused him to slip, we do not know. But what is clear, his near death caused the death of a policeman who tried to pull him back up on the roof. Thus Scotty, like other noir heroes, is a victim of guilt from a past which cannot be redeemed. He too is a confused World War II vet, perhaps the last one of the period. Just how confused we only realize as the film progresses. In the meantime, he is unemployed until called by Gavin Elster (Tom Helmore), an old college chum who, in accord with noir conventions, hires him as a private eye to investigate Mrs. Elster. Like many other such contracts, the job turns out to be a bogus one that masks the real plot. Only Scotty, unlike Sam Spade, does not get wise to the deception until too late. He's not even suspicious.

Instead, he becomes Elster's victim. Knowing of Scotty's disability, Elster has concocted a perfect crime. Of course we too are taken in by the deceit and do not know this until two thirds of the way through the film. Scotty does not trail Mrs. Elster. Rather he trails Elster's mistress, Judy Barton (Kim Novak), who pretends to be Madeleine Elster. According to Elster, Madeleine is suicidal, seemingly possessed by the spirit of her dead great grandmother, Carlotta Valdez. In the good old days of the Barbary Coast when men could wander and be free, the beautiful Carlotta became the mistress of a wealthy scoundrel who abandoned her, causing her to wander poor and forlorn through the Western Addition until she took her own life. The fake Madeleine pretends to go into trances, lose track of time and place, and become Carlotta. Thus she visits Carlotta's grave in the Mission Dolores cemetery; she drives to the Palace of the Legion of Honor where she sits before a portrait of Carlotta (I wish the museum would acquire the original of this portrait!);[21] she rents a room in the old gothic looking McKittrick House, one of Carlotta's former homes and now a hotel; and after many days of leading Scotty around San Francisco, she finally goes to the Old Fort, just beneath the Golden Gate Bridge, where she leaps into the bay. As was predictable, Scotty dives in and rescues her, takes the unconscious beauty to his apartment (on the corner of Jones and Lombard streets), removes her wet clothing—she all the while feigning to be unconscious—and waits for her to recover. Now that they have met, he does not reveal that he works for her husband. Instead he falls in love.

On the next day, as he again follows her, the trail winds back to his own apartment where she has gone to thank him, no doubt certain that he is not far behind. The two meet, and from this point on Scotty is hooked. They begin to spend their days together, wandering. Like Jeff Bailey in *Out of the Past*, Scotty not only attempts to save the woman in question but also betrays his client by making love to her. A true noir hero, he violates a moral and professional code, takes a false step, and enters a darker world from which he may or may not be able to extricate himself. Putting together the hints Madeleine has planted about her past, he figures out that as a child she must have visited the mission at San Juan Bautista, not far down the Peninsula from San Francisco. If, he imagines, she could see that it is a real place, not a spirit vision of Carlotta's childhood, she might be cured. Unaware this is Elster's plan, he takes her to the mission. Now lovers, they embrace in the old stable across the plaza from the church, but she breaks from him, runs to the church tower (a studio fabrication) and before Scotty, still afflicted with his vertigo, can stop her, she climbs to the top and leaps to her death. At the inquest, the coroner (Henry Jones), mercilessly rules the death a suicide while blaming Scotty for negligence of duty. Elster consoles him and disappears "scot" free, never to be seen again.[22] So ends the first half of the film, almost like an intermission.

The second half begins like the first with a kind of dream sequence, another noir convention, the hallucinatory nightmare, only now in Technicolor. Like Madeleine and Carlotta, Scotty too falls through space into a grave, and, like a Cornell Woolrich hero, he wakes up insane[23]—a victim of a fate over which he has no control. No longer free to wander, he is taken to a mental hospital where he remains for a long period of time in a catatonic state. Once released, he begins to wander again, only now Scotty confines his journeys to the itineraries previously set by Madeleine, longing for her miraculous return. He now enters into the psychopathic phase of his persona.

Walking along a busy San Francisco street, he spots a pretty red head who resembles the blonde Madeleine. He follows her to her hotel and asks permission to speak to her. No clear headed young woman would ever allow such a creepy type, even if he looked like Jimmy Stewart, to enter her hotel room, but this girl does. At first we suspect she is just a lonely bimbo, Judy Barton from Salina, Kansas, who is comforted by Scotty, an older man with money who wants to befriend her. As he gains her confidence, and he is frank about his lost love, he begins transforming her into Madeleine. In her famous article "Visual Pleasure and Narrative Cinema," Laura Mulvey describes very well how Scotty's actions fuse fetishism with erotic sadism,[24] though curiously she fails to give Hitchcock much credit for noticing this as well. New clothes, new make-up, dyed hair, slowly, as in the creation of a movie star, Judy turns into Madeleine, and only then can Scotty consummate his love for the ghostly departed.

Figure 6.6. Just Judy Barton from Salina, Kansas. Kim Novak in *Vertigo*

But then, after the swirling 360-degree camera movement and the *Liebestod* music of Bernard Herrmann—all of which signify the ecstatic completion of Scotty and Madeleine's union—Judy makes a mistake. Secure in her possession of him, prior to their return to Ernie's (the restaurant where Scotty first set eyes on Madeleine), she carelessly asks him to help her put on the Carlotta/Madeleine necklace which figured prominently in Carlotta's portrait. At once Scotty realizes that Judy hasn't become Madeleine, she *is* Madeleine and he has been duped. Changing tack, he decides to return to the past and uncover the ghost and the crime which has driven him mad. With a frightening look on his face, he insists that they drive back down the Peninsula to San Juan Bautista. Once there, he drags her up the bell tower's stairs, repeating phrases such as, "You were an apt pupil, weren't you, Judy?" and forcing her into a confession of her role in Elster's crime. As "Madeleine" ascended, Elster waited in the belfry, then threw off the dead body of the true Madeleine, knowing full well that Scotty would never be able to make it to the top of the ladder to see this. But now cured of his vertigo, Scotty arrives at the top where Judy pleads with him to accept her as she is. But still ambivalent, at once moral and pathological, he rejects her. Suddenly from out of the shadows like a specter, a nun appears and frightens Judy, who loses her balance and falls to a second death.

Judy, of course is a femme fatale. Like all the other film noir femme fatales, she must die for her crimes. But just as Scotty is the most fully developed noir hero, so Judy herself becomes a three dimensional character. Femme fatales are a sexy bunch, but greed drives them much more than Eros. They use their sex appeal to get money and to control the men who can get it for them. Think of Phyllis Dietrichson (Barbara Stanwyck) in *Double Indemnity*. She admits to her accomplice Walter Neff (Fred MacMurray) that she never loved him—at least till the moment when he is about to kill her. Or in *Out of the Past*, to take the other most interesting of these women, Kathie Moffat (Jane Greer) seems fond of Jeff Bailey (Robert Mitchum), but she's a chronic liar, a totally duplicitous personality, who abandons him as easily as she shoots her gangster lover Whit (Kirk Douglas). Comfort and protection motivate her much more than romantic attachments. But Judy Barton really loves Scotty. Her tragic flaw is weakness and vulnerability to the male will. She cannot extricate herself from Elster's plot. As she says, knowing the real Madeleine is already dead and that if she tells Scotty the truth, she will become an accomplice to murder, "It's too late." But then if she thought only of her own well being, she would never have submitted to Scotty's fetishism and madness. According to all accounts, Hitchcock and his writers seriously considered saving the revelation that Judy was Scotty's Madeleine until the very end, but wisely they decided otherwise. At the moment Scotty leaves the hotel room after first encountering Judy, the audience learns the truth of the situation through a subjective flashback of Judy's memory, an example of noir like un-classical narrative. Reason would tell her to flee, and she begins packing, but then her genuine love for Scotty persuades her to remain and take her chances. This startling knowledge not only heightens the dramatic irony of Scotty's behavior, it transforms Judy from a mere sex object and male fantasy into a thinking and feeling character. Instead of looking at her and admiring her beauty, we sympathize with her. Like the heroines in women's films, she has been trapped between two inadequate men, the domineering and clever Elster, and the gullible and domineering Scotty. And at the same time, through her genuine love, we become more aware of Scotty's pathology and indifference to a real flesh and blood woman. If Hitchcock created Scotty to act out his own sadistic crimes against women, then in this film he self-consciously indicts himself. As Katie Trumpener put it, *Vertigo* is "a movie that at once participates in exploitative desire and unmasks it."[25]

Femme fatales require a foil, not just the males they deceive, but a prim and proper good girl, less mysterious and erotic, but morally superior. This arrangement of course reverses the conventions of the 1930s in which the good girl had all the pluck, energy, and sex appeal while the femme fatale wannabes served merely as comic foils. Think of Carol Lombard or Ginger Rogers vs. Gail Patrick. *Vertigo* supplies this character in the person of Midge Wood (Barbara Bel Geddes). Wood implies "wooden" but also "would" in the sense that she would marry Scotty and be an exceptionally devoted wife if he would but give her a chance. As is true of Judy, the role gives depth to the type. She is a commercial artist and designer, educated and talented. She and Scotty were once engaged—in the past, in college days. Scotty does not seem to know why, but now, they are just friends, at least he in his myopia and self-centeredness, seems to think so. While she looks longingly at him, he mindlessly banters about potentially sexual subjects such as brassieres and his being a big boy now, that is, knowing about sex and women, though in fact he's still an adolescent, as vulnerable as Judy to the guile of a mature male. Though he is as blind to Midge's love as he is to Judy's deception, Midge is not blind to him and realizes he has fallen in love, only not with her. As he trails Madeleine, so she trails the two of them. Once she perceives the truth, she even tries to shock him out of his obsession by painting herself into a version of Carlotta's portrait. She wants to be the object of his male gaze, but her attempt backfires and he gloomily departs only to see her one more time, still oblivious, as she visits him in the mental hospital.

Technicolor prevents the portrayal of a dark city. Yet no black and white film noir can match *Vertigo*'s vision of a haunted San Francisco. Los Angeles, by virtue of its being contained within Hollywood, naturally takes precedence among noir's favorite locations. Yet the city of choice, the one most filmed apart from Los Angeles, surpassing even New York, is San Francisco, "Noir City "as its annual noir festival bills itself. Philip Marlowe walked the mean streets of L.A., but his mentor, Sam Spade, worked in San Francisco. As Madeleine wanders about, and Scotty slowly and painfully follows her, we are given a virtual tour of America's most beautiful city. Hitchcock liked to position his characters in well known and iconic places: the dome of the British Museum Reading Room, the Firth of Forth Bridge, the Statue of Liberty, and Mount Rushmore to name the most obvious. But never did he explore a city, neither London nor New York, as he did in *Vertigo*. From Nob Hill to Union Square, from the Dolores Mission to Pacific Heights, from Coit Tower and Telegraph Hill to the Golden Gate, and then to the area south of the city, closer to Santa Cruz where Hitchcock had his second home, to Big Basin and the redwoods—*sempervirens*, like Carlotta, always living—to Monterey Bay, where Scotty and Madeleine first embrace. When one visits San Francisco, one can arrange for a *Vertigo* tour.

Was Hitchcock just taking advantage of picturesque locations, a kind of urban Monument Valley, with which he happened to be familiar? Or was he, as with his characters, further developing and enriching the conventions of film noir? I suspect the latter. For in *Vertigo*, the city has become a puzzle, a maze, a labyrinth like human sexuality which have no easy ways out. It invites wandering, but where does one go? What does it mean? The two doomed lovers are anything but free. Scotty calls the architect Maybeck's pavilion for the Panama Pacific Exposition (1915) "The Pillars of the Past." This occurs at one of the calmest moments, accompanied by lyrical music, in their relationship, but the past, the ghostly past of Carlotta and the criminal past of the fake Madeleine are about to crash down upon Scotty's head and to destroy Judy utterly. It would seem that the beauteous city but serves as an objective correlative to Madeleine's own beauty. Instead it's a whited sepulcher that masks the tragedies of human existence buried beneath. It's a look into the abyss, the "mise en abyme" of Katie Trumpener's article "Fragments of the Mirror." As she points out, the film so repeats itself and doubles back on itself that it is likely that after Scotty leaves the tower he will once again commence his search for the Madeleine who never existed.[26]

As if to trump all other film noirs, *Vertigo* derives not from American pulp fiction or Weimar expressionism, but from France, from a kind of *serie noir* French thriller, *D'entre les morts* (1954) by Pierre Boileau and Thomas Narcejac who also wrote the novel on which Clouzot's *Diabolique* (1955) was based. As with other great films based on novels, *Vertigo* is far superior to its source. In the novel, the Scotty character sees the second Madeleine in a newsreel. He knows from the start who she really is and nags her into confessing before he finally strangles her. As the novel begins in 1940 and concludes in 1945 or 1946, it concerns itself not with the romantic agony that haunts Scotty, like a character in Proust or Hawthorne, but with the trauma of France's collapse in World War II. The Elster character, actually the chief suspect in his wife's death, dies during the war. So the screenwriters Samuel Taylor, Alec Coppell, and also Hitchcock, have completely transformed the idea of being between two deaths and reinterpreted it in accord both with Hitchcock's own vision of life and art and with the most fundamental conventions of film noir: the confused and erring protagonist, the crime, the femme fatale, multiple investigations, the good girl, the multiple double crosses, and the labyrinthine city. It remains as the best example of the genre ever made and the triumph and climax of a brilliant period.

Hitchcock never made a better film. The next year, in *North by Northwest* (1959), he followed *Vertigo* with a return to his other favorite branch of the thriller, the romantic spy genre. It marks the pinnacle of his career. Almost as if to exorcise the tragedy of *Vertigo*, he and screenwriter Ernest Lehman employ many of the same situations but reverse their outcomes. The hero, Roger Thornhill (Cary Grant) is another good looking movie star type, who happens to be as emotionally immature as Scotty Ferguson, only shallower. Unlike Scotty, who resists femininity except on his terms of perfection, Roger has been married several times and is currently dating his mother. He too falls into a plot not of his own making and encounters another femme fatale, Eve Kendall (Eva Marie Saint) who like her namesake plays a double role in the story. Like Judy, she has become the mistress of a suave and evil man Phillip Vandamm (James Mason), note the satanic connotations. Also like Judy, she falls for the ironic hero, yet still goes through with the nefarious plot to destroy him. But unlike Judy, and unlike Scotty, Eve and Roger redeem themselves, prove to be heroic, and on the head of George Washington at Mt. Rushmore achieve their genuine identities of Mr. and Mrs. Thornhill. The love tragedy of *Vertigo* has been rewritten into the romantic comedy of *North by Northwest*, both of them to the accompaniment of Bernard Herrmann's score.

It's no mystery that Hitchcock's works hang together. From *The Lodger* on one finds recurring motifs in both style and substance. At the same time, for various reasons critics divide the films into groups such as the British period, the Selznick period, the Hollywood period, or the late period. Within such groupings, critics also discover trilogies such as *Vertigo, North by Northwest*, and *Psycho*. Because of the coherence of Hitchcock's diverse works, anyone can play the game. For my part, as mentioned, I see a strong relationship between *Vertigo* and *North by Northwest*, but *Psycho* represents a new direction and a break with film noir. It begins as a film noir, even to the extent of being filmed in black and white when Technicolor had become the norm. At the outset, we find its protagonist, an attractive blond, Marion Crane (Janet Leigh) in a hotel room in bed half naked (a nod to the Production Code) with her handsome lover Sam Loomis (John Gavin). She wants to get married. He, like L. B. Jeffries and Scotty Ferguson wants to remain single, for the time being. He pays too much alimony to his ex-wife and he makes too little money. Marion threatens to Platonize their relationship and the two part, he back to Fairview, California (an imaginary town) and she to the real estate office in Phoenix where she works. A drunken dirty old man, Mr. Cassidy (Frank Albertson), comes in to the office to close a deal on a house he has bought as a wedding present for his daughter. He makes some lewd and suggestive remarks to Marion, whose boss then asks her to deposit Cassidy's boastful $40,000 cash payment in the bank before it closes for the weekend. Marion, however, obviously until this time a loyal and dutiful worker, without warning, packs her bag and the money and drives out of town, presumably headed toward Sam and Fairview. Like all the noir heroines before her, she has stepped or fallen into crime.

There follows three deservedly much-praised sequences, not classically filmed at all, but depicted as a dream sequence or nightmare. In the first as she drives through the night fighting the glare of oncoming traffic, all to the haunting score by Bernard Herrmann, she imagines the voices of her coworker and sister talking about her flight. In the second, now in broad daylight, she is trailed by a suspicious highway patrolman and foolishly swaps cars while he looks on. In the third, she drives again through the rain and the night, disoriented and lost, until she turns into the Bates Motel. All this is perfect noir. But then, only half-way through the film, after Norman's "mother" kills her in the famous shower scene, the film makes a radical 90-degree turn and leaves noir altogether, despite a subsequent investigation of her disappearance. Just as *Blackmail* began as a police procedural and turned into a film noir, so *Psycho* begins as a film noir and turns into a horror film. If I were into trilogies I would group it with *The Birds* (1963) and *Marnie* (1964), both with female protagonists; the first a horror film, the second dealing with psychosis.

EPITAPH

In Plato's *Symposium*, Socrates remarks that if a dramatist really understood life, he would be able to write both tragedies and comedies. Homer allegedly wrote a comic epic, but Sophocles and Aristophanes stuck to their preferred genres. Not until Shakespeare do we witness the complete realization of

Socrates' insight. In the history of film, I can think of no other auteur, not even Ford or Renoir, Hitchcock's greatest contemporaries, who achieved such brilliance in these opposing genres. That Hitchcock reached his greatest heights during the period of film noir but confirms what film lovers already know, namely that the genre of film noir contains some of the best films ever made, films rich in meaning and enduring values. It is common to refer to the 1930s as the Golden Age of Hollywood. But the 1940s and 1950s probably produced more masterpieces. Unlike *The Maltese Falcon* whose dark exterior hid the lead beneath, the darkness of film noir revealed a second Golden Age.

NOTES

1. Robin Wood, *Hitchcock's Films* (New York: A. S. Barnes, 1965).
2. Andrew Sarris, *The American Cinema: Directors and Directions, 1929–1968* (New York: Dutton, 1968).
3. James Naremore, "Hitchcock at the Margins of Noir," in *Alfred Hitchcock: Centenary Essays*, ed. Richard Allen and S. Ishli-Gonzalez (London: BFI Publishing, 1999), 263–78.
4. Naremore, 263.
5. Naremore, 265.
6. Naremore, 266–76.
7. Naremore, 276.
8. Naremore, 264.
9. Bettina Rosenbladt, "Doubles and Doubts in Hitchcock: The German Connection," in *Hitchcock: Past and Future*, ed. Richard Allen and Sam Ishii-Gonzalez (London: Routledge, 2004), 41–51.
10. Rosenbladt, 41; Lesley Brill, "Hitchcock's *The Lodger*," in *A Hitchcock Reader*, 2nd edition, ed. Marshall Deutelbaum and Leland Poague (Chichester: Wiley-Blackwell, 2009), 75–84.
11. Vincent Brook, *Driven to Darkness*, 72.
12. Thomas Elsaesser, "Too Big and Too Close: Alfred Hitchcock and Fritz Lang," in *The Hitchcock Annual Anthology*, ed. Sidney Gottlieb and Richard Allen (London: Wallflower Press, 2009), 146–72.
13. Later, perhaps ironically, he calls film noir, "everyone's favourite genre," 152.
14. See the superb essay by Charles L. P. Silet, "Through a Woman's Eyes: Sexuality and Memory in *The 39 Steps*," in *A Hitchcock Reader*, 114–25.
15. See James M. McLaughlin, "All in the Family: Alfred Hitchcock's *Shadow of a Doubt*," in *A Hitchcock Reader*, 145–55.
16. See Richard Abel, "*Notorious*: Perversion par Excellence," in *A Hitchcock Reader*, 164–71.
17. Others include Sylvia Sidney in the pre-noir *You Only Live Once* (1937), Joanne Woodward in a *Kiss Before Dying* (1956), and Glenn Close in the neo-noir *Fatal Attraction (*1987).

18. Jonathan Rosenbaum, "Introduction to the Chinese edition of *More than Night*," Jonathanrosenbaum.com. Available at www.jonathanrosenbaum.com/?p=15842 (accessed June 11, 2009).

19. Rich, *San Francisco Noir*, 12.

20. Hirsch, *The Dark Side of the Screen*, 167.

21. Dan Aulier in *Vertigo: The Making of a Hitchcock Classic* (New York: St. Martin's Press, 1998), 83, suggests that the portrait by John Ferren may no longer exist.

22. To protect the film from censorship, Hitchcock filmed a coda in which Midge and Scotty hear a radio report of Elster's arrest.

23. Tom Gunning points out that Scotty is in fact in love with three women, Carlotta as well as Madeleine and Judy, and that his fall into the grave is a nightmarish attempt to fuse himself, in death, with his feminine opposite. "The Desire and the Pursuit of the Hole: Cinema's Obscure Object of Desire," in *Erotikon*, ed. Shadi Bartsch and Thomas Bartscherer (Chicago: University of Chicago Press, 2005), 272–73.

24. Mulvey, "Visual Pleasure and Narrative Cinema" [1975], in *Film Theory and Criticism*, 841–43.

25. Katie Trumpener, "Fragments of the Mirror: Self Reference, Mise en Abyme, *Vertigo*," in *Hitchcock' Rereleased Films: From Rope to Vertigo*, ed. Walter Raubicheck and Walter Srebnick (Detroit, MI: Wayne University Press, 1991), 175–87.

26. Trumpener, 182.

Chapter Seven

Meanings

THE BLACK HOLE

One of the more energetic attacks on the concept of film noir comes from Thomas Elsaesser. He complains that:

> A case, therefore of a doubly over-determined historical fantasy, firmly located in the 1950s rather than the 1940s, and firmly located in Europe rather than in America. A first conclusion then, would be to contend that essentially film noir has no essence, that its most stable characteristic is its "absent centeredness," its displacements, its over determinedness, whose ghostly existence as too many discourses, instead of cancelling each other out, merely seems to amplify the term's resonance and suggestiveness. Most noticeable is the term's historical imaginary as deferred action (*Nachfraglichkeit*). Film noir is thus in a sense a textbook example of how *not* to write film history, considering that never have so many causes explained so few effects, and never have so many heterogeneous determinants made so little difference in invalidating other, seemingly equally plausible lines of arguments: all of them leading to that relatively limited corpus of films made between *The Maltese Falcon* (1941), *Kiss Me Deadly* (1955) and *Touch of Evil* (1958).[1]

Amidst the mistakes—located in the 1950s in Europe, an afterthought, a limited corpus of films—Elsaesser does make one accurate observation: the resonance and suggestiveness of film noir. That its many discourses and multiple causes act as a "black hole"[2] is not altogether an inaccurate metaphor. The complexity of film noir and the many important historic issues which it reflects are the very things that pull multiple interpretations into it, including even the negative ones he represents. As we have been arguing, film noir was anything but a simple phenomenon. To repeat Paula Rabinowitz, it *was* the context and that explains its "resonance and suggestiveness." So it is only natural then that like other important cultural events, such as the rise of the novel, film noir has justly, inevitably, attracted numerous, varying, even contradictory interpretations, none of which invalidate either its importance or the fact of its being. Let us examine some of them.

RACE, GENDER, AND CLASS

Race

Commentators often point out how film noir pushed the envelope in matters of sex and violence. There's no argument here: film noir cracked open the Production Code. Yet the most significant "advance" of film noir occurs in the treatment of blacks. As Stanley Crouch said, "One of the most characteristic elements of film noir is its avoidance of racial stereotypes."[3] In the 1930s Hollywood in the depths of the Depression only whites had the dignity to be unemployed. The blacks all worked, but in subservient roles

Figure 7.1. At the Harlem Club. Robert Mitchum, Theresa Harris, and Ted Collins in *Out of the Past*

as housemaids, shoeshine boys, and buffoon-like servants in the manner of Step'n Fetchit. For anyone familiar with these stereotypes, anyone like me who grew up on them, the brief scene in *Out of the Past* when Jeff Markham seeks out Kathie's former maid Eunice (Theresa Harris) comes as something of a shock. The setting is the Harlem club, where the band plays the theme song of the movie "The First Day I Met You" in a semi-jazz style, needless to say the best rendition of it in the film. But they are not wearing jungle outfits or engaged in Cab Calloway antics. And Theresa Harris, instead of being a Mammy type such as Hattie McDaniel or Louise Beavers, is a good-looking, slim young woman who speaks normative American English. Her escort is also well dressed. The whole atmosphere is middle class. Crouch also noticed this scene and remarked, "the black bit players seem to be people with individual dreams and individual lives, not human whoopee cushions ever ready to shriek and guffaw while being humiliated."[4] It's just a moment, yet it signifies a profound transformation in Hollywood's treatment of blacks.

An even more telling moment occurs in *The Breaking Point* (1950), the second Warner Brothers' version of Hemingway's *To Have and Have Not*. This time John Garfield plays Harry Morgan and the setting shifts from Key West to Southern California. Garfield has a faithful black assistant played by Juano Hernandez, depicted as a subordinate, not a caricature. The film adds to the novel and the convention a small part for Hernandez's young son. The boy goes to school with Garfield's white daughters as though such racial mixing were ordinary. As is typical in American literature and film, he gives good advice to his white boss and, when Garfield's boat is commandeered by gangsters, dies trying to help him. One of the gangsters, aided by Garfield, dumps Hernandez's body overboard. At the end of the film, as Garfield, having defeated the crooks, is being carried off the boat on a stretcher, his small daughters run to greet him. We also see the little black boy approaching the scene looking for *his* dad. The crowd leaves, and the film ends, the camera pulling back on a boom, as the little boy is left alone on the dock. Pathos, to be sure, yet it conveys in one shot the indifference of an entire culture.[5]

Such a shift in perspective, such a rise in consciousness, had to be caused by the war. How could we oppose the racist Nazis and maintain a segregated caste system society? In 1949 James Edwards played a GI in *Home of the Brave*, one of the first Hollywood films to expose racial prejudice. That same year saw the release of both *Pinky* starring Jeanne Crain as a light skinned black woman who passed for white and *Lost Boundaries* in which Mel Ferrer also plays a black who can pass. Then in 1950 Sidney Poitier, who to Hollywood was as Jackie Robinson was to baseball, began his distinguished career in a film called *No Way Out*, directed by Joseph Mankiewicz. Poitier

Figure 7.2. Indifference. The concluding shot of *The Breaking Point*

plays a young doctor who is accused by Richard Widmark, a racist redneck, of killing his brother. Of course, he is innocent, as well as competent and dignified, and he is not a white playing a black doctor. Dignified blacks had appeared before, usually in Uncle Tom or Mammy roles, but I cannot recall in any Hollywood film before this a black actor playing an MD or any upscale professional role in a dominantly white society.

Gender

Everyone, except children, appreciates film noir, but often for different reasons. Feminists enjoy the femme fatale and see her as an empowered woman. It's hard to argue with feelings, but I have trouble with this sense of the films, first, because the femme fatale invariably is killed or imprisoned, and second, because the heroines of the 1930s were much more empowered, gutsy, professionally competent, and witty than these dangerous women who for the most part are kept. True, noir gave the femme fatale a gun and the freedom to kill; it made her more aggressively sexual and it certainly made her more interesting than the confused and amnesiac men with whom she dealt. Such shifts in convention crossed heretofore generic boundaries, to feminists a pleasing phenomenon despite its negative results in the films. Furthermore the femme fatale/good girl split cast the conventional woman and her conventional wife and mother roles into a corner of dull respectability, another-welcome development. Nevertheless, following Molly Haskell's analysis in *From Reverence to Rape*, one could just as easily see this development as a move toward increased misogyny—the weakening of the Production Code allowed women to be beaten and slapped around as never before. In a famous pre-Code scene James Cagney pushes a grapefruit into the face of Mae Clark. In *The Big Heat* Lee Marvin throws boiling hot coffee into the face of Gloria Grahame.

Received opinion tells us that the femme fatale is an essential character in film noir.[6] But in fact, despite her importance in many films, she is no more essential than the hard-boiled detective. Too many film noirs lack femme fatales. Think of *The Asphalt Jungle, The Big Clock, The Dark Corner, In a Lonely Place, Laura, Rope, Scandal Sheet, Strangers on a Train,* and *This Gun for Hire.* Received opinion also regards film noir as a male genre. Yet in a significant number of film noirs, the main character is a woman. It is she who investigates, she who makes the false step, she who becomes tarnished, and in general follows the same pattern as the male protagonists. Think of *the Phantom Lady, Mildred Pierce, The Accused, The Reckless Moment*

Figure 7.3. Gloria Grahame and Lee Marvin in *The Big Heat*

among the often canonized films, but also *The Blue Gardenia* (1953), *The Damned Don't Cry* (1950), *Deception* (1946), *Destination Murder, Dial M for Murder* (1954), *Dishonored Lady* (1947), *Hell's Half Acre* (1954), *The Lady Gambles, Leave Her to Heaven, Make Haste to Live* (1954), *My Name is Julia Ross* (1945), *No Man of Her Own* (1950), *Possessed, The Second Woman* (1950), and *Unfaithful*. A few of these are B movies, but most of them feature major stars, such as Anne Baxter, Joan Crawford, Hedy Lamarr, Grace Kelly, Barbara Stanwyck, and Gene Tierney. They are not gothics or primarily women's films, but genuine film noirs. I give brief sketches of them in the Appendix, but such films deserve a book of their own, which should do much to dispel the false notion that noir is confined to a boy's game.

One should also not overlook the fact that there's a female gaze as well as a male one. Typically it counters the advances of a male masher, as when Claudette Colbert tells off Roscoe Karns in *It Happened One Night*. 1930s heroines were especially good at this kind of put-down. Think of the contempt with which Ginger withers Fred in *Top Hat* (1935), but it appears in film noir as well, starting with Mrs. Kane's expressions as she looks at her husband Charles in the famous breakfast montage. It usually accompanies salty and wisecracking dialogue, for instance this from *I Wake Up Screaming*:

> *Carole Landis (a waitress taking an order from Allyn Joslyn):* Will that be all?
>
> *Joslyn (leering at her):* No, but the rest of it isn't on the menu.
>
> *Landis:* You couldn't afford it if it was.

Or this from *The Dark Corner*:

> *Mark Stevens:* How do you do that (swing a bat) after all that chop suey?
>
> *Lucille Ball:* My father was a major league umpire. Well, what else can I beat you at?
>
> *Stevens:* What kind of games do you like to play? You know, we've got some great playgrounds up around 52nd Street.
>
> *Ball:* Among them your apartment?
>
> *Stevens:* Ah, just a coincidence.
>
> *Ball:* I haven't worked for you long, Mr. Galt, but I know when you're pitching a curve at me, and I always carry a catcher's mitt.
>
> *Stevens:* How fancy. A guy's gotta try to score hasn't he?
>
> *Ball:* Not in my league. I don't play for score. I play for keeps, said she with a smile.

The prize for such female squelches of the male, however, goes to Marie Windsor in *The Narrow Margin* (1952), as she directs a stream of witty invective against Charles McGraw. There's also the gaze of the female audience, which from the outset of cinema from Edison's Sandow The Strong Man through Rudolph Valentino to Brad Pitt, is allowed to look upon the naked torsos of Hollywood's matinee idols. If your shirt stays on, you are not a romantic hero.

Class and Psyche

Film noir also crossed the boundary between Marx and Freud. As Colin McArthur put it, "if the Thirties, for American cinema, was the era of popularized Marx, the Forties was the time of diluted Freud."[7] I cannot recall a single 1930s film that does not delve into issues of class. However much the film might in the end, as in screwball comedies and musicals, ameliorate class conflict, the oppressive oligarchs converted to tapping their feet to the Broadway melody, the conflict is there to be ameliorated. There's no more striking instance of this change in perspective than the scene in *Double Indemnity*

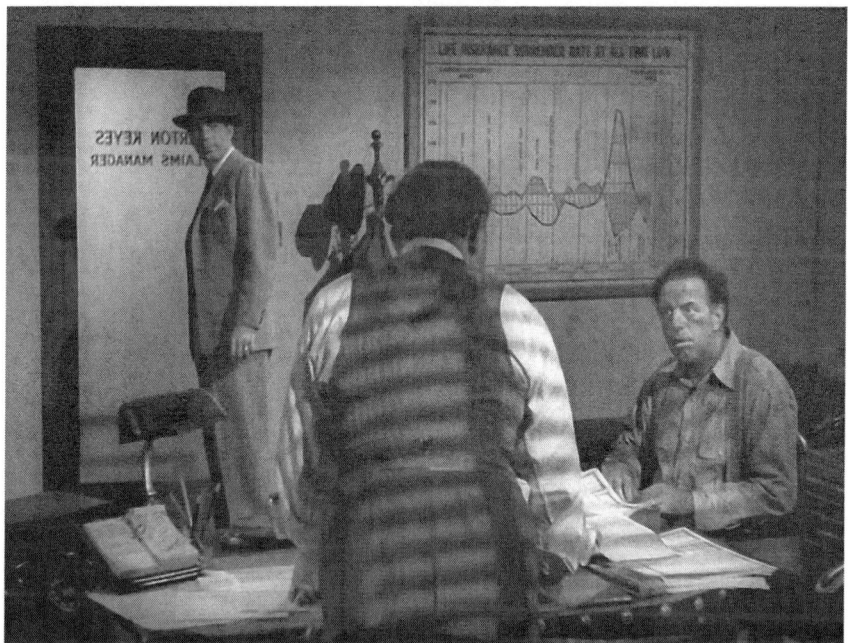

Figure 7.4. The end of the class war. Fred MacMurray, Edward G. Robinson, and Fortunio Bonanova in *Double Indemnity*.

in which Keyes (Edward G. Robinson), the insurance claims investigator, confronts Mr. Garlopis (Fortunio Bonanova) and exposes his scheme to cheat Pacific All Risk. In a 1930s film, Mr. Garlopis, an ethnic blue collar worker with an accent, would be treated sympathetically as one of the oppressed.[8] But here the film uses the poor truck farmer as a fumbling incompetent in order to reveal the brilliance of Keyes and "the little man" inside him who warns about attempted fraud. Keyes unceremoniously ushers Mr. Garlopis to the door and out he goes along with class issues. He's like Thersites in *The Iliad*, who raises the concerns of the common soldier only to be kicked out of camp and the aristocratic considerations of the poem.

Instead film noir dwells on psychological states and conflicts. Nathaniel Rich believes that dread is the subject of noir,[9] but I think guilt is the better term. In the past, a crime has been committed, and it comes back to haunt, not only the protagonists, but the entire film. Guilt better explains the boomerang effect of many of the best noirs in which the investigator must seek his own guilty self, as in *Scandal Sheet* and *The Crooked Way;* or in which the not so innocent protagonist becomes associated with the actual criminal, as in *Tension*; or in which his (or her) attempt to clear himself of crime provides the clues which lead the investigators back to himself, as in *Nora Prentiss* and *Impact*. The whole narrative device of the flashback or the death scene frames the entire film and accentuates the guilt from which one cannot escape, the past which catches up with you. Again, to make an analogy to the classics, all the returning veterans in film noirs are like Agamemnon, the leader of the Greeks against the Trojans, triumphant yet somehow culpable. For the victory, stained as it was in blood, involved crimes which had to be atoned. He of course returns to find a femme fatale, in the person of his adulterous wife, Clytemnestra, who kills him and then is murdered by her son, Orestes, who then flees pursued by the avenging Furies. Like Orestes, noir characters are also "running away from themselves," their psyches troubled and fragmented. It is not that the noir protagonist is a war criminal. Agamemnon's crime, the sacrifice of his daughter, took place prior to the war, and besides, a previous crime, cannibalism no less, had put a curse on his House. Likewise in film noir, only rarely, as in *Act of Violence*, does a serviceman commit the crime during the war. More often the crime occurred when the vet was away or when he returns or in the distant past. Yet the films seldom fail to mention his veteran status. Admittedly most mature men of the time were in fact veterans, but why bother to bring this detail into the narrative if there were not some emotional link between the pervasive guilt of the films and the recent war?[10] Even as late as 1958, in *Vertigo*, we are told that Scotty (Jimmy Stewart) is a veteran.

None of these vets suffer from class discrimination or poverty but rather from amnesia, stolen identities, fragmented knowledge, or false accusations that somehow ring true. That their problems are psychological brings the psychiatrist to the fore. When a psychiatrist appears in a 1930s film, he is usually suspect or an object of ridicule, as in *Mr. Deeds Goes to Town* (1936). Noir however no longer perceives him as a comic figure but a healing one, and a positive contributor to the investigation. Lee J. Cobb plays a police psychiatrist in *The Dark Past*, and Lew Ayres plays one in *The Dark Mirror*. In *Conflict* Sydney Greenstreet, also a psychiatrist, becomes the detective who solves the murder, while Morris Carnovsky takes on the usual role, a healing mentor, to Hedy Lamarr in *Dishonored Lady*. In *Nightmare Alley* Helen Walker plays a double-crossing, crooked, femme fatale psychiatrist, appropriately named Lilith. Telotte cites a paper by Laurence Miller which notes "approximately 260 forms of psychopathology have been identified, all of them surfacing at various points in the noir canon."[11] Marlisa Santos goes so far as to believe that the contradictions of psychiatry, on the one hand its ability to "eliminate the mysteries of the human psyche," and on the other "to expose [its] depths of unknowability . . . is the driving force of the elusive *noir* sensibility. . . . The very philosophies at the heart of psychoanalysis, then, are also at the very heart of noir: human motivations and behavior tend to shades of gray, not black and white, and while it is worth pursuing their sources, such pursuit can be dangerous or even futile."[12]

We have already mentioned how *Spellbound* is the most psychiatric of all noirs. The tormented hero (Gregory Peck) is himself a psychiatrist; he is loved by another (Ingrid Bergman) whose psychiatrist mentor (Michael Chekhov) helps her to cure him and lead her to the villain of the piece, still another analyst (Leo G. Carroll). And we have noted how the film and its four psychiatrists, none of them aware of the Oedipus complex, might have been an in-joke on the part of Hecht and Hitchcock. At the time, however, its pop-Freudianism, its Dali sets, and its haunting, romantic score by Miklos Rozsa, proved enormously popular. All this interest in emotional states, identity crises, and distressed males naturally opened the door of the homosexual closet. Just as it succeeded in showing the nightmarish depths of the city, film noir, implicitly at least, introduces a new perspective on homosexuality. The Production Code and the official innocence of the New Deal forbad any direct treatment of homosexuality. So 1930s films abound with comic gay figures, prissy hotel managers and floor walkers, best portrayed by Franklin Pangborn or Eric Blore. In *Top Hat* Blore welcomes Fred Astaire to "our ménage," the one he has with Horace Hardwicke (Edward Everett Horton). In *Follow the Fleet* (1936), Fred Astaire's shipboard band, which plays for the sailors dancing together, is named "Bake Baker's Navy Blue Blowers."

Did Joe Breen deliberately overlook this, or was the age more innocent? The Code continued in force throughout the noir period, but as in other categories, the perspective on homosexuals shifted. Instead of comic gays who remain sexless, in *Johnny Eager* (1942) we see Van Heflin hopelessly in love with Robert Taylor, a role that won him an Oscar. In *Double Indemnity* we see MacMurray and Robinson lighting each other's cigarettes, and saying, "I love you too." Or in *In a Lonely Place* we see Ruth Elliot as an obvious lesbian masseuse advising Gloria Grahame to dump Humphrey Bogart. In *Gilda*, Rita Hayworth is sexy, but no femme fatale; rather she's an innocent screen between the homoerotic relationship of Glenn Ford and George Macready. Noir abounds with such transgressive situations and characters, which from a gay perspective can be seen as augurs of liberation, despite the criminal and abnormal contexts in which they appear. At least they exist with somewhat more recognizable features, or a wider range of them, than previously, yet as Richard Dyer points out, what really characterizes gays, their sex lives, these films never mention.[13]

For all the above reasons, left-leaning spectators appreciate film noir. Recently Buhle and Wagner have claimed noir "as the cinematic triumph of the Left's filmmakers."[14] Since Hollywood filmmakers as a group have always been liberal, no one can dispute this claim, but for Buhle and Wagner left usually means certified left winger, or radical, which is a different matter. McCarthyism and blacklisting did not end film noir; too many of its best examples occur after the HUAC hearings and the Waldorf agreement of the producers not to hire Communists. A great deal of talent was lost as a result of this unfortunate turn of events, but the genre survived, and the period, like all periods, died of exhaustion, old age, and the need for change. None of the great noir masters, Hitchcock, Lang, Siodmak, Wilder, Preminger and company were certified left wingers. What did mesh with a radical outlook was noir's vision of a corrupt society, a pervasive dark underworld, and alienated, fragmented, and victimized protagonists. If overt class conflict disappeared, the implicit sense of an evil system in which everyone is entrapped replaced it. As Jack Shadoian puts it, "society is the gangster."[15] The villains, however, were not bankers, as in the 1930s, or corporate chiefs and high government officials as now. In fact the majority of noirs were apolitical, focused far more on individual crises and domestic issues than on institutional evil. There were, of course exceptions, such as *The Big Clock* in which Charles Laughton plays an evil media mogul, *The Strange Love of Martha Ivers* (1946), which links crime and business, or *Force of Evil* (1948) which attempts to make the numbers racket a symbol of free enterprise. There were also anti-Capra anatomies of Middle American towns without pity, such as the lynching movie *Try and Get Me* (1950). But on the other side, a few noirs were overtly anti-

Communist, notably the underrated *I Married a Communist* (1950), whose title was changed on later releases to *The Woman on Pier 13*, and *Pick Up on South Street* (1953). More than a few, especially in the 1950s, concentrated on the hard work and efficiency of law enforcement agencies that eliminated the threats of racketeers, plagues, psychopaths, and communist agents. On the whole, rather than deliberately focusing on late capitalism as the source of its malaise, film noir presented a whole world drenched in anxiety, a kind of war induced post-war trauma that had as many implicit causes as there were changes in the American way of life, to which we should add not only those mentioned on page one, but also the new prosperity which brought both higher expectations and greater risks of personal failure.

THE PHILOSOPHY OF FILM NOIR

Each film noir presents its own vision and merits its own interpretation. As a group however, dealing as they do with crime and fallibility, noirs invariably convey dark and troubling visions, bordering on a nightmarish view of life. We have mentioned Robert Porfiro's view of the existential gloom embodied in film noir, a concept that has become the prevailing one. Recently however, a refreshingly revisionist view has come to the fore, one which emphasizes positive or redemptive patterns to be found in the corpus of film noir. In more than a few films, as pointed out by R. Barton Palmer, the characters work their way out of the labyrinth.[16] Among these, we find such notable films as *Spellbound, Notorious*, as well as excellent B movies such as *Desperate, Tension*, and *Crime Wave* (1954). Thomas S. Hibbs believes that films such as *Double Indemnity, The File on Thelma Jordan*, and of course *I Confess* align themselves as much if not more to Pascal's sense of the human condition than they do to Nietzschean nihilism and existentialism.[17] As Pascal stated, "Man's greatness comes from knowing he is wretched." Thus Hibbs sees the protagonists of film noir not as mere mechanical victims to the dark powers of fate but as sympathetic characters who in Pascal's phrase "seek with groans" some kind of redemption or understanding. Their voiceover narrations, for instance, contribute to this double sense of both failure and comprehension. To Hibbs, film noir is like the novels of Flannery O'Connor and those religious narratives "that do not circumvent tragedy and the unsavory features of the human condition, but rather pass through them."[18]

For many critics, this aspect of noir results from the Production Code and accords neither with the genuine vision of the films nor with reality. The triumph of justice and the happy ending are but a *deus ex machina* imposed on art by a compromising censorship created by all the wrong people. Yet for many others, the moral endings come as a sort of relief and are not merely tacked on. Rather they arise naturally out of the moral dilemmas and confusions of the characters. Apropos of such endings, Aeon Skoble claims:

> So where's the moral ambiguity, the inversion of traditional values that is supposed to pervade film noir? We've got the lonely settings; we've got the strange camera angles; we've got the unsettling use of light and shadow; we've got the hard-boiled dialogue; we've got the femmes fatales. But we also have, it turns out, a body of films which showcase practical reason and ethical decision making, in settings that affirm moral realism and explicitly reject nihilism. Perhaps surprisingly, films noirs end up being more about moral clarity.[19]

How one views film noir obviously corresponds to a large extent on how one views life, so that the films become dark mirrors of ourselves. But our responses to them and the justifications we make for them fall into familiar and traditional aesthetic and psychological patterns. Here we can return to Northrop Frye. Needless to say the dark vision of film noir, its fallen protagonists, its betrayals and double crosses, its corrupt cities, the time each film spends in the "mad" world, that analogy to hell which marks the lower boundary of the human imagination, lends itself best to plots of irony and tragedy. The films most often canonized, the ones that have generated the greatest amount of discussion, employ the plot of tragedy. I confess these are my own favorites too: *Double Indemnity*, *Out of the Past*, *Sunset Boulevard*, *Gun Crazy*, *D.O.A.*, *Criss Cross*, *The Killers*, *The Asphalt Jungle*, and *Vertigo*.

Other important films use the plot of irony, the one in which the protagonist ends up pretty much where he/she started, sometimes sadder and wiser. Among them, one finds *Mildred Pierce*, who, cleared of a murder charge walks off into the shade with her inadequate first husband. Unlike *The Asphalt Jungle* in which the sympathetic Dix (Sterling Hayden) dies tragically, *The Killing* treats a group of losers, not gangsters, whose success at robbing the Santa Anita racetrack is foiled when the suitcase containing the loot falls off of a baggage cart and is blown away by the motors of the airplane as Johnny Clay (Sterling Hayden again) looks helplessly on. In *In a Lonely Place*, Humphrey Bogart is cleared of a murder, but he loses Gloria Grahame and ends up just as lonely as he was at the outset of the film. In *Detour* Tom Neal never escapes from the labyrinth of fate. In *Scarlet Street* this same fate pins Edward G. Robinson's murder of Joan Bennett on her pimp, Dan Duryea, but leaves him destitute and a wanderer. And then in *The Maltese Falcon* Sam Spade solves the murder of his partner, but only at the cost of losing his lover.

Film noir offers very few plots of romance. These are those stories which begin in a green world and in which the innocents, though threatened, triumph in the end. A notable exception is *The Big Sleep*. As Chandler himself said, his hero Philip Marlowe is "untarnished," a knight on a quest. He begins in a *green* house, no less, but that opens into the fallen world of the Sternwood family and from there to the corruption of the mad world of the dark city which holds his two daughters in bondage. Comic plots, surprisingly prove more common. By this I do not mean ha ha funny comedy, but that plot structure in which a fallen character or *eiron* by chance or virtue or a combination of the two makes his way out of the labyrinth into some hope of happiness, as in *The Divine Comedy*. *Murder, My Sweet* reconstructs Chandler's novel in this way. Marlowe (Dick Powell) begins the film imprisoned, blinded by the light of the third degree. Still blinded at the end, he's released into a taxi and the arms of his new and now liberated girlfriend Ann Grayle (Anne Shirley) appropriately named as the goal of the quest. In *Laura* detective Dana Andrews becomes obsessed with a dead woman, his investigation of her murder revealing only his own fetishism. When Laura (Gene Tierney) turns up alive, we see that she is also fettered, bound to two inadequate men, one a womanizing cad (Vincent Price) to whom she is engaged, the other a controlling aesthete (Clifton Webb) who dominates her psychologically. In solving the crime, the two find one another and a better life. Plots such as these are the ones Palmer and Hibbs refer to. A black T shirt given to supporters of The Film Noir Foundation has written on it, "No Happy Endings." Actually, there are many, but I think the point to be made, as Hibbs says, they are earned, not the unconvincing tacked and improbable so called "Hollywood ending."

THE REWARDS OF FILM NOIR

We are back with Hume and Aristotle and the paradox of tragedy or realism, the world as it is, which is to say fallen, being entertaining. With the death of Jeff Bailey in *Out of the Past*, we may undergo *some* kind of catharsis which purges us of pity and fear as we transfer such debilitating emotions onto the scapegoat hero. Or, following Longinus, we may experience *ecstasis*, a kind of heightening of emotion through our identification with doomed characters such as Swede in *The Killers*, with troubled characters such as Mildred Pierce, or with characters such as Marlowe who make their way out of the darkness into the light, all of these types enabling us to feel more deeply and, perhaps, cope better with our own troubles. Horace defended poetry by claiming it delighted while it instructed, giving it an edge no doubt over the tougher going of philosophy. In terms of delight, one can argue that the great year of 1939, the apogee of the studio system and the classical style, was but the prelude to a more interesting and in many ways aesthetically superior baroque development. Never were black and white films more beautifully created and stunning to watch, so much so that one still laments their passing into the banalities of wide screen Technicolor. The greatest directors, the best actors, the wittiest screenwriters all participated. Even the credits improved. Instead of using title cards, standard throughout the 1930s, noirs from the outset integrate the credits with the narratives and themes of the films, thereby enhancing interest and meaning from the outset.[20]

Like *Citizen Kane*, film noir offered a fascinating double vision—a gloomy, tragic or ironic tale fraught not with pathos or sentimentality but vibrant with exuberance and bravura. No one has captured this double aspect better than James Harvey, here writing about *Out of the Past*:

> *Out of the Past* shows the familiar noir mixture of depressive content and exhilarated style. And if it's even grimmer than most such movies (noir heroes are more likely than not to survive at the end, and especially so if they are private eyes like Jeff), it's also *more* exhilarated. It's not just those romantic scenes in the flashback: the whole movie has an oddly elated rhythm and spirit. It offers the familiar noir ambience of the nighttime city, with its clubs and apartments, its enclosing dark spaces and looming shadows—but then it keeps leaving town, breaking into light and open and sweeping views, from Acapulco to Lake Tahoe to Telegraph Hill. . . . But it's also the visual rhythm, the fluidity of Tourneur's camerawork and editing, that make the film feel so high spirited and expansive—as if it were riding some magical inner current, sweeping toward its ending almost as if it were going to be a happy one.[21]

Although the scores of 1930s musicals have never been surpassed, those of dramatic films improved during the 1940s and 1950s. This was the period of Hollywood's greatest composer, Bernard Herrmann, who began noir with his score for *Citizen Kane* and ended it with *Vertigo*. Miklos Rozsa's score for *Spellbound* became a best-selling record. Then too, all those wicked nightclubs employed singers and bands, so that many noirs add musical numbers to their attractions, such as the hot jazz in *Phantom Lady* and *D.O.A.*, but also "Hit Parade" songs and other popular tunes and performers of the era.

"These Are the Things I Love," *I Wake Up Screaming*
"I've Got You," sung by Veronica Lake (dubbed by Martha Mears), *This Gun for Hire*
"Remember," *Moontide* (1942)
"I Had the Craziest Dream" *Time to Kill*
"Spring Will Be a Little Late This Year" sung by Deanna Durbin, *Christmas Holiday*
"Tangerine" and "My Ideal" playing in the background of *Double Indemnity*
"Laura," theme song of *Laura*

"I Can't Believe That You're in Love with Me," *Detour*
"The More I See You," "Mood Indigo," and Eddie Heywood's band in *Dark Corner*
"Her Tears Flowed like Wine," sung by Lauren Bacall, *The Big Sleep*
"Put the Blame on Mame," sung by Rita Hayworth, *Gilda*
"Either It's Love or It Isn't," *Dead Reckoning*; also in *The Big Heat*
"It's Just Too Wonderful," *Dark Passage* (1947)
"The First Time I Met Her," *Out of the Past*
"Isn't It Romantic," "My Ideal," "Two Sleepy People," *I Walk Alone* (1948)
Esy Morales and his Rumba Band. *Criss Cross*
"Blue Moon," *East Side, West Side* (1949)
"Laughing on the Outside," *Gun Crazy*
"You'd Be So Easy to Love," *Side Street*
"I Never Loved Before," *In a Lonely Place*
"That Old Black Magic," "I Don't Want to Walk without You," *Dark City* (1950)
"Give Me a Kiss to Dream On," *The Strip*
"I Get Along Without You Very Well," sung and played by Hoagy Carmichael and sung by Jane Russell, *Las Vegas Story* (1952)
"Blue Gardenia," sung by Nat King Cole, *Blue Gardenia*
"I Know Why and So Do You," *Vicki* (1953)
Songs by Connie Russell and the Billy May Orchestra in *Nightmare* (1956)
"You'll Never Know," *The River's Edge* (1957)

In terms of instruction, realism, even the very stylized and arty realism of film noir, can be justified on several moral grounds. For instance, by presenting an all too human or fallen world, film noir acts as a Gull's Hornbook, a cautionary tale that warns the audience not to take false steps and fall into the nets which entangle the protagonists. They teach by example, not good example, but warning examples that show us what not to do. Then too, as Warshow claimed in his essay about gangster films, they gratify us in showing the libidinous life of illicit sex and violence while warning us of its dangers. In his study of hard-boiled fiction and film noir, John T. Irwin adopts a similar view. "For in the lives of many readers, hard-boiled detective fiction has served for decades now as precisely that vicarious experience of the exceptional . . . that releases readers temporarily from the humdrum and routine of their own lives and then returns them to their lives with a renewed appreciation of the pleasures of the humdrum and routine."[22] We think of the two Baileys. Through Jeff (*Out of the Past*), we're purged of former mistakes. With George (*It's a Wonderful Life*), we embrace our ordinary, dutiful lives. If such moral clarity were merely imposed by the Production Code Office, then neo-noir by having more freedom of expression should result in better,

Figure 7.5. Deanna Durbin in *Christmas Holiday*

more satisfying films. But is that the case? As much as I admire *Chinatown*, for instance, I come away disappointed that John Huston can get away with incest and murder. Am I alone in feeling this? I thought *The Long Goodbye* (1973) the very worst of all Raymond Chandler's adaptations. And I detested the triumph of evil in *Se7en* (1995). I liked *Body Heat* because although Kathleen Turner executes the perfect crime, her gull like accomplice William Hurt ends up in jail. *Kill Me Again*, another favorite, conforms to Code morality, as does *Out of Time*. But as I go from neo-noir to neo-noir, despite their talent and cinematic virtuosity, I usually am unimpressed. *Basic Instinct* is a good example. Camille Paglia[23] loves the film because Sharon Stone takes on goddess-like power over men—and gets away with murder—but watching it, though admiring director Paul Verhoeven's homage to Hitchcock, I end up feeling polluted. Attribute this to geriatric conservatism if you will, but as said earlier, I am a member of the audience for whom film noir was first created. Despite such drawbacks, I suspect these neo-noirs disappoint other viewers as well and do not achieve great popularity because our moral instincts are just as strong as our voyeuristic ones. In his analysis of *Crime and Punishment*, R. P. Blackmur concluded that for Dostoyevsky the crime was to be born, the punishment was to live.[24] Crime and Punishment go together and are basic to life itself. Just as the Code forced writers into wit rather than profanity, so its imposed moral framework, however superficially or clumsily applied, satisfied more than the Legion of Decency. It satisfied a basic human understanding that a crime implied a punishment. Anything less struck a false note. It is escape that's emotionally artificial, not poetic justice and the Hollywood ending. Ultimately, it's the uneasy balance between libidinousness and morality, between the id and the super-ego that makes film noir satisfying. So rather than deplore the complexity, the ambiguity, the resonance and suggestiveness of film noir, we should, like most critics, despite their opposing interpretations, and like all audiences, applaud it.

NOTES

1. Elsaesser, *Weimar Cinema and After*, 423.
2. Elsaesser, 424.
3. Stanley Crouch, "Noir America," *Slate* (March 15, 2007), www.slate.com/id/2161815/.
4. Crouch, ibid.
5. Dan Flory, *Philosophy, Black Film, Film Noir* (University Park: Pennsylvania State University Press, 2008), 33–35, discusses this scene. His book explores the relationship between film noir and black films and literature.
6. See for instance Marian E. Keene, "A Closer Look at Scopophilia: Mulvey, Hitchcock, and *Vertigo*," in A *Hitchcock Reader*, 234–49. Keene corrects some of Mulvey's basic assumptions, but she also says, "But by allying himself with and privileging the woman's story in *Vertigo* in a way no *film noir* has ever done, Hitchcock breaks with the genre's characteristic absorption in the man's dilemma (falling in love with a villainous woman)."
7. Colin McArthur, *Underworld USA* (London: Secker & Warburg, British Film Institute, 1972), 67.
8. Daniel M. Hodges, "The Rise and Fall of the War Noir," in *Film Noir Reader 4*, 214, considers the crime films of World War II (1940–1944) as a "displacement" of class conflict caused by the need for national solidarity during the war.
9. Rich, *San Francisco Noir*, 8.
10. J. P. Telotte, "Voices from the Deep: Film Noir as Psychodrama," in *Film Noir Reader 4*, 146, believes that approaching film noir itself as a kind of psychodrama "provides a useful metaphor for linking cultural and individual explorations."
11. Telotte, 146, 158.
12. Marlisa Santos, *The Dark Mirror: Psychiatry and Film Noir* (Lanham, MD: Rowman & Littlefield, 2010), xii–xiii.
13. Richard Dyer, *The Matter of Images: Essays on Representation* (London: Routledge, 1993), 61.
14. Paul Buhle and David Wagner, *Radical Hollywood: The Untold Story Behind America's Favorite Movies* (New York: New Press, 2002), xvi. Dennis Broe, *Film*

Noir, American Workers, and Postwar Hollywood (Gainesville: University Press of Florida, 2009), despite the absence of working class figures from mines and factories in the films (51) sees film noir as "cultural formation" that expressed working class hopes and finally a "lament for a desired change that was not to be," xvi.

15. Jack Shadoian, *Dreams and Dead Ends: The American Gangster Film*, 2nd ed. (New York: Oxford University Press, 2003), 177.

16. R. Barton Palmer discusses this aspect of noir in "Moral Man in the Dark City," *The Philosophy of Film Noir*, 187–206.

17. Thomas S. Hibbs, *Arts of Darkness: American Noir and the Quest for Redemption* (Dallas, TX: Spence Publishing Company, 2008), 28–82.

18. Hibbs, xviii.

19. Aeon J. Skoble, "Moral Clarity and Practical Reason in Film Noir," *The Philosophy of Film Noir*, 47–48.

20. Robert Porfiro, "The Noir Title Sequence," in *Film Noir Reader 4*, 276–85.

21. James Harvey, *Movie Love in the Fifties*, 20–21.

22. John T. Irwin, *Unless the Threat of Death Is behind Them: Hard-Boiled Fiction and Film Noir* (Baltimore: Johns Hopkins University Press, 2006), 29.

23. In her running commentary on the DVD.

24. R. P. Blackmur, *Eleven Essays in the European Novel* (New York: Harcourt, Brace & World, 1964), 119–40.

Chapter Eight

Last Words

In conclusion, our investigation has discovered not devised Four Axioms.

FILM NOIR WAS NOT AN AFTERTHOUGHT

Unlike most artistic categories, film noir was named as such almost immediately after it commenced, as early as 1946, only two years after *Double Indemnity*, the film that brought the genre into consciousness. That Hollywood did not adopt the name until the 1970s does not mean that it was unaware. On the contrary, all the evidence, including parodies, indicates the opposite. You cannot imitate something of which you are unaware.

FILM NOIR IS A GENRE

Film noir consists of a fallible protagonist, a crime, an investigation, and a contemporary setting. In literature, such a combination is nothing new, and film history reveals early examples, notably in the work of Hitchcock and Lang. But it did not become a type, that is, a group of recognizably similar films, until the early 1940s. Its production declined in the 1960s, but the 1970s and the elimination of the Production Code gave it new life, immediately recognized by critics as "neo-noir."

FILM NOIR WAS ALSO A STYLE

Film noir is unique in film history as being the only genre that was also a style. Components of the style existed in the silent era, notably in the German films of the 1920s, but Orson Welles brought them together in *Citizen Kane* (1941). Its combination of chiaroscuro, depth of focus, oblique camera angles, a disjointed and fragmented narrative, all supporting an appropriately gloomy world view, initiated the style. It suited the new genre of film noir perfectly and was used in hundreds of crime films throughout the 1940s and 1950s. Thus, popular usage of the term film noir as any urban crime film of the era is understandable, if not entirely accurate.

FILM NOIR WAS ALSO A PERIOD

The style of film noir, its gloomy outlook, its narrative conventions, may be seen and felt in all of Hollywood's genres from the 1940s well into the 1950s. As such it was the dominant or period style of World War II and the immediate post-war decade, primarily but not exclusively in Hollywood. The violence of the war, the weakening of the Production Code, guilt over victory, the fear of success, the difficulty of readjustment, political witch hunts, the flight to the new suburbs, and the fear of the bomb all contributed to the phenomenon. Technicolor, television, the collapse of the Studios and with them the Production Code, the Cold War, its spies and agents, and primarily the rise of a new audience, the Baby Boomers, which we call the 1960s, all put an end to the period, but, as we have seen, the genre survived.

Appendices

Rich Altman pokes a bit of fun at genre makers by pointing out that they typically describe one or two examples (perhaps the only ones that truly fit their category) and conclude with a list (24). True to form, I described *Vertigo*. Now comes the list.

Taxonomy, any sort of classification, inevitably becomes frustrating. Altman gave the example of nuts. Here I think of birds. They fly. But then so do bats, squirrels, and a variety of toads and frogs. Neither Ostriches nor Penguins fly. Just in my lifetime of bird watching, the American Birding Association and the American Ornithological Union have shifted categories on numerous birds, ones as common as Flickers, Orioles, and Thrushes, not to mention the moving in and out of species and sub-species of several kinds of Sparrow. Intrepid explorers of the last wild spaces continue to discover new species, whose assignments must be debated, and as in film, there's the problem of hybrids, which at any moment can become species in their own right.

At times all this effort at categorization seems useless. Why not just chew the nuts, watch the birds, and enjoy the movies? The trouble is that we are thinking beings, and as I stated earlier, thinking depends largely on categories, inadequate as they inevitably prove to be. We need them. Without them, we could not recognize either identity or change. Nevertheless, I worry that all the previous discussion has but muddled the issues. In addition to arguing about what is or what is not film noir, I have extended the concept into three categories, genre, style, and period. As a final effort at clarification then, I add not one but several lists. The films are those from the classic period, roughly 1940 to 1960, included in Silver and Ward's *Film Noir: An Encyclopedic Reference to the American Style*, Keaney's *Film Noir Guide*, Duncan's *Film Noir: Films of Trust and Betrayal*,[1] the third edition of Hirsch's *Film Noir: The Dark Side of the Screen*, and all the films categorized as film noir by the

Internet Movie Database. Altogether they make up almost 800 titles. Of these I have seen over 500 and the following are the ones I include.

In Appendix A I have placed all those films that belong to the *genre* of film noir, as I defined it in chapter 2. Every one of them can be considered within other categories, but I think film noir is the best fit. Under each title I have included a short note or comment which helps to explain my decision. The majority of these films employ the *style* of film noir, but a few do not, and that too shall be noted. As previously mentioned, the style, which was primarily studio based, gave way in the 1950s to the more documentary approach used most frequently in the law and order procedurals. As a bonus or distraction, after each title I have rated the films. In honor of France, I use the Michelin Guide system, three stars for "worth a trip," two stars for "worth a detour," one star for "of interest," and no star simply to record the film's belonging to the genre of film noir. All such ratings are subjective. As a scholar, I felt I had to list them all as generic film noirs, but as a critic I had to make some value judgments.

In Appendix B, I have placed a number of films which I consider borderline, films which have moved from the center of film noir and might just as well be considered as best belonging to other genres. By making such a list, I am not conceding that film noir is too amorphous to be defined as a genre, but only acknowledging what is typical of all genres, namely that they mutate and form hybrids as they differ from those films central to the concept. As oft stated, every film belongs to several genres.

In Appendix C, I have merely listed those crime films of the classic *period* which others have identified as film noir. To be sure, since most of them partake of the *style* of film noir, I cannot argue with the designation. But they do not, as I have defined it, belong to the *genre*. To me, they fit better into other well known categories such as gangster films, police procedurals, spy thrillers, and women's films involving crime. That the *style* extended not just to the great family of crime films but to all other genres, I discussed in chapter 5. That is where *period style* applies.

NOTE

1. Paul Duncan, *Film Noir: Films of Trust and Betrayal* (Harpendon, UK: Pocket Essentials, 2006).

Appendix A

Within the Genre

99 River Street (1953) **
   Phil Karlson: John Payne, Evelyn Keyes.
   John Payne, an ex-boxer, has an anger management problem. When his unfaithful wife is murdered, he becomes the chief suspect. Nobody is on the level, even Keyes, an actress, who fakes a murder to get a part in a play. Jack Lambert, an icon of a hood, makes the proceedings even more sinister. That male anxieties can only be allayed by women's return to domesticity gets full support in this film. Keyes gives up her profession as an actress to be the happy wife of her gas station operator husband. The title has little to do with the film, but it must have sounded good at the time.

The Accused (1949) **
   William Dieterle: Loretta Young, Robert Cummings, Wendell Corey.
   As in a women's film, Loretta Young, a professor of psychology, is torn between two suitors, but instead of being suffering, noble, and morally superior to the males, here she is a murderer attempting to cover her tracks.

Act of Violence (1948) *
   Fred Zinnemann: Van Heflin, Robert Ryan, Janet Leigh, Mary Astor.
   Ryan seeks revenge on Heflin, suburban, successful, and tormented, who while a POW betrayed his buddies. A sacrificial twist concludes the film after some vintage noir scenes in the vicinity of L. A.'s Flight of Angels. All the women, including Phyllis Thaxter, are motherly understanding types, sympathizing with the tormented ex-GIs running away from themselves.

Among the Living (1941) *
   Stuart Heisler: Albert Dekker, Susan Hayward, Harry Carey.
   An insane twin brother, a rotting old southern mansion, a company town whose factory is closed down, townspeople turned mob, all of these motifs

lend themselves to several genres. But the treachery of Dr. Carey, the acquiescence of the sane Dekker, the murders committed by his brother, the manipulations of Hayward, and the cinematography all indicate an early film noir, before the genre came into consciousness.

Angel Face (1952) **

Otto Preminger: Robert Mitchum, Jean Simmons, Mona Freeman.

The hapless Mitchum takes a job as chauffeur to Herbert Marshall, the father of angelic faced Simmons, who is not what she appears to be. Murder and tragedy follow.

The Arnelo Affair (1947)

Arch Oboler: Frances Gifford, John Hodiak, George Murphy.

"Jungle Girl" Gifford plays a neglected housewife whom Hodiak first lures into decorating his apartment and then frames for a murder. There's no affair, but all the principals act as if there were one: a flaw of the Code or of the writer/director?

The Asphalt Jungle (1950) ***

John Huston: Sterling Hayden, Louis Calhern, Sam Jaffe, Jean Hagen, Marilyn Monroe.

This film could also be considered a caper film or a gangster film. But in addition to its many night scenes of a wasted city, it focuses on no less than five fallen protagonists done in by chance and their own bungling, plus two or three other tarnished types. An investigation of crime in the dark unnamed city frames the entire work.

Beyond a Reasonable Doubt (1956) **

Fritz Lang: Dana Andrews, Joan Fontaine, Sidney Blackmer.

As an argument against capital punishment, Andrews allows himself to be framed for the murder of a stripper and condemned to die, but twists of fate ruin the plan to reveal his innocence. Fontaine, Andrews's fiancée, leads an investigation to exonerate him until the ultimate noir revelation: he actually did it.

The Big Clock (1948) **

John Farrow: Ray Milland, Charles Laughton, George Macready.

Milland finds himself implicated in a murder, becomes the chief suspect, and is ordered by Laughton, a megalomaniacal tycoon and the real villain, to find the alleged killer, namely himself. One of the few noirs that concentrates on a corporation, here a media giant, no doubt inspired by Time/Life and Henry Luce.

The Big Combo (1955) **

Joseph H. Lewis: Cornel Wilde, Richard Conte, Brian Donlevy, Jean Wallace.

This might be considered a cop film, but here Wilde breaks the rules, in part because he falls in love with Conte's mistress, Jean Wallace. Conte, obsessed with himself and his power, gets equal attention, while John Alton's extraordinary cinematography, noir from start to finish, provides a grammar of the style.

The Big Heat (1953) ***

Fritz Lang: Glenn Ford, Gloria Grahame, Lee Marvin, Alexander Scourby. More than a policier: in this film an obsessed cop, Ford, departs from ordinary lawful police procedures—and the police—in his vendetta against the killers of his wife, Jocelyn Brando. The women become the chief victims, especially Grahame, a kind of noir icon, the mistress of hit man Marvin, in one of her best roles.

The Big Knife (1955) *

Robert Aldrich: Jack Palance, Ida Lupino, Shelley Winters, Rod Steiger. A satirical, tragic Hollywood on Hollywood version of noir. Wendell Corey plays the villain, Winters, as usual, the victim, in this play turned movie by Clifford Odets.

The Big Sleep (1946) ***

Howard Hawks: Humphrey Bogart, Lauren Bacall. A slightly more tarnished Marlowe, as portrayed by Bogart, and the totally corrupt and seedy Bay City, as invented by Chandler, bring this film into the genre of noir. But it might just as easily be seen as a whodunit that goes awry or a romantic love story that doesn't.

Black Angel (1946) **

Roy William Neill: Dan Duryea, June Vincent, Peter Lorre, Broderick Crawford. A whodunit from Cornell Woolrich. Dan Duryea is an alcoholic, rejected husband with memory problems. Peter Lorre is the chief murder suspect and owner of the nightclub where most of the film takes place. In order to save her unfaithful husband, Vincent becomes a tarnished investigator.

Black Widow (1954)

Nunnally Johnson: Ginger Rogers, Van Heflin, Peggy Ann Garner. So bad, it's almost interesting. Hollywood looks at a fallen Broadway world in a Big Studio, Technicolor, Cinemascope production. It's an *All About Eve* transformed into a noir, complete with murder, betrayals, and an investigation.

Blind Spot (1947) *

Robert Gordon: Chester Morris, Constance Dowling, Steven Geray. Drunken author Morris claims he could easily write a locked room potboiling mystery novel. When his indifferent publisher is found dead in a locked room, Morris becomes the chief suspect. Dowling plays the potential femme fatale, while Geray serves as the sybaritic art connoisseur. A borderline whodunit, B all the way, but one of Morris's best roles.

The Blue Dahlia (1946) **
George Marshall: Alan Ladd, Veronica Lake, William Bendix.
More noirish than his novels, this screenplay by Raymond Chandler features a returning veteran (Ladd) accused, and seemingly guilty, of killing his unfaithful wife. He's helped to clear himself by Lake (who says to him, "So we meet again") who is the wife of Howard da Silva, the lover of Ladd's wife. One wishes it had been directed by Edward Dymytrk.

The Blue Gardenia (1953) **
Fritz Lang: Anne Baxter, Raymond Burr, Richard Conte, Ann Sothern.
What starts out as an office sit-com soon turns into a noir and Lang nightmare, as not entirely innocent Baxter finds herself trapped into believing she has killed office masher Burr. Nat King Cole sings the indifferent theme song.

A Blueprint for Murder (1953) *
Andrew L. Stone: Joseph Cotten, Jean Peters, Gary Merrill.
Joseph Cotten investigates the death of his niece, seemingly at the hands of her step-mother, Jean Peters, to whom he is attracted. Unable to prove the case against her, he attempts to poison Peters in order to prevent her from killing his nephew as well. The film teases you into suspecting Cotten himself as the murderer.

Blonde Ice (1948)
Jack Bernhard: Leslie Brooks, Robert Paige.
Brooks is really a femme fatale—she kills at least three guys, then for no reason confesses in this sub-B noir, just a cut above Ed Wood.

Born to Kill (1947) *
Robert Wise: Lawrence Tierney, Claire Trevor, Elisha Cook, Jr.
Tierney is a deranged killer who proves irresistible to women, particularly Claire Trevor, who becomes a jealous, confused accomplice. Walter Slezak plays a sleazy investigator, while Esther Howard repeats the garrulous drunk role first seen in *Murder My Sweet*.

The Bribe (1949) *
Robert Z. Leonard: Robert Taylor, Ava Gardner, John Hodiak, Vincent Price.
Taylor, an investigator in Latin America, falls for Gardner, who is married to Hodiak. Unusual for MGM, this film employs a noir visual style as well as a noir plot. It ends with a great fireworks scene.

The Brothers Rico (1957) *
Phil Karlson: Richard Conte, Dianne Foster, James Darren.
Like *Kiss of Death*, the film centers on an ex-gangster (Conte) who has gone straight, but in an effort to save his younger brother from the mob, he

re-enters the underworld. Darren, the brother, faces his doom like Swede in *The Killers*. The screenplay was adapted from a novel by Georges Simenon of *serie noir* fame.

The Burglar (1957) *

Paul Wendkos: Dan Duryea, Jayne Mansfield, Martha Vickers.

Based on a novel by David Goodis, the film begins with the theft of a diamond necklace and proceeds through a series of double crosses to a climax on Atlantic City's Steel Pier. Dan Duryea, Mansfield's guardian, plays a good bad guy who attempts to protect his ward.

The Case Against Brooklyn (1958) *

Paul Wendkos: Darren McGavin, Warren Stevens, Margaret Hayes.

A late entry that should be better known. Filmed in a crisp documentary style, it begins as a police procedural, but turns into noir when married rookie cop McGavin falls into the arms of Hayes, the widow of a mobster.

The Chase (1946) *

Arthur Ripley: Robert Cummings, Michele Morgan, Steve Cochran, Peter Lorre.

A Cornell Woolrich story that mixes up nightmare and reality. Cummings, a confused vet with emotional and memory problems, becomes involved with unhappy gangster's wife Morgan and attempts to rescue her. When she's stabbed in the back by someone else, he removes the knife.

Chicago Deadline (1949) *

Lewis Allen: Alan Ladd, Donna Reed, Arthur Kennedy, June Havoc.

Written by Herman Mankiewicz, this film has many *Citizen Kane* narrative devices. It also borrows from *Laura* the concept of the beautiful dead woman at the center of a web of intrigue and murder, but Donna Reed is no Gene Tierney. Alan Ladd plays the investigator, a reporter who stays one step ahead of the police and along the way seduces June Havoc.

Christmas Holiday (1944) ***

Robert Siodmak: Deanna Durbin, Gene Kelly, Gale Sondergaard, Richard Whorf, Dean Harens.

One of the best. Gene Kelly is a Freudian disaster, dominated by his mother Sondergaard. Deanna Durbin, a singer at a New Orleans club (bordello) plays a faithful and abused wife. The scene which introduces her as she sings "Spring Will Be a Little Late This Year" and which also announces that she is no longer a child star, is a masterpiece of mise-en-scene. This is an early noir whose only investigation consists of a series of flashbacks and voiceovers. It is also a women's war film, only the absent husband is in prison, a noir twist provided by screenwriter Herman Mankiewicz.

City That Never Sleeps (1953) *
John H. Auer: Gig Young, Mala Powers, William Talman.
This film goes far beyond the documentary police procedural. Gig Young plays a cop going bad, having an affair with Powers, a stripper, and accepting money from Edward Arnold to arrest Talman who's having an affair with Marie Windsor, Arnold's wife. It was shot in Chicago at night. Wally Cassell plays The Mechanical Man, a mime who witnesses the murders and also loves Powers.

The Clay Pigeon (1949) *
Richard Fleischer: Bill Williams, Barbara Hale, Richard Quine.
Fleischer, like Enil Karlson and Anthony Mann, belongs in the Pantheon of B movie directors. In this film, Williams plays an amnesiac vet accused of a wartime murder. He escapes the military only to discover he's also the chief suspect in an even earlier crime, the murder of his best friend. There's a wonderful chase scene through LA's Chinatown.

Conflict (1945) *
Curtis Bernhardt: Humphrey Bogart, Alexis Smith, Sidney Greenstreet.
For once Greenstreet is a good guy, here a psychiatrist investigator who leads the police into trapping wife-killer Bogart, obsessed with his love for Smith, his wife's sister. Robert Siodmak, Bernhardt's brother, wrote the original story.

Cornered (1945) *
Edward Dymytrk: Dick Powell, Walter Slezak.
Powell is an ex-POW out to revenge the murder of his French wife. Relentless and tough, but also imprudent, he harms some of the good guys before he murders, in self defense, the insidious Slezak, a Nazi collaborator. Buenos Aires is the dark city.

Crack-Up (1946) *
Irving Reis: Pat O'Brien, Claire Trevor, Herbert Marshall, Ray Collins.
Pat O'Brien is another 1930s stalwart converted to noir. Here he's a museum curator and amnesiac, accused of crime in his own museum. It demonstrates how an old fashioned whodunit is transformed by noir conventions. There's a very good scene in a pinball arcade.

Crime of Passion (1957) *
Gerd Oswald: Barbara Stanwyck, Sterling Hayden, Raymond Burr.
Stanwyck, a former journalist, has become a frustrated housewife. Attempting to advance the career of her detective husband, Hayden, she resorts to adultery which in turn leads to murder. The noir twist: Hayden must investigate the crime.

Crime Wave (1954) ***

André De Toth: Sterling Hayden, Gene Nelson, Phyllis Kirk.

One of the best B noirs. Nelson, an ex-con trying to go straight, gets involved with his former buddies again in order to protect Kirk, his wife. Hayden plays a sadistic detective who has it in for him. The cinematography by Bert Glennon is outstanding.

The Crimson Kimono (1959) *

Sam Fuller: James Shigeta, Christine Downs, Glenn Corbett.

A late entry. Detective Shigeta mistakes his partner's jealousy for racism and almost beats him to death in a Kendo match. Solving the murder of a stripper helps him overcome his paranoia. More dated than most noirs.

Criss Cross (1949) ***

Robert Siodmak: Burt Lancaster, Dan Duryea, Yvonne De Carlo, Stephen McNally.

Shot almost entirely in the day, this film is as dark as it gets. It has the works: multiple double crosses, the iconic Dan Duryea, flashbacks, a genuine femme fatale, a script to die for.

The Crooked Way (1949) **

Robert Florey: John Payne, Ellen Drew, Sonny Tufts.

This is pure noir, featuring an amnesiac vet with a criminal past that seeks him out. John Alton's superb cinematography amplifies the noir plot.

Crossfire (1947) ***

Edward Dmytryk: Robert Ryan, Robert Mitchum, Robert Young.

Not just a social conscience movie about anti-Semitism, this film includes a psychologically disturbed killer, a sustained investigation, a dark city, and other noir essentials, including Gloria Grahame in a small part and her ex, Paul Kelly, who, in a memorable exchange, expresses the confusion and disorientation of the returning vets.

Cry Danger (1951) ***

Robert Parrish: Dick Powell, Rhonda Fleming, Richard Erdman.

Dick Powell returns from prison and attempts to recover the money he was framed for stealing. No one in this film is on the level except Regis Toomey, a good cop. The rest all lie and cheat. Set in a tacky trailer park overlooking downtown LA.

A Cry in the Night (1956) *

Frank Tuttle: Natalie Wood, Raymond Burr, Edmond O'Brien.

A child liberation noir. Wood is dominated by heavy father O'Brien, a police captain, and Burr, the pathological kidnapper of Wood, dominated by his insane mother.

Cry Vengeance (1954) *
Mark Stevens: Mark Stevens, Martha Hyer, Skip Homier.
Stevens plays an ex-detective and ex-con whose face was deformed when the mob tried to kill him. Instead they killed his wife and child and framed him for the crime. Free from prison, he's obsessed with revenge and grimly pursues the wrong man to Alaska.

D.O.A. (1950) ***
Rudolph Maté: Edmond O'Brien.
Noir taken to its extreme: an investigation of a murder by the murdered man. His flight from domesticity and a propensity to philander cost O'Brien his life.

The Damned Don't Cry (1950) *
Vincent Sherman: Joan Crawford, David Brian, Kent Smith.
Another Joan Crawford noir. As in a women's film, she is superior to all four men in her life, but as in a noir she is a kind of femme fatale, an immoral social climber seemingly indifferent to the murders and crimes of her lovers.

Danger Signal (1945) *
Robert Florey: Zachary Scott, Faye Emerson, Bruce Bennett.
Scott was an upper class Dan Duryea. Here a writer and murderer, he charms Emerson and her younger sister, Mona Freeman. Emerson's own pathology and her attempts to kill Scott turn this melodrama into a film noir. Bennett is the good man; Rosemary De Camp the psychiatrist.

Dangerous Profession (1949) *
Ted Tetzlaff: George Raft, Ella Raines, Pat O'Brien, Jim Backus, Bill Williams.
Raft, an ex-cop, now a bail bondsman, puts up his own dough to bail out Williams, the husband of Raines, his old somewhat dishonest flame. When Williams is murdered, Raft's investigation places him between the law and the criminals.

Dark City (1950) *
William Dieterle: Charlton Heston, Lizabeth Scott, Viveca Lindfors, Dean Jagger.
A gangster role has often catapulted new actors to stardom. Here it works for Charlton Heston, a small-time grifter and war hero who veers to the good as he tries to extricate himself from his criminal past. He and Jagger both conduct investigations, but neither Scott nor Lindfors are femme fatales, just faithful girlfriend and loyal widow.

The Dark Corner (1946) **
   Henry Hathaway: Mark Stevens, Lucille Ball, Clifton Webb.
   Lucille Ball plays the savvy wisecracking secretary to a somewhat confused private eye, Mark Stevens. He utters the archetypal lament, "I feel all dead inside. I'm backed up in a dark corner, and I don't know who's hitting me." Clifton Webb performs a variation of his role in *Laura*.
The Dark Mirror (1946) **
   Robert Siodmak: Olivia de Havilland, Lew Ayres, Thomas Mitchell.
   Two investigations of a murder: one psychiatric, the other criminal. The innocent twin becomes an accessory to the crime by playing mum with the police. Whodunit becomes which one is it?
Dark Passage (1947) **
   Delmar Daves: Humphrey Bogart, Lauren Bacall, Agnes Moorehead.
   Though Bogart is innocent of killing a hated wife, he's had an affair with Moorehead, and as an escaped and hunted con, he causes the death of two people and cannot prove his innocence. The first person camera point of view, unlike that in *The Lady in the Lake*, is fortunately abandoned when the bandages from the plastic surgery are taken off to reveal Humphrey Bogart. Bacall is the good woman.
Dead Reckoning (1947) *
   John Cromwell: Humphrey Bogart, Lizabeth Scott, Morris Carnovsky.
   Bogart, trying to be tough, becomes trapped in the fallen world he sets out to investigate. Scott plays the duplicitous but doomed femme fatale. Snappy dialog by Steve Fisher.
Deadline at Dawn (1946)
   Harold Clurman: Bill Williams, Susan Hayward, Paul Lukas.
   Sailor Williams can't remember whether or not he's murdered Lola Lane in this noir based on a Woolrich novel and written for the screen by Clifford Odets. Neither Hayward nor the camera work of Nicholas Musuraca and Vernon Walker's special effects can rescue this film from a sententious script and a miscast Lukas as Maxi the Taxi.
Deception (1946) *
   Irving Rapper: Bette Davis, Claude Rains, Paul Henreid.
   Davis, like other heroines of melodrama, is caught between two inadequate men, her jealous husband Henreid, and her sadistic former lover Rains. She lies about her past and finally kills the lover, a great composer, to save the career of her cellist husband. Rains steals the film as he deliberately drives Davis to kill him. This film demonstrates how noir can even penetrate the concert hall. It contains an original cello concerto by Erich Wolfgang Korngold, who also composed the score.

Decoy (1946)
Jack Bernhard: Jean Gillie, Robert Armstrong, Edward Norris.
Only one step above Ed Wood. Gillie is a real femme fatale, but the plot borders on a ludicrous science fiction resurrection from the dead.

Desperate (1947) **
Anthony Mann: Steve Brodie, Audrey Long, Raymond Burr.
Brodie is an innocent truck driver forced into crime by a gang, whom he then must flee to save his pregnant wife. Although essentially innocent, he makes a number of questionable decisions along the way. In a scene notable for its violence, Burr beats him in a dark stairway as a ceiling light swings back and forth, etching noir chiaroscuro.

Destination Murder (1950) **
Edward L. Cahn: Joyce Mackenzie, Albert Dekker, Hurd Hatfield.
Edward Cahn made one of the best westerns, *Law and Order*, then got lost as a studio hack. Here he shows his talents in this much better than average B film. Joyce Mackenzie, in search of her father's killer, seems, if we decipher the Code, to sleep her way to the top of the mob and revenge. All the characters are double crossers. The Redcaps, an Ink Spots–like group, provide the musical numbers.

Detour (1945) ***
Edgar G. Ulmer: Tom Neal, Ann Savage.
Everyone's favorite B movie. Neal stumbles from one mistake to another, as the song, "I Can't Believe That You're in Love with Me" accompanies him to his doom. Too short for an investigation; it's just implied.

Dial M for Murder (1954) **
Alfred Hitchcock: Grace Kelly, Ray Milland, Robert Cummings.
Even Grace Kelly could not escape being tarnished. Unfaithful to her husband, Milland, a rotter who wants her dead, she kills her intended assassin and is then framed for murder.

Dishonored Lady (1947) *
Robert Stevenson: Hedy Lamarr, Dennis O'Keefe, John Loder.
Another example of a women's film transformed into a noir. Lamarr is a successful editor haunted by the tragic death of her father and too easily seduced by rich man Loder. Her office enemy, William Lundigan, frames her for his murder of Loder and robbery of Loder's safe. Good man (like the usual good girl) O'Keefe helps clear her. Morris Carnovsky plays the wise psychiatrist who is the moral center of the film.

Double Indemnity (1944) ***
Billy Wilder: Fred MacMurray, Barbara Stanwyck, Edward G. Robinson.
This film is one of two essential noirs, and the one that brought the genre into consciousness. No study, course, or article can do without it. Based on

a novel by James M. Cain, its screenplay is the purest noir ever concocted by Raymond Chandler.

A Double Life (1947) ***

George Cukor: Ronald Coleman, Shelley Winters, Signe Hasso, Edmond O'Brien.

Coleman's Oscar role as a murderous Othello (onstage and in real life). Winters portrays a lower class victim again, while O'Brien, an agent accused of having an affair with Hasso, Coleman's ex-wife, investigates.

Drive a Crooked Road (1954) *

Richard Quine: Mickey Rooney, Dianne Foster, Kevin McCarthy.

Mickey plays a mechanic/race car driver who's seduced into driving a souped up getaway car by Foster, the mistress of McCarthy. Noir has begun to wane: The film employs bright daylight location shots, particularly at Malibu; the femme fatale turns good girl; and the investigation only begins at the end.

Edge of Doom (1950) *

Mark Robson: Farley Granger, Dana Andrews, Joan Evans, Paul Stewart, Adele Jergens.

Film noir owes a great debt to the naturalistic novel, in which social and psychological forces bring about the tragic fate of a lower class protagonist, in this case Farley Granger, who murders an unsympathetic priest with a crucifix. Dana Andrews in a Bing Crosby priest role delivers all the pious platitudes. Joan Evans plays the good girl who loves Granger. Stewart is a petty thief whose robbery of a movie box office leads to Granger's arrest, and Adele Jergens, his floozy girlfriend, serve as contrasts.

Fall Guy (1947)

Reginald LeBoy: Clifford Penn, Teala Loring, Robert Armstrong.

Another Woolrich story in which the hero suffers memory problems and is framed for a murder. Elisha Cook, Jr., is present again, operating the elevator.

Fallen Angel (1945) **

Otto Preminger: Dana Andrews, Linda Darnell, Alice Faye, Charles Bickford.

Dana Andrews, a drifter, arrives on the central coast of California and, like all the men in the movie, falls for Linda Darnell, in one of her best roles as the temptress of the local diner. Alice Faye, the presumed star, plays the rich good girl who unfortunately does not even sing. After Andrews marries Faye, he becomes the chief suspect in Darnell's murder.

The Family Secret (1951)

Henry Levin: John Derek, Lee J. Cobb, Jody Lawrance.

John Derek, a law student, accidentally kills his best friend and admits the crime to his lawyer father, Cobb, but refuses to tell the D.A. Cobb then takes on the defense of the man falsely accused, who dies before the trial is over. This is a great idea for a film noir, but it gets murdered on the way to the screen.

Fear in the Night (1947)
Maxwell Shane: Paul Kelly, De Forrest Kelley.
In this Cornell Woolrich inspired film, Kelley dreams of a murder which turns out to be real. This B movie was upgraded and remade as *Nightmare* (1956).

The File on Thelma Jordan (1950) **
Robert Siodmak: Barbara Stanwyck, Wendell Corey.
Stanwyck is as bad as you can get: liar, thief, murderer, and Wendell Corey, a DA, falls for her. Less cold hearted than Phyllis Dietrichson, though, she redeems herself by murdering her former lover in a car crash, which also kills her.

Flaxy Martin (1949) *
Richard L. Bare: Virginia Mayo, Zachary Scott, Dorothy Malone.
Virginia Mayo plays a 100 percent femme fatale who double crosses both her gangster keeper and her lover Scott, a mob lawyer who wants out. Instead of a being a cad, he turns into a fall guy and takes the rap for Mayo, a suspect, not the perpetrator, in a murder case. Dorothy Malone plays the good girl, a redemptive librarian. The not quite omnipresent Elisha Cook, Jr. plays a role similar to that of Wilmer in *The Maltese Falcon*.

Force of Evil (1948) **
Abe Polonsky: John Garfield, Thomas Gomez, Marie Windsor, Beatrice Pearson.
This is more overtly political than most noirs. Using very stylized dialogue, Polonsky, who was soon after blacklisted, equates the numbers racket with capitalism. George Barnes provided superb cinematography, but today, certain scenes, such as Garfield's farewell to Pearson, provoke unintended laughter.

Framed (1947) *
Richard Wallace: Glenn Ford, Janis Carter, Barry Sullivan.
Carter, a femme fatale, seduces unfocused vet Ford and involves him in her plots for robbery and murder. By falling for Ford and betraying and killing Sullivan, her former lover, she proves fatal to herself.

Gilda (1946) **
Charles Vidor: Rita Hayworth, Glenn Ford, George Macready.
Hayworth is right as she sings "Put the Blame on Mame," for she is not a femme fatale but a well-meaning gal caught in a homoerotic tug of war between her neurotic husband, Macready, and her former lover, Ford. This is

still another example of how a women's film turns into noir as it ventures into crime and the underworld.

The Glass Key (1942)
Stuart Heisler: Alan Ladd, Veronica Lake, Brian Donlevy.
Except for the corny ending, the film remains true to the Hammett novel. Ladd plays a sleazy henchman to political boss Donlevy in this tale of big city corruption, murder, and double crossing. Lake is a seeming femme fatale.

The Great Flamarion (1945)
Anthony Mann: Erich von Stroheim, Mary Beth Hughes, Dan Duryea.
A carnival noir in the Continental manner. Von Stroheim plays an Emil Jannings type obsessed with the unlikely Hughes, his lover and femme fatale, who is married to the alcoholic Dan Duryea. It includes betrayals, murder, flashbacks, and revenge.

The Guilty (1947)
John Reinhardt: Bonita Granville, Don Castle, John Litel.
Nancy Drew and her father are here immersed in the nightmare world of Cornell Woolrich. This is a genuinely B Monogram film that is too short for its convoluted plot. Granville plays a double role.

Guilty Bystander (1950)
Joseph Lerner: Zachary Scott, Faye Emerson, Mary Boland.
This film, shot in New York, has a Chandleresque plot in which ex-detective Scott, a hopeless alcoholic, must rise to the occasion of his son's kidnapping.

Gun Crazy (1950) **
Joseph H. Lewis: Peggy Cummins, John Dall.
A young couple on a crime spree would not seem to qualify as film noir, but when the male in the case falls into banditry through his love for the crazed femme fatale, the film enters noir territory. The film's most famous sequence, a bank robbery, consists of one long shot taken from the back of the getaway car.

Hell's Half Acre (1954) *
John H. Auer: Evelyn Keyes, Wendell Corey, Marie Windsor.
Noir comes to Hawaii, Hell's Half Acre being a Honolulu crime zone. Despite poor execution, the film has a great noir plot by Steve Fisher who also wrote *I Wake Up Screaming*, among others. Corey has faked his death at Pearl Harbor. Keyes, his widow, comes in search of him. Multiple murders, sinister doings, and three investigations keep the film moving before Corey sacrifices himself, releasing Keyes from the past so she can marry her wimpy boyfriend.

He Ran All the Way (1951) **
   John Berry: John Garfield, Shelley Winters, Wallace Ford.
   Garfield is a confused punk who didn't mean to kill a guard in a hold up. The best scene takes place in a "plunge," a public swimming pool, where Garfield meets the ever gullible Winters. She shelters him, but his neuroses delay any escape and lead to his death in the gutter. The last half of the film seems like a naturalistic stage play. It was Garfield's last film.

He Walked by Night (1948) **
   Alfred L. Werker: Richard Basehart, Scott Brady.
   Despite the police procedural and magisterial voiceover narration of Reed Hadley, the twisted noir protagonist Basehart, aided by the brilliant noir cinematography of John Alton, place this film into the genre.

Her Kind of Man (1946) *
   Frederick De Cordova: Zachary Scott, Janis Paige, Dane Clark, William Bendix.
   Scott, ever the cad, plays an unreformed bootlegger who now runs a casino and slaps around the help. Paige is his girl until Clark, a Broadway columnist, competes for her affection. Faye Emerson, Scott's sister, tries to put him on the right track and is killed for her efforts. Howard Smith plays the good cop investigating Bendix's suspicious disappearance.

High Wall (1947) **
   Curtis Bernhardt: Robert Taylor, Audrey Totter, Herbert Marshall.
   Taylor is a brain-damaged vet accused of killing his wife, but confined to a mental hospital. Totter, good for a change, plays a sympathetic Ingrid Bergman–like psychiatrist who helps to heal him and solve the crime.

His Kind of Woman (1951) *
   John Farrow: Robert Mitchum, Jane Russell, Vincent Price.
   Vincent Price hams it up as a ham actor in this camp noir. Jane Russell plays his world-weary mistress until she meets more world-weary, ex-con Mitchum, who, when he's bored, irons his money. A thin Raymond Burr plays the heavy.

Hollow Triumph (1948) *
   Steve Sekeley: Paul Henreid, Joan Bennett.
   Another John Alton film, written by Daniel Fuchs. Henreid plays a double role as a crook and as a not too perfect psychiatrist. Henreid 1 kills Henreid 2 in order to steal his identity. Bennett sleeps with both. Fate makes his triumph hollow.

Human Desire (1954) **
   Fritz Lang: Glenn Ford, Gloria Grahame, Broderick Crawford.
   A remake of Renoir's *La Bête Humaine*, itself based on Zola's novel. Ford, returned from the Korean War, becomes involved with Grahame,

Crawford's wife. The train tracks and locomotives in both films serve as metaphors for the force of destiny, but Ford, unlike Gabin in the French film, escapes.

I Confess (1953) **

Alfred Hitchcock: Montgomery Clift, Anne Baxter, Karl Malden, Brian Aherne.

Set in a cloudy gray Quebec, the film examines from a noir perspective the obligation of a priest never to reveal what he has heard in the confessional, even if silence makes him the prime suspect of a murder investigation. He's not completely innocent.

I Married a Communist (1949) **

Robert Stevenson: Robert Ryan, Laraine Day, Thomas Gomez, John Agar. Rereleased as *The Woman on Pier 13*, no doubt over political embarrassment with the title, this is one of the most underrated noirs. Here the dark past is Ryan's former membership in the Communist Party. Married to Day, the boss's daughter, he attempts to become a shipping executive, but the Party, like mobsters, wants to take over the docks. Parallel and interlocking subplots give the film more than usual depth.

I Wake Up Screaming (1941) ***

H. Bruce Humberstone: Betty Grable, Victor Mature, Carole Landis, Laird Cregar.

If this film had flashed across the French screen in 1946, it would have played a greater role in the early discussions of film noir, for it is in fact the first full Hollywood A movie realization of what would become a genre. It is the film that weds the style and structure of *Citizen Kane* to the crime melodrama. Laird Cregar plays the creepy detective, Carol Landis the bad sister. It's all here, even Elisha Cook, Jr.

I Walk Alone (1948) **

Byron Haskin: Burt Lancaster, Kirk Douglas, Lizabeth Scott.

Returning from a long prison sentence, similar to returning from the war, Lancaster confronts his old partner in crime, Douglas, who is as sinister as in his previous film, *Out of the Past*. Scott is a pawn, who sings. The nightclub and rackets are now run like big business, and accountant Wendell Corey, Lancaster's brother, works for Douglas.

Illegal (1955) *

Lewis Allen: Edward G. Robinson, Nina Foch, Hugh Marlowe, Albert Dekker.

Robinson, a great DA, sends an innocent man to the chair, resigns, and becomes a criminal lawyer with ties to the mob. Foch, his faithful secretary, is accused of murdering her crooked husband Marlowe. To defend her, Robinson must go against his employers. Jayne Mansfield, in her first role, is a key witness.

Impact (1949) **

Arthur Lubin: Brian Donlevy, Ella Raines, Helen Walker, Charles Coburn. This has the double twist of plot which makes so many noirs fun. Walker, Donlevy's wife, arranges for her lover to kill him, but the lover dies instead, his charred body mistaken for Donlevy's, who fakes amnesia and leaves the crime scene. Walker is then condemned for his murder. Donlevy disappears into Idaho and falls for good girl Raines, but when he returns to his previous life, he's accused of killing the lover. Coburn, with an Irish brogue, plays the investigator.

In a Lonely Place (1950) ***

Nicholas Ray: Humphrey Bogart, Gloria Grahame.
Long a sleeper, only now is it recognized as one of the best noirs. Ray prided himself on taking a gun away from Bogart and depicting him as a neurotic screenwriter, an ex-GI with a temper, who becomes a murder suspect while courting a more innocent and sympathetic Grahame.

Inner Sanctum (1948)

Lew Landers: Charles Russell, Mary Beth Hughes.
A short B movie not unlike the radio program that gave the film its name. In a flash forward, a strange clairvoyant tells a young woman on a train a murder story. Russell, the murderer, like Tom Neal in *Detour*, cannot escape his own doom. But then neither can the young woman, whose story it was.

Inside Job (1946)*

Jean Yarbrough: Preston Foster, Alan Curtis, Ann Rutherford.
Curtis's attempt to go straight fails when his past catches up with him in the form of Foster, his former partner in crime and now a big shot racketeer. Rutherford, the not so good wife, has little trouble becoming an accomplice in robbing the department store where she and Curtis work. The last scene reverses what looked to be a happy ending.

Jail Bait (1954)

Edward D. Wood, Jr.: Timothy Farrell, Lyle Talbot, Steve Reeves.
Exhibit B in the case for Ed Wood as Hollywood's worst director. Yet, noir it is, complete with plot twists brought about by plastic surgery and stolen identities. The title refers not to a Lolita but to the danger of carrying a gun.

Jigsaw (1949)

Fletcher Markle: Franchot Tone, Jean Wallace, Myron McCormick, Marc Lawrence.
Unimaginative direction and banal dialogue spoil this noir in which Tone, a womanizing DA, investigates the murder of journalist McCormick who had been investigating a right wing hate group. Wallace is the femme fatale whom Tone romances.

Johnny O'Clock (1947) *
Robert Rossen: Dick Powell, Evelyn Keyes, Ellen Drew, Lee J. Cobb, Thomas Gomez.
Robert Rossen's directorial debut. Dick Powell, who helps run a gambling casino owned by Gomez, becomes implicated in no less than three murders and kidnaps police inspector Cobb before the Code wins in the end.

The Killer Is Loose (1956) *
Budd Boetticher: Wendell Corey, Joseph Cotten, Rhonda Fleming.
Corey a pathetic, myopic bank clerk acts as the inside man in a bank robbery. He's caught, but not before Cotten, the cop, accidentally kills his wife. When Corey escapes from the prison farm, he sets out to avenge her murder by killing Fleming, Cotten's unhappily married wife.

Killer's Kiss (1955) **
Stanley Kubrick: Davy Gordon, Irene Kane, Frank Silvera.
A superb diploma work by the young master; its original title was "Kiss Me, Kill Me." As often in Kubrick's films, time plays a conscious role. Low budget, shot mostly at night, the film concludes with a brutal fight in a mannequin warehouse.

The Killers (1946) ***
Robert Siodmak: Burt Lancaster, Ava Gardner, Edmond O'Brien.
The film begins with Hemingway's short story and then creates the story behind it, complete with femme fatale Gardner, investigator O'Brien, and chief victim, Lancaster, a not too bright boxer who more closely resembles a character from a naturalistic novel than a Hemingway hero. In every respect, this film is dead center noir.

The Killing (1956) ***
Stanley Kubrick: Sterling Hayden, Elisha Cook, Jr., Marie Windsor.
Coming early in Kubrick's career and late in the noir period, *The Killing* has a documentary visual style and, being a caper film, might well be placed on the cusp of noir. But its gallery of noir stalwarts, none of them here playing gangsters but rather desperate people drawn into crime by their circumstances, plus Kubrick's disjunctive narrative style bring the film into the genre. The actual robbery sequence is a masterpiece of film art, one that Eisenstein would have approved of. And then there's Timothy Carey, the horse assassin, talking to James Edwards in the parking lot of the track: "Who do you like?" "Red Lightening in the seventh."

A Kiss Before Dying (1956) **
Gerd Oswald: Robert Wagner, Joanne Woodward, Virginia Leith, Jeffrey Hunter.
Based on an Ira Levin novel, it could be considered a murder mystery. Wagner kills the pregnant Woodward, covers up the crime, murders a witness, and then courts Leith, Woodward's sister and daughter of tycoon

George Macready. But Wagner's pathology, his sick relationship with his mother, Mary Astor, and Leith's investigation of her sister's murder all nudge this into a generic noir. Jeffrey Hunter plays the good boy and helper.

Kiss Me Deadly (1955) ***

Robert Aldrich: Ralph Meeker, Cloris Leachman, Albert Dekker.

The film departs from the Mickey Spillane original, deepening the portrait of Mike Hammer and placing him in a much murkier and more apocalyptic criminal world. For many critics it marks the end of the classic period.

Kiss the Blood Off My Hands (1948) *

Norman Foster: Burt Lancaster, Joan Fontaine.

Set in London. Lancaster, a troubled vet, falls deeper into crime, and nurse Fontaine, who attempts to kiss the blood off his hands, kills Robert Newton, his tempter. Russell Metty shot the film, and Miklos Rozsa composed the score.

The Lady from Shanghai (1947) **

Orson Welles: Rita Hayworth, Orson Welles.

In this film an innocent Welles is drawn into the web of femme fatale Hayworth. The nightmarish plot reaches a climax in the justly famous Hall of Mirrors shoot-out.

Lady in the Lake (1946)

Robert Montgomery: Robert Montgomery, Audrey Totter, Lloyd Nolan.

An interesting idea that doesn't work: the first person camera point of view. One wishes that this great Chandler novel had been given more conventional noir treatment. Montgomery (Marlowe) of course is innocent, but Nolan plays a very vicious rogue cop.

The Las Vegas Story (1952)

Robert Stevenson: Victor Mature, Jane Russell, Vincent Price.

The noir plot gets waylaid by the back and forth relationship between Mature and Russell, which here lacks the chemistry between her and Mitchum. Nevertheless, there's a murder, two investigators, and a nightclub starring Hoagy Carmichael. The Code blinked at the ending as Price, the inadequate husband, but not the murderer, goes off to jail, and Russell off to Mature.

Laura (1944) ***

Otto Preminger: Gene Tierney, Dana Andrews, Clifton Webb, Vincent Price.

Rather than in the dark city, it takes place in an arty media and publishing world presided over by Webb (Waldo Lydecker), a spin-off of Alexander Woollcott. But its noir style, its creepy detective who becomes obsessed with an allegedly dead beauty, its seedy though sophisticated characters, its narrative reversals, voiceover and flashback, make it more than the usual whodunit. It has an outstanding score by David Raksin, turned into a popular song after the release of the film.

The Letter (1940) ***
William Wyler: Bette Davis, Herbert Marshall, James Stephenson.
This is a superior noir made just before the genre came into consciousness. Set in the tropics rather than in a city and based on a story by W. Somerset Maugham, it nevertheless centers on a femme fatale, a murder, an investigation, fallible protagonists, and a final blow of fate.

Loan Shark (1952) *
Seymour Friedman: George Raft, Dorothy Hart, Paul Stewart.
A better than average B noir. After his brother-in-law is murdered, Raft, an ex-con, agrees to infiltrate the mob that victimizes the factory workers. Joseph Biroc's noir cinematography gives the film some distinction.

The Long Night (1947)
Anatole Litvak: Henry Fonda, Barbara Bel Geddes, Vincent Price, Ann Dvorak.
A remake of *Le jour se leve*. Like the original, this is a studio set film that attempts poetic realism. Narrated as a flashback, its naturalistic plot concerns a doomed proletarian who has killed the charlatan who seduced his not entirely innocent girlfriend. Vincent Price is no Jules Berry.

Loophole (1954) **
Harold Schuster: Barry Sullivan, Charles McGraw, Dorothy Malone.
Noir stalwart Sullivan plays a bank teller who is tricked out of his cash box. When he neglects to report the crime immediately, McGraw, a bond insurance investigator, makes his life miserable.

Macao (1952) **
Josef Von Sternberg: Robert Mitchum, Jane Russell, William Bendix, Gloria Grahame.
Grahame plays the villain's girlfriend in this thriller of mixed identities, criminal pasts, and double crosses. Mitchum and Russell bond again, and an oriental nightclub presents unlimited opportunities for Von Sternberg's visual touches, though the film was reshot by Nicholas Ray.

Make Haste to Live (1954) *
William A. Seiter: Dorothy McGuire, Stephen McNally, Edgar Buchanan, Mary Murphy.
Dorothy McGuire, a successful newspaper editor in a small New Mexico town, finds the past catches up with her when her mobster husband, McNally, after eighteen years in the pen for allegedly killing her, seeks out vengeance. To further complicate her troubles, she pretends he's her brother. And as "Uncle," he romances Murphy, their daughter.

The Maltese Falcon (1941) ***

John Huston: Humphrey Bogart, Mary Astor, Sydney Greenstreet, Peter Lorre.

The default first film noir. It's the third version of the Hammett novel done by Warner Brothers in less than ten years. But unlike most remakes, it is the most memorable, primarily because of Huston's faithfulness to the novel and the film's superb cast. It made Bogart a star and created the screen's first true hard-boiled detective.

The Man on the Eiffel Tower (1949)

Burgess Meredith: Franchot Tone, Charles Laughton, Burgess Meredith.

Mental case Tone implicates a hapless Meredith in a murder, and then plays cat and mouse with Inspector Maigret, here portrayed by Laughton. The climax takes place on the famed tower.

Manhandled (1949) *

Lewis Foster: Dorothy Lamour, Dan Duryea, Sterling Hayden.

A man tells his psychiatrist that he dreamt of killing his wife. When she's found dead and her jewelry found missing, investigator Hayden and crooked private eye Duryea enter the plot, which along the way attempts to incriminate Lamour, who was fool enough to have Duryea as a boyfriend.

The Mask of Dimitrios (1944)

Jean Negulesco: Peter Lorre, Sidney Greenstreet, Faye Emerson.

Peter Lorre is miscast as a novelist hero investigating the death of the still living Dimitrios (Zachary Scott). All the good noir elements get sidetracked by the personal quirks of Greenstreet and Lorre. Eric Ambler wrote the novel.

Mildred Pierce (1945) ***

Michael Curtiz: Joan Crawford, Zachary Scott, Ann Blyth, Jack Carson, Bruce Bennett.

The best of the women's films turned noir. Screenwriter Ranald MacDougall transforms Cain's Dreiser-like novel, which dealt only with the rise and fall of a middle class housewife, into a murder mystery, the whole film consisting of a flashback. Crawford won an Oscar for this, and it gave her a whole new career as a mature woman.

Moonrise (1948) *

Frank Borzage: Dane Clark, Gail Russell, Ethel Barrymore.

A swamp noir. Dane Clark, a confused young man haunted by the past, kills his taunter, Lloyd Bridges. That a director of romances such as Borzage could make a credible film noir indicates the power of the period. Always ominous, an amusement park and its Ferris wheel provide the best scene.

Murder Is My Beat (1955)
Edgar G. Ulmer: Barbara Payton, Paul Langton.
Disappointing after *Detour*, though it has a more complicated noir plot. It begins with detective Langton being arrested for letting alleged murderess Payton loose. Then the flashbacks take over as he and Payton become a "comedy of remarriage" couple tracking down the real killers.

Murder, My Sweet (1944) ***
Edward Dymytrk: Dick Powell, Claire Trevor, Anne Shirley.
This is the second screen adaptation of Chandler's *Farewell My Lovely;* the first was a Falcon movie. The producers, afraid that because Dick Powell was the star audiences would think it a musical, changed the name. They also tampered with the plot, immersing Marlowe deeper into the fallen world, yet giving the film a comic structure. It is drenched in noir atmosphere, and cinematographer Harry Wild gave it the full RKO treatment, previously seen in *Stranger on the Third Floor* and *Citizen Kane*.

My Favorite Brunette (1947) *
Elliot Nugent: Bob Hope, Dorothy Lamour, Peter Lorre.
One of the few comic noirs. It's the film that proves that film noir was not an afterthought. Because the French gave the genre its name does not mean that Hollywood was not aware of it. Once more, how can you make a parody of something that does not exist?

Naked Alibi (1954) **
Jerry Hopper: Sterling Hayden, Gene Barry, Gloria Grahame.
Hayden dismissed from the Force for brutality, goes south of the border to get cop killer Barry who two-times his wife with Grahame. Cinematographer Russell Metty gives the film the same look as he did his later work, *Touch of Evil*.

Niagara (1953) **
Henry Hathaway: Joseph Cotten, Marilyn Monroe, Jean Peters.
Two couples on a honeymoon at Niagara Falls, one conventional, the other noirish and doomed. Cotten plays the older, still disturbed former GI husband to the unfaithful Monroe. Peters is a somewhat repressed investigator who becomes involved in the *amour fou* murders.

Night Editor (1946) *
Henry Levin: William Gargan, Janis Carter.
A night editor tells the story, in flashbacks, of a famous 1920s murder case. Gargan, a good detective, is having an affair with Carter, a bad society woman. When they witness a brutal murder, he must pretend he was not a witness, but the investigation in this boomerang plot leads back to him. The Code may have forced the writers to set the film back a generation so as to provide the happy contemporary ending.

Nightfall (1957) **
Jacques Tourneur: Aldo Ray, Anne Bancroft, Brian Keith, James Gregory.
Aldo Ray, though innocent, makes the ever dangerous noir mistake of walking off in the snowy wasteland with hot money. Bancroft first appears as a femme fatale, but switches to good girl. Gregory plays the investigator and Keith the crook, both pursuing Ray. David Goodis wrote the original story on which the film is based.

Night Has a Thousand Eyes (1948) **
John Farrow: Edward G. Robinson, Gail Russell, John Lund.
Another noir from the imagination of Cornell Woolrich. Robinson is a fake psychic who starts getting real premonitions. His attempts to alter the future lead to tragic consequences.

No Man of Her Own (1950) *
Mitchell Leisen: Barbara Stanwyck, John Lund, Lyle Bettger.
More Cornell Woolrich. When Phyllis Thaxter dies in a train wreck, Stanwyck takes her identity. Both were eight months pregnant. When the past catches up with her, murder follows.

Nobody Lives Forever (1946)
Jean Negulesco: John Garfield, Walter Brennan, Faye Emerson.
Ex-gangster and disoriented ex-GI, Garfield decides to save Geraldine Fitzgerald from his former criminal buddies. Emerson plays the femme fatale in a film whose chief location is a creaky pier at night.

No Questions Asked (1951) **
Harold F. Kress: Barry Sullivan, Arlene Dahl, George Murphy, Jean Hagen.
A complete film noir. Sullivan, an insurance lawyer turns fence and goes bad through his love for treacherous Dahl. Good girl Jean Hagen stands by. Murphy investigates. How many Hollywood films, like this one, end with the wounded hero being driven off in an ambulance, his sins atoned for?

Nora Prentiss (1947) **
Vincent Sherman: Ann Sheridan, Kent Smith, Bruce Bennett, Robert Alda.
Dead center noir. Kent Smith is really the central character, who by way of an accident fakes his own death, and then, when he's disfigured in another accident, is successfully prosecuted as his own murderer. Sheridan plays the nightclub singer for whom he gives up family and career.

Notorious (1946) ***
Alfred Hitchcock: Cary Grant, Ingrid Bergman, Claude Rains.
This hybrid of a gothic melodrama (the imprisoned woman), a women's film (a heroine caught between two unworthy men), and a spy thriller turns into a noir. The woman is sexually notorious and proves a femme fatale to her husband; her husband is dominated by his possessive mother; and her lover is a pimp for the CIA. Truffaut thought this Hitchcock's best film.

Odds Against Tomorrow (1959) **

Robert Wise: Robert Ryan, Harry Belafonte, Ed Begley.

A very late noir, possibly the last of the period, complete with Shelley Winters and Gloria Grahame. A bunch of losers attempt a bank robbery and everything goes wrong. A saxophone score accompanies the anti-racism of the film.

On Dangerous Ground (1952) *

Nicholas Ray: Robert Ryan, Ida Lupino. Ward Bond.

Directed by Ray, produced by John Houseman, written by A. I. Bezzerides, featuring the noir icon Ryan supported by Lupino, as well as a score by Bernard Herrmann, this should have been one of the greatest film noirs, but the ingredients don't fit well enough to make a fully satisfying whole.

One Way Street (1950)

Hugo Fregonese: James Mason, Marta Toren, Dan Duryea, William Conrad. Despite the presence of Duryea and Conrad, all the characters are clichéd or implausible. What starts out as good noir in the dark city degenerates into a sentimental stay in a Mexican village where crooked doctor Mason reforms, though Fate will not be cheated.

The Other Woman (1954) *

Hugo Haas: Hugo Haas, Cleo Moore.

Married to the daughter of a studio chief, Haas plays a continental film director who wants to make art films, ones that don't have happy endings. In this cheapie he narrates his own unhappy story of blackmail and murder, caught in the plot of Moore, a revengeful and over the top femme fatale. Set in a Hollywood studio, the film self-consciously comments on the relationship between noir and classic Hollywood.

Out of the Past (1947) ***

Jacques Tourneur: Robert Mitchum, Jane Greer, Kirk Douglas.

This is the other essential noir. The hard-boiled detective double crosses his client, falls in love with a duplicitous, lethal woman, and discovers he cannot escape his past. Based on contrasts: Bridgeport vs. San Francisco; Virginia Huston (the good girl) vs. both Jane Greer *and* Rhonda Fleming, the film consists of so many lies that it takes a final lie from the mute Dickie Moore to close it. For pilgrims, Jeff Bailey's gas station is no longer there, but otherwise Bridgeport, sixty years later, looks the same.

The Paradine Case (1947) *

Alfred Hitchcock: Gregory Peck, Alida Valli, Ann Todd.

This courtroom noir is noteworthy only because Hitchcock directed it. A distinguished supporting cast—Charles Coburn, Charles Laughton, Leo G. Carroll, Louis Jourdan, Ethel Barrymore—plus the cinematography of Lee Garmes, the costumes of Travis Banton, and the music of Franz Waxman cannot save a film that has no sympathetic characters.

The People Against O'Hara (1951) *
John Sturgis: Spencer Tracy, Diana Lynn, John Hodiak, James Arness.
Tracy, a lawyer recovering from alcoholism, comes out of retirement to defend Arness against a murder charge. Though he began his career as a gangster, the older Tracy carries too much Father Flannigan with him to be a tough noir hero, but John Alton shot the film whose plot includes relapses, betrayals, and investigations.

Phantom Lady (1944) ***
Robert Siodmak: Ella Raines, Franchot Tone, Alan Curtis.
This is Siodmak's first film noir. Its investigator is a woman, Raines, the faithful secretary who seeks the Phantom Lady in order to clear her boss, Curtis, from the chair. Based on a Woolrich novel, it shows the dark city, a crazed artist killer, Tone, and best of all Elisha Cook, Jr. at the drums, beating out his desire for an encouraging Raines.

Pickup on South Street (1953) **
Sam Fuller: Richard Widmark, Jean Peters, Thelma Ritter.
Widmark is a three-time loser who runs afoul of the mob, in this case the Communist Party, when he pickpockets microfilm from courier Peters. Ritter is a stool pigeon and informer who rises to tragic heroism. Patriotism triumphs over the class struggle.

Pitfall (1948) ***
André De Toth: Dick Powell, Lizabeth Scott, Jane Wyatt, Raymond Burr.
Film noir delights in disrupting the conventional life and showing the pitfalls of escape from a humdrum existence. Powell errs with Lizbeth Scott, who is not a femme fatale but a woman unlucky in the men in her life. Burr, in one of his best roles, plays a P.I. who stalks her. Wyatt, the good wife, also has a dark side. The uncredited screenwriter William Bowers no doubt provided the snappy dialogue.

A Place in the Sun (1951) ***
George Stevens: Montgomery Clift, Elizabeth Taylor, Shelley Winters.
Dreiser's long naturalist novel, *An American Tragedy*, provides a simple and effective noir plot. An upwardly mobile Clift, while courting the upper class Taylor, stumbles into an affair with the lower class Winters and causes her death. An investigation follows and leads to the ultimate conclusion.

Possessed (1947) **
Curtis Bernhardt: Joan Crawford, Van Heflin, Raymond Massey.
Imagine Mildred Pierce really killing Monte Beragon, losing her memory, and wandering the empty early morning streets of L.A. It wasn't a dream, and psychiatry cannot save her.

The Postman Always Rings Twice (1946) **
Tay Garnett: John Garfield, Lana Turner, Cecil Kellaway.
MGM had trouble getting the noir look. But despite its glossy veneer and the absence of the dark city and chiaroscuro, the presence of a femme fatale, a flashback narrative, investigations, double crosses, and twists of fate place the film in the genre. It does not hold up as well as other classics. Too many reversals between Garfield and Turner and a sappy Production Code ending spoil the story, which was done better by Visconti in *Ossessione* (1943).

Private Hell 36 (1954) *
Don Siegel: Ida Lupino, Steve Cochrane, Howard Duff.
Two frustrated cops recover stolen money. Duff, married to Dorothy Malone, wants to return it; Cochrane, stuck on nightclub singer Lupino, wants to keep it. Lupino coauthored the screenplay.

The Prowler (1951) **
Joseph Losey: Van Heflin, Evelyn Keyes.
Heflin is a cop who seduces Keyes and kills her husband. It's a perfect noir situation which Losey develops very well. With life insurance money the two buy a motel in Vegas, but her pregnancy (her husband was sterile) might tip someone off to their crimes, or so Heflin supposes.

Pushover (1954) *
Richard Quine: Fred MacMurray, Kim Novak, Dorothy Malone, Philip Carey.
Walter Neff meets Madeleine Elster. MacMurray, now a cop, falls for gun moll Novak and succumbs to her scheme to run off with stolen money. Good cop Phil Carey and good girl Malone act as a counterweight to MacMurray's fall.

Quicksand (1950) **
Irving Pichel: Mickey Rooney, Peter Lorre, Jeanne Cagney, Barbara Bates.
Poor Andy Hardy, now a mechanic who "borrows" $20 from a till, falls into a quicksand of deeper crime, blackmailing, and double crossing. It has the documentary look common to many later film noirs.

Race Street (1948) *
Edwin L. Marin: George Raft, William Bendix, Marilyn Maxwell, Harry Morgan.
George Raft plays an upscale bookie and nightclub owner who wants to retire and settle down with femme fatale Maxwell. When his best friend Morgan is murdered by a new syndicate, he refuses to cooperate with another friend, police investigator William Bendix, and seeks to avenge the death himself. His tragic death resolves his dilemmas.

Raw Deal (1948) **

Anthony Mann: Dennis O'Keefe, Marsha Hunt, Claire Trevor, Raymond Burr.

Nobody's on the level. Social worker Hunt helps O'Keefe escape and shoots a man for him but he betrays her, as does the jealous Trevor. Burr of course has double-crossed O'Keefe. John Alton was the cameraman.

The Reckless Moment (1949) **

Max Ophuls: Joan Bennett, James Mason, Geraldine Brooks, Shepperd Strudwick.

Since You Went Away done as a film noir. An upper middle class wife and mother keeps her family together by hiding bodies, coping with blackmailers, and inspiring love in the heart of a petty crook. Three men die while hubby is away.

Red Light (1949)*

Roy Del Ruth: George Raft, Virginia Mayo, Raymond Burr.

George Raft attempts to avenge the murder of his brother, a priest. Raymond Burr at his villainous best, attempts to bring evil out of evil, but Providence, in the form of the red light—"24 Hour Service"—wins out in the end.

Ride the Pink Horse (1947) *

Robert Montgomery: Robert Montgomery, Wanda Hendrix.

This is Ben Hecht's essay into existentialism. Montgomery plays an enigmatic character with but one name, Gagin, who, pursued by the police, seeks revenge in a New Mexico town that has a symbolic carousel. Hendrix, in brown face, plays an Indian girl who wants to save him.

Roadblock (1951) *

Harold Daniels: Charles McGraw, Joan Dixon.

Some nice twists. McGraw an insurance investigator turns crook through his love for femme fatale Dixon, a racketeer's mistress. She turns good, but not good enough to save McGraw.

Rogue Cop (1954) *

Roy Rowland: Robert Taylor, George Raft, Janet Leigh, Steve Forrest.

Just what the title says. Taylor is comfortable with all the corruption until it leads to the death of his kid brother Forrest, whereupon he seeks revenge and redemption.

Rope (1948) **

Alfred Hitchcock: James Stewart, John Dall, Farley Granger.

A tour de force of an entire film consisting of one shot, this Technicolor production begins with a murder and then becomes a long investigation. It twists into noir because the investigator, Stewart, is also the instigator of the crime.

Scandal Sheet (1952) ***
   Phil Karlson: Broderick Crawford, Donna Reed, John Derek.
   Karlson would make any pantheon of 1950s directors. This film takes a very satisfying noir twist in that an aggressive yellow journalism editor (Crawford) with a take-no-prisoners attitude toward getting the story accidentally kills his estranged wife. Derek, his star reporter, starts the investigation which Crawford must encourage, though it leads ultimately to himself.

Scarlet Street (1945) ***
   Fritz Lang: Edward G. Robinson, Joan Bennett, Dan Duryea.
   This is a remake of Renoir's *La Chienne* (1931), and a sequel to *The Woman in the Window*. Robinson, a pathetic and henpecked clerk, falls in love with Bennett, a scarlet woman who brings out his talent for portraiture. Her pimp/lover, Duryea, attributes the paintings to her. When Robinson finds her in Duryea's arms, he kills her. The lover is convicted of the crime, and Robinson ends up wandering the dark streets jobless and unable to paint. This is how noir treats the plot of the worm turns.

Screaming Mimi (1958) *
   Gerd Oswald: Anita Ekberg, Philip Carey, Gypsy Rose Lee.
   A maniac with a knife attacks Ekberg in the shower, and she turns psycho. Reporter Carey tries to solve the case and falls for Ekberg. She becomes an exotic dancer in a nightclub, The Madhouse, run by Gypsy Rose Lee, who gives a hint of what made her famous by her own rendition of "Put the Blame on Mame." This is a late classic noir, filmed by Burnett Guffey in hard edged black and white.

The Second Woman (1950) *
   James V. Kern: Robert Young, Betsy Drake, John Sutton.
   This *Rebecca*-like woman's film becomes a noir, as Betsy Drake, in love with the seemingly paranoid and self-destructive Young, attempts to cure him of his tragic past by investigating the causes of the "accidents" which plague him. The film, set at Pebble Beach, begins with Young's attempted suicide and then becomes a sustained flashback, until the whodunit-like conclusion.

The Secret of the Whistler (1946) **
   George Sherman: Richard Dix, Leslie Brooks.
   A radio series here turned into a noir film. Dix plays a painter with an invalid wife. He falls in love with Brooks, his gorgeous model, and to free himself attempts to kill his wife, but does not. Somewhat recovered, the wife discovers his intentions and kills herself, incriminating him. Brooks becomes suspicious, investigates, and when she finds evidence of murder, Dix kills her. All of the events in this plot result from chance, or is it a moralistic fate which the Whistler, like the Shadow, "knows"?

Shadow of a Doubt (1943) ***

Alfred Hitchcock: Joseph Cotten, Teresa Wright, Macdonald Carey, Henry Travers.

A psychotic serial killer comes to Santa Rosa and disrupts the dull and conventional ordinary life. The noir twist occurs because his niece, who has the same name, also has homicidal tendencies and catches on to him. A closer look at the climax suggests that she actually kills him.

Shadow on the Wall (1950) *

Patrick Jackson: Ann Sothern, Zachary Scott, Nancy Davis.

Noir can turn even Maisie into a killer. Scott, who suffers loss of memory, is accused of killing his wife who was having an affair with Tom Helmore, who later became Gavin Elster. Child psychiatrist Nancy Davis (Reagan) unravels the crime through her treatment of Gigi Perreau, who saw the murderer's distinctive shadow on the wall.

Shield for Murder (1954) **

Edmond O'Brien and Howard W. Koch: Edmond O'Brien, John Agar, Marla English.

This is a rogue cop noir. O'Brien, dissatisfied with his pay, kills a crook and steals his loot and is then assigned to investigate the murder. John Agar plays his good cop protégé who gets wise to him. Now hunted by both the police and the mob, O'Brien shoots it out with the mob at a public gym, a great scene, and then is gunned down by the police at the suburban home he wanted to buy and where he has buried the stolen money.

Shockproof (1949) **

Douglas Sirk: Cornel Wilde, Patricia Knight.

Sam Fuller coauthored the screenplay. Wilde, a parole officer, decides not to turn in his parolee wife for shooting a man but instead takes it on the lam with her. In this film, the parole officers have bugged a police psychiatrist's office.

Shoot to Kill (1947) *

William A. Berke: Luana Walters, Edmund MacDonald, Russell Wade.

Noir all the way. Wade investigates a car crash and uncovers a crooked DA, lots of double crosses, fake marriages, a dark city, a nightclub where Gene Rodgers performs, all narrated through disjointed flashbacks.

Side Street (1950) **

Anthony Mann: Farley Granger, Cathy O'Donnell; James Craig, Paul Kelly.

Unlike *Naked City*, the location shooting of New York in this film truly serves a generic film noir. Picking up a satchel of dough always proves disastrous, even when one is well intentioned.

Slightly Scarlet (1956) *
  Allan Dwan: Rhonda Fleming, Arlene Dahl, John Payne.
  What a great idea to put these two beauties together in glorious Technicolor, shot by John Alton. Loosely based on a James M. Cain novel, it's the story of two sisters, one not too good, one bad, both attracted to the morally ambivalent Payne.

The Sniper (1952) *
  Edward Dymtryk: Arthur Franz, Marie Windsor, Adolphe Menjou.
  Like the pre-noir *M*, this film centers on a mentally disturbed serial killer, abused as a child by his mother. Windsor is his first victim; Menjou the cop who gets him. It contains lots of San Francisco's local color as well as some Stanley Kramer social awareness about mental illness and the flaws of society.

Somewhere in the Night (1946)
  Joseph L. Mankiewicz: John Hodiak, Nancy Guild.
  1946 was a big year for amnesiac veterans. Hodiak plays one in this film looking for a mysterious character who turns out to be himself. Richard Conte owns the nightclub and Lloyd Nolan plays the investigator. All the conventions are here, but in this early version of them, they look dated.

Spellbound (1945) ***
  Alfred Hitchcock: Gregory Peck, Ingrid Bergman, Leo G. Carroll.
  The most self-consciously Freudian of all the noirs, except for ignoring that Freudian basic, the Oedipus complex. Ben Hecht wrote the screenplay; Miklos Rozsa wrote the haunting score, his best; and Salvador Dali created the dream. There's no dark city but all the other ingredients are present, including an amnesiac veteran, plus Ingrid Bergman in one of her most appealing roles. She gives it the extra star.

The Strange Affair of Uncle Harry (1945) **
  Robert Siodmak: George Sanders, Geraldine Fitzgerald, Ella Raines.
  In attempting to murder his incestuous sister Fitzgerald, Sanders poisons his other sister by mistake, whereupon Fitzgerald is condemned for the crime. They won't believe his confession, or was it all a dream? Ella Raines is the girl he wants to marry.

Strange Bargain (1949) *
  Will Price: Jeffrey Lynn, Martha Scott, Harry Morgan.
  Lynn, an unfortunate suburbanite who falls into trouble when his ex-boss involves him in a scheme to make a suicide look like a murder. Scott is Lynn's wife and Morgan the investigator. Truly, a B movie, but lots of pitfalls and twists hold one's attention.

Strange Triangle (1946) *
Ray McCarey: Preston Foster, Signe Hasso, Shepperd Strudwick.
Foster, a former bank cop, returns from the war to be promoted to bank examiner. On his first night on the town he's seduced by the mysterious Signe Hasso, who turns out to be the wife of bank manager Strudwick who's embezzling money to please his unfaithful wife. Foster attempts to straighten things out and ends up accused of murder.

Stranger on the Third Floor (1940) **
Boris Ingster: Peter Lorre, John McGuire, Margaret Tallichet, Elisha Cook, Jr.
A candidate for the original Hollywood film noir. Cinematographer Musuraca and special effects master Walker provide a complete noir look to this noir plot of one innocent man, Elisha Cook, Jr., condemned for murder. McGuire, the key witness, also becomes a suspect. His nightmares are so noirish they almost become a parody of film noir at its very outset.

Strangers on a Train (1951) ***
Alfred Hitchcock: Farley Granger, Robert Walker.
As in *Shadow of a Doubt*, the seeming innocent becomes a mirror image of the psychopath, and as often in noir and in Hitchcock the innocent man becomes the chief suspect. It's not just the *doppelgänger* plot that makes this film great, it's Hitchcock's treatment of it.

Street of Chance (1942) *
Jack Hively: Burgess Meredith, Claire Trevor, Louise Platt.
The first of many Cornell Woolrich noirs. Meredith is an amnesiac; Trevor the femme fatale. It joins the film noir plot with the film noir look.

The Strip (1951) **
Laszlo Kardos: Mickey Rooney, Sally Forrest, James Craig.
Amour fou on Sunset Strip, as drummer Mickey Rooney's attempts to advance Sally Forrest's career only lead to her death and his arrest for murder. Mickey drums, convincingly, for Louis Armstrong's band.

Sunset Boulevard (1950) ***
Billy Wilder: Gloria Swanson, William Holden, Erich von Stroheim.
Like *D.O.A.*, this film takes noir to the extreme. Here the narrator is not a dying man, as in *Double Indemnity*, but a dead man, floating face down in the pool, who tells his story of selling out and becoming a gigolo, a male entrapped in the gothic prison usually reserved for females. Norma Desmond's visit to the set of *Samson and Delilah* is one of the many highpoints of the film. Another is her bridge game with old stars Buster Keaton, Anna Q. Nilsson, and H. B. Warner. Erich von Stroheim portrays a parody of himself as Swanson's former director, Max von Mayerling, and Swanson screens scenes from *Queen Kelly* (1932), the film they actually made together.

Suspense (1946) **
>Frank Tuttle: Barry Sullivan, Belita, Albert Dekker, Bonita Granville.
>Noir goes to the Ice Capades and allows some excellent skating by Belita, whose adulterous romance with Sullivan leads to murder.

Tension (1949) **
>John Berry: Richard Basehart, Audrey Totter, Barry Sullivan, Cyd Charisse.
>MGM was the studio most impervious to noir, yet it made this excellent B version. Basehart plays a mild mannered pharmacist who, when Totter, his wife, leaves him to go live in Malibu with a flashy lover, decides to take on another identity in order to kill them both. Charisse is the good girl who falls for identity #2. Of course, someone else kills the lover, but Sullivan, the not overly scrupulous detective, suspects Basehart, and wants him to snap, like the rubber band he's always fingering.

They Won't Believe Me (1947) ***
>Irving Pichel: Robert Young, Susan Hayward, Jane Greer.
>All told in a flashback, this film has the twists of plot that characterize the best film noirs. When Young's mistress, Hayward, dies in a car crash and is mistaken for his wife, Young decides to kill the real wife, only to discover she's already dead. When her body is discovered, he's charged for murder. Still more twists. Greer plays one of the sleazy Young's former girlfriends.

The Thief (1952) *
>Russell Rouse: Ray Milland, Rita Gam, Martin Gabel.
>Milland is an anguished, guilt-ridden atomic scientist passing secrets to the Communists. Without dialogue the film is extremely effective until the unconvincing conclusion. The best scene is a chase on the 86th floor of the Empire State Building.

This Gun for Hire (1942) ***
>Frank Tuttle: Alan Ladd, Veronica Lake, Laird Cregar, Robert Preston.
>This is one of the earliest noirs. Ladd plays a psychologically disturbed assassin hired by an executive of a criminal corporation that is selling a poison gas formula to the Axis. When the corporation double crosses him, the investigations begin. Lake plays the girl between the law and the killer. The film has a full-fledged noir look to it, the work of John Seitz. Frank Tuttle, who previously shone as the director of 1930s musicals such as *Waikiki Wedding* (1937), like the rest of the industry, here enters into the period of noir.

T-Men (1947) **
>Anthony Mann: Dennis O'Keefe, Alfred Ryder.
>Despite the overlay of law and order, the perverse lives of the undercover agents and their own descent into criminal-like behavior place this film

within the genre. It is also one of the best examples of John Alton's film noir cinematography.

Too Late for Tears (1949) **
Byron Haskin: Lizabeth Scott, Arthur Kennedy, Dan Duryea.
Scott at her most dangerous. When she and husband Kennedy accidentally recover some criminal loot, to keep the money she kills Kennedy, then Duryea, who has come after them. He's almost the only honest person in the film, and a victim as well. Don Defore plays the investigator who sets things right.

Touch of Evil (1958) ***
Orson Welles: Charlton Heston, Janet Leigh, Orson Welles.
As Welles created the noir style with *Citizen Kane*, here he ends it. The film is so baroque that one has trouble taking it seriously, except as a camp send up of film noir itself. Charlton Heston, unable to consummate his marriage to Janet Leigh, begins the fun. Cameos by old pals Marlene Dietrich and Joseph Cotten all add to it. Venice, California never looked so ominous.

Try and Get Me (1950) **
Cy Enfield: Frank Lovejoy, Lloyd Bridges, Richard Carlson.
Leftist writers and directors always enjoy exposing the underlying corruption of a bourgeois community. In this example, Lovejoy, a despairing veteran, falls in with petty-criminal Bridges in order to obtain consumer goods for his family. Their robbery ends in a murder which leads to their being lynched by the good townsfolk.

The Turning Point (1952) **
William Dieterle: William Holden, Edmond O'Brien, Alexis Smith.
This film illustrates how a police procedural, shot on locations, becomes a film noir. Instead of concentrating on the step-by-step victory of the law over the syndicate, it focuses on the problems of O'Brien, the chief investigator, whose idealized father turns out to be a mob informant, and whose fiancée, Smith, leaves him for the cynical reporter Holden. It ends not triumphantly but tragically.

The Unfaithful (1947) *
Vincent Sherman: Ann Sheridan, Zachary Scott, Lew Ayres.
Sheridan kills a man who attacks her. Marital troubles deepen as the past is revealed. She knew the dead man earlier; he was a sculptor who had made a bust of her. Lew Ayers plays the sympathetic family lawyer and Scott her inadequate husband. David Goodis wrote the story.

The Unknown Man (1951)*
Richard Thorpe: Walter Pidgeon, Barry Sullivan, Keefe Brasselle, Ann Harding.

Not much in the way of style, but the film employs the noir twist. Pidgeon, a super-respectable lawyer successfully defends Brasselle, who it turns out is actually guilty of the murder and then must defend him again, when he is innocent, for the murder that Pidgeon himself committed.

The Velvet Touch (1948) *

John Gage: Rosalind Russell, Leo Genn, Sidney Greenstreet, Claire Trevor.

Russell plays a noir heroine, in this case a Broadway star, who kills Leon Ames, her producer and former lover. Sidney Greenstreet investigates the murder, and Claire Trevor, another actress and ex-Ames mistress, becomes the chief suspect. Genn is a UN architect who wishes to save Russell. It's another Hollywood look at sophisticated Broadway in which Ibsen's *Hedda Gabler* serves as the play within the play.

Vertigo (1958) ***

Alfred Hitchcock: James Stewart, Kim Novak, Barbara Bel Geddes.

The perfect film noir, which also concludes the period. This is one of the best films of all time. It gives a depth of character not only to the obsessed investigator who double crosses his client and becomes involved in the murder, but also creates great sympathy for the femme fatale who becomes enmeshed through genuine love as she tries to escape her dark past. It also features a great love/death score by Bernard Herrmann, who began his career with *Citizen Kane*.

Vicki (1953) *

Harry Horner: Jeanne Crain, Jean Peters, Elliot Reid, Richard Boone.

A remake of *I Wake Up Screaming*. Not bad, but no one is up to the original, though Boone is properly creepy in the Laird Cregar role.

The Web (1947) *

Michael Gordon: Edmond O'Brien, Vincent Price, Ella Raines, William Bendix.

O'Brien, a two-bit lawyer, gets conned into defending Price and then gets framed for his efforts. He and Bendix, the detective in the case, both conduct investigations. Raines is the love interest.

When Strangers Marry (1944) *

William Castle: Kim Hunter, Robert Mitchum, Dean Jagger.

Woolrich again. This is his version of the women's film. Hunter becomes suspicious of husband Jagger and is attracted and seemingly helped by old boyfriend Mitchum in the first of his sinister roles.

Where Danger Lives (1950) *

John Farrow: Robert Mitchum, Faith Domergue, Claude Rains.

Dr. Robert Mitchum should have stayed with nurse girlfriend Maureen O'Hara (the director's wife) instead of being ensnared by Faith Domergue (the producer's girlfriend). She murders her husband, Claude Rains, much too soon; he has but one scene. False steps and chance lead to the predictable descent down at the border.

Where the Sidewalk Ends (1950) ***

Otto Preminger: Dana Andrews, Gene Tierney, Gary Merrill, Karl Malden. One of the first rogue cop noirs. Detective Andrews unintentionally kills a suspect and then disposes of the corpse. As he falls in love with Tierney, the police pin his crime on her innocent father. Ben Hecht provides a tight plot with some neat twists.

While the City Sleeps (1956) **

Fritz Lang: Dana Andrews, Ida Lupino, Thomas Mitchell. The big cast also includes George Sanders, Rhonda Fleming, Vincent Price, Sally Forrest, Howard Duff, James Craig, and John Barrymore, Jr. There's a murder, a serial killer in fact, but in a slight twist on the noir formula, none of the principals is involved in the crime, but most of them are busy double crossing or using one another in an attempt to solve it and win the prize position of media mogul.

Whirlpool (1949) *

Otto Preminger: Gene Tierney, Richard Conte, Jose Ferrer. The two unworthy men in her life do not make this a women's film. The kleptomaniac wife of psychiatrist Conte, Tierney seeks aid from the charlatan Ferrer. He frames her for the murder of one of his former patients who had transferred to Conte. Detective Charles Bickford heads the investigation. Ben Hecht wrote the screenplay during his Freudian period.

The Woman in the Window (1944) ***

Fritz Lang: Edward G. Robinson, Joan Bennett, Dan Duryea. Edward G. Robinson murders Bennett's lover, and then is blackmailed by Duryea as the police draw ever closer to solving the crime. Robinson poisons himself just before Bennett discovers that the police pinned the murder on Duryea. But, like film noir, it was all a dream—the nightmare from which you awake when the lights go up.

The Woman on the Beach (1947) **

Jean Renoir: Joan Bennett, Robert Ryan, Charles Bickford. Why shouldn't Renoir, one of the sources of noir, get to make a noir while he sojourned in Hollywood? Ryan is at his most confused in this love triangle with Bennett and her blind husband Bickford.

World for Ransom (1954) *

Robert Aldrich: Dan Duryea, Gene Lockhart, Patric Knowles. An oriental noir. Duryea is a private investigator in Singapore who becomes enmeshed with international criminals when he tries to rescue Knowles, the husband of his former mistress, Marian Carr, a nightclub performer whose name in the film is Frennessey. A Galahad takes a chance in a world governed by Fate.

You Only Live Once (1937) ***

Fritz Lang: Henry Fonda, Sylvia Sidney, William Gargan.

This is Hollywood's first film noir, made by one of the co-creators, Lang, before Hollywood and then the French became conscious of the genre. Fonda, an alleged three time loser, cannot believe in his redemption, and with his bride Sidney escapes to their doom.

Appendix B
Borderline

The 3rd Voice (1960) *
  Hurbert Cornfield: Edmond O'Brien, Larraine Day, Julie London.
  A late entry. Set at a Mexican resort, it's a Cinemascope black and white film, but with stark contrasts, not noir chiaroscuro. O'Brien is a con man impersonating a rich man whom femme fatale Day has murdered. He becomes more culpable as the plot unfolds, but he's crooked at the outset.

Affair in Trinidad (1952) *
  Vincent Sherman: Rita Hayworth, Glenn Ford, Alexander Scourby.
  Part *Gilda*, part *Notorious,* and only part noir. A murder, an investigation, but Rita only seems to be an adultress, while Glenn Ford is genuinely sullen and grumpy. The film turns into a spy thriller as Scourby, Rita's alleged lover, aids Nazi scientists set up Soviet missiles in the Caribbean—all this a decade prior to the Cuban missile crisis.

Between Midnight and Dawn (1950) *
  Gordon Douglas: Edmond O'Brien, Mark Stevens, Gale Storm.
  O'Brien and Stevens are cop buddies and Marine vets, both sweet on Storm. When Stevens is killed by Donald Buka, the disillusioned O'Brien starts turning rogue cop and beating up witnesses. His behavior and the brutality of the scenes almost counter the police procedural framework.

Beware My Lovely (1952) *
  Harry Horner: Robert Ryan, Ida Lupino.
  Would you really want Robert Ryan to be your handyman? True noirs are set in the contemporary world, not as here just after World War I. This film is rather a psychological melodrama in which mentally unbalanced murderer Ryan imprisons widow Lupino in her own house. Or did he?

The Brasher Doubloon (1947)
 John Brahm: George Montgomery, Nancy Guild.
 This film makes the list primarily because it is based on Raymond Chandler's novel, *The High Window.* Montgomery is a very stiff Marlowe, and the screenwriters seem to have been unaware of Chandler's literary gifts. The supporting characters are true to form in this near whodunit. *Time to Kill* (1942) was an earlier pure whodunit version of the novel.

Cause for Alarm (1951) *
 Tay Garnett: Loretta Young, Barry Sullivan.
 An innocent but fallible Young becomes implicated in the death of her jealous paranoid husband Sullivan. A modest domestic but incomplete noir.

Cry of the City (1948) *
 Robert Siodmak: Victor Mature, Richard Conte, Debra Paget.
 Half gangster film, half cops and robbers, it's the familiar tale of two boyhood friends, who like Cagney and O'Brien in the 1930s, take different paths, both obstructed by betrayals.

East Side, West Side (1949) **
 Mervyn LeRoy: Barbara Stanwyck, Van Heflin, James Mason, Ava Gardner.
 This A production qualifies as a women's film or melodrama, but it is a film noir as well. It contains an unhappy marriage, deception, infidelity, but also a femme fatale, lots of nightclub scenes, a murder, and then an investigation that focuses on an innocent who had a motive. Park Avenue substitutes for the dark city.

Hangover Square (1945) *
 John Brahm: Laird Cregar, Linda Darnell, George Sanders.
 A follow-up to the 1944 version of *The Lodger,* using the same set and some of the same actors. Here, instead of playing the Ripper, Cregar is a disturbed Mr. Hyde type of composer (his music provided by Bernard Herrmann) who goes on killing binges. Sanders plays an anachronistic police psychologist, while Darnell supplies the temptations.

High Sierra (1941) ***
 Raoul Walsh: Humphrey Bogart, Ida Lupino, Joan Leslie.
 Based on a W. R. Burnett novel with a screenplay by John Huston, this seeming gangster film concentrates on a good bad guy who wants to "crash out" and go straight. There's neither a murder nor an investigation, just a heist that goes bad for this existential, tragic protagonist. Remade as *I Died a Thousand Times* (1955).

Kansas City Confidential (1952) *
 Phil Karlson: John Payne, Preston Foster, Coleen Gray.
 Payne a bit too innocent. He's framed for a crime committed by rogue cop Foster. Foster in turn is too sympathetic and ultimately sacrificial for the sake of his daughter, Gray, who has fallen for Payne.

Keeper of the Flame (1942) **
George Cukor: Katharine Hepburn, Spencer Tracy.
A *Citizen Kane* spin off. Like *Kane* it contains no direct murder, just crypto-fascist political ambitions. Tracy comes to report on the great man's life and discovers the dark secrets which led Hepburn, the faithful wife, to cause his accidental death—out of loyalty to his name or loathing for what he was becoming.

Knock on Any Door (1949) *
Nicholas Ray: Humphrey Bogart, John Derek, George Macready.
The film splits between a doomed noir protagonist, represented by Derek, and a social consciousness film, represented by reforming defense attorney Bogart. The kid goes to the chair, but society sent him there.

A Lady without a Passport (1950) *
Joseph H. Lewis: Hedy Lamarr, John Hodiak.
Hodiak is an incompetent cop who is nearly corrupted by the almost femme fatale Lamarr in this tropical atmospheric pro-immigration (legal of course) film.

The Lodger (1944) ***
John Brahm: Laird Cregar, Merle Oberon, George Sanders.
Had this been set in contemporary rather than Edwardian London, it would be a perfect example of the psychopathic serial killer noir. Sanders plays the investigator and Oberon the intended victim. Laird Cregar never falls into camp, and the direction by former German Braham and the cinematography by Lucien Ballard supply textbook examples of the noir look at its best.

Man in the Vault (1956) **
Andrew McLaglen: William Campbell, Karen Sharpe, Anita Ekberg.
Campbell, a locksmith, gets forced by a gang of crooks (Berry Kroeger and Mike Mazurki) into robbing a safe deposit box. There's no investigation and the murders all cluster at the climax. But William Clothier's cinematography provides a documentary look at LA in the late 1950s and includes a superb chase through a deserted bowling alley.

Moontide (1942) *
Archie Mayo: Jean Gabin, Ida Lupino, Thomas Mitchell, Claude Rains.
Poetic realism and Jean Gabin come to Hollywood. Ida Lupino was never lovelier. Although conceived as a naturalistic proletarian melodrama, the film includes a night spot (the Red Dot), a murder, a suppressed investigation, lots of fog and chiaroscuro, and a memory losing, fallible but redeemed hero. Mitchell plays Tiny, the homoerotic villain.

The Naked Kiss (1964) *
Sam Fuller: Constance Towers, Anthony Eisley, Michael Dante.
This is a candidate for the first neo-noir: the prostitute heroine, turned nurse to handicapped children, murders her fiancé when she catches him

molesting one of her wards. The Code died a natural death before it was abolished in 1968.

The Narrow Margin (1952) ***

Richard Fleischer: Charles McGraw, Marie Windsor, Jacqueline White.

This film departs from a police procedural and centers on McGraw's attempts to bring to trial and save the life of Marie Windsor, a seemingly fallen woman and gangster's widow, who in fact is an undercover cop investigating McGraw's integrity. In the process he loses her and his partner.

Night and the City (1950) **

Jules Dassin: Richard Widmark, Gene Tierney, Francis X. Sullivan.

The dark underworld and the naturalistic plot all indicate film noir, but though there's a death, there's neither murder nor investigation, just the pitiless fall of a loser.

Nightmare Alley (1947) ***

Edmund Goulding: Tyrone Power, Colleen Gray, Joan Blondell, Helen Walker.

More an exercise in naturalism than film noir, the film depicts the rise of a fraudulent mentalist and his foredoomed fall into a "geek." Power, playing against his popular image, commits involuntary manslaughter as well as fraud; Walker plays a femme fatale; and Lee Garmes' cinematography captures the dark underside of the carney and nightclub worlds.

Nocturne (1946) *

Edwin L. Marin: George Raft, Lynn Bari, Virginia Huston.

Raft plays a determined investigator who almost gets too involved with seeming femme fatale Bari who's really protecting her younger sister, a suspect in the murder of a womanizing composer. Noir liked the arty world almost as much as it did the dark city.

No Way Out (1950) **

Joseph L. Mankiewicz: Sidney Poitier, Richard Widmark, Linda Darnell.

A social consciousness, anti-racism film that enters into noir territory through its depiction of crime, revenge, and a fallen society. This was Sidney Poitier's first featured part, a doctor who becomes victimized by red-neck racist Widmark.

Party Girl (1958) *

Nicholas Ray: Robert Taylor, Cyd Charisse, Lee J. Cobb, John Ireland.

This is a late Technicolor noir, in which crippled, crooked lawyer Taylor and dancer Charisse struggle to get free from the mob run by Cobb. Because it is set in the past, Chicago in the 1930s, it departs from noir's basic contemporary vision.

Rear Window (1954) ***
Alfred Hitchcock: James Stewart, Grace Kelly, Raymond Burr, Thelma Ritter.
A murder, an investigation, a fallible protagonist, and a story by Cornell Woolrich would certainly qualify a film as noir, but it is more a romantic thriller shot in Technicolor and featuring the erotic chemistry of two super stars.

Secret Beyond the Door (1947) *
Fritz Lang: Joan Bennett, Michael Redgrave, Ann Revere.
Lang's version of *Rebecca* and *Suspicion*. Some Freudian twists and murderous impulses on the part of Redgrave do not prevent his healing by Bennett, in the room seemingly intended for her murder.

The Sleeping City (1950) *
George Sherman: Richard Conte, Coleen Gray.
This would be a law and order film were it not that Conte, the undercover agent investigating crime in a big city hospital (NY), falls for nurse Gray, who is one of the perpetrators. It's an example of the shift in the 1950s to a more documentary style.

The Suspect (1944) *
Robert Siodmak: Charles Laughton, Ella Raines, Henry Daniell.
Like *Crime and Punishment*, this film has a very noir plot, but its setting in Victorian London removes it too far from the contemporary scene, which is one of the essentials for the genre not the period.

They Live by Night (1949) ***
Nicholas Ray: Farley Granger, Cathy O'Donnell, Howard Da Silva, Jay C. Flippen.
Two star-crossed lovers, on the run. Granger escapes from prison, but wants to go straight, encouraged by O'Donnell, but Howard Da Silva forces him to participate in a robbery that goes bad. He borders on innocence; there's really no investigation; and the film is set in the 1930s.

The Trap (1959)*
Norman Panama: Richard Widmark, Tina Louise, Lee J. Cobb, Earl Holliman.
Arriving late, shot in Technicolor, and set in the desert, this film is a candidate for neo-noir. Widmark plays a lawyer fallen into the web of the mob led by Cobb. To save his own skin, he persuades his sheriff father to allow Cobb to escape at the local airport, but the plans all go awry. Ultimately Widmark redeems himself, but his father and brother, Holliman, die in the process, and en route he makes love to Louise, his brother's wife. Part noir, part gangster film, part law and order, part Arthur Miller–like play.

Trapped (1949) **
  Richard Fleischer: Lloyd Bridges, Barbara Payton, John Hoyt.
  Almost a noir, as Bridges, a con, is released in hopes he will uncover a counterfeit ring. Despite the double crossing and the archetypal nightclub scenes, the power of the law in the form of a government agency proves too powerful for a generic noir. There's a superb climax in a trolley car barn. The screenplay is by Earl Felton, who also wrote *Narrow Margin*.

Undercurrent (1946) *
  Vincente Minnelli: Katharine Hepburn, Robert Taylor, Robert Mitchum.
  Hepburn sleeps with the enemy, who has a criminal past and a mysterious brother. Despite many noir elements, this remains a women's film.

Walk Softly, Stranger (1950) *
  Robert Stevenson: Joseph Cotten, Alida Valli, Paul Stewart.
  Cotten, a strange returning vet with a criminal past, falls in love with the crippled heiress Valli. Stewart, his criminal past, appears and takes him back into crime. Despite the gloom, the excellent noir title, and screenplay by noir pro Frank Fenton, there's no murder, and no investigation.

Wicked as They Come (1956) **
  Ken Hughes: Arlene Dahl, Philip Carey, Herbert Marshall.
  Dahl uses her beauty to climb out of the slums at the expense of gullible males and victims. When, three-quarters through the film, she finally reaches the top, this bad girl melodrama turns into a noir, as she mistakenly kills her husband thinking he is a stalking former lover. Philip Carey, her amused and devoted observer, carries on a brief investigation which releases her from death row. Retitled *Portrait in Smoke*.

Appendix C
Period Pieces

CRIME FILMS OFTEN ASSOCIATED OR IDENTIFIED AS FILM NOIR

Police Work–Law and Order

Appointment with Danger (1951) Lewis Allen
Armored Car Robbery (1950) Richard Fleischer
Boomerang (1947) Elia Kazan
Border Incident (1947) Anthony Mann
Borderline (1950) William A. Seiter
A Bullet for Joey (1955) Lewis Allen
Chicago Confidential (1957) Sidney Salkow
City of Fear (1959) Irving Lerner
Cry of the Hunted (1953) Joseph H. Lewis
Cop Hater (1958) William Berke
Dragnet (1954) Jack Webb
The Enforcer ((1951) Bretaigne Windust
Experiment in Terror (1962) Blake Edwards
Follow Me Quietly (1949) Richard Fleischer
House of Bamboo (1955) Sam Fuller
The House on 92nd Street (1945) Henry Hathaway
Johnny Angel (1945) Edward L. Marin
Johnny Stool Pigeon (1949) William Castle
The Killer That Stalked New York (1950) Earl McEvoy
*The Lineup (*1958) Don Siegel
Lured (1947) Douglas Sirk
The Mob (1951) Robert Parrish

Mystery Street (1950) John Sturges
Naked City (1948) Jules Dassin
The Night Holds Terror (1955) Andrew L. Stone
Panic in the Streets (1950) Elia Kazin
Parole, Inc. (1948) Alfred Zeisler
The Phenix City Story (1955) Phil Karlson
Port of New York (1949) Laslo Benedek
The Racket (1951) John Cromwell
Southside 1-1000 (1950) Boris Ingster
Slaughter on Tenth Avenue (1957) Arnold Laven
The Stranger (1946) Orson Welles
The Street with No Name (1948) William Keighly
The Tattooed Stranger (1950) Edward Montagne
The Threat (1949) Felix Feist
The Undercover Man (1949) Joseph H. Lewis
Union Station (1950) Rudolph Maté
Walk a Crooked Mile (1948) Gordon Douglas
Walk East on Beacon (1952) Alfred Werker

Better Investigators

Abandoned (1949) Joseph M. Newman
Behind Locked Doors (1948) Budd Boetticher
Call Northside 777 (1948) Henry Hathaway
The Captive City (1952) Robert Wise
Deadline USA (1952) Richard Brooks
Woman on the Run (1950) Norman Foster

Caper Films

Five Against the House (1955) Phil Karlson
Plunder Road (1957) Hurbert Cornfield

Cloak and Dagger

Berlin Express (1948) Jacques Tourneur
Escape in the Fog (1945) Budd Boetticher
Fly-By-Night (1942) Robert Siodmak
Journey into Fear (1943) Norman Foster
Ministry of Fear (1944) Fritz Lang
Confidential Agent (1945) Herman Shumlin

Shack Out on 101 (1955) Edward Dein
The Hand Whip (1951) William Cameron Menzies

Gangsters and Heels

711 Ocean Drive (1950) Joseph M. Newman
Ace in the Hole (1951) Billy Wilder
Baby Face Nelson (1957) Don Siegel
Crashout (1955) Lewis Foster
Cry Terror (1958) Andrew Stone
Cry Tough (1959) Paul Stanley
The Dark Past (1948) Rudolph Maté
The Devil Thumbs a Ride (1947) Felix Feist
Dial 1119 (1950) Gerald Mayer
The Gangster (1947) Gordon Wiles
The Hitch-Hiker (1953) Ida Lupino
I Died a Thousand Times (1955) Stuart Heisler
Johnny Eager (1942) Mervyn LeRoy
Key Largo (1948) John Huston
Larceny (1948) George Sherman
New York Confidential (1955) Russell Rouse
Shakedown (1950) Joe Pevney
Split Second (1953) Dick Powell
Suddenly (1954) Lewis Allen
Two of a Kind (1951) Henry Levin
White Heat (1949) Raoul Walsh

Prison Films

Brute Force (1947) Jules Dassin
Caged (1950) John Cromwell
Canon City (1948) Crane Wilbur
Convicted (1950) Henry Levin
Lady Gangster (1942) Robert Florey (as Florian Roberts)
Riot in Cell Block 11 (1954) Don Siegel
The Story of Molly X (1949) Crane Wilbur

The Boxing Racket

Body and Soul (1947) Robert Rossen
Champion (1949) Mark Robson

City for Conquest (1940) Anatole Litvak
The Harder They Fall (1956) Mark Robson
The Set-Up (1949) Robert Wise

Whodunits

Backfire (1950) Vincent Sherman
Dr. Broadway (1942) Anthony Mann
The Falcon Takes Over (1942) Irving Reis
The Girl in Black Stockings (1957) Howard W. Koch
Grand Central Murder (1942) S. Sylvan Simon
The Kid Glove Killer (1942) Fred Zinnemann
Lady on a Train (1945) Charles David
The Spiral Staircase (1945) Robert Siodmak
The 13th Letter (1951) Otto Preminger
Time to Kill (1942) Herbert I. Leeds
Two O'Clock Courage (1945) Anthony Mann
The Unsuspected (1947) Michael Curtiz
The Verdict (1946) Don Siegel

Innocents in Trouble

The Big Night (1951) Joseph Losey
Dark Waters (1944) André De Toth
The Glass Wall (1953) Maxwell Shane
Fingers at the Window (1942) Charles Lederer
My Name is Julia Ross (1945) Joseph H. Lewis
Railroaded! (1947) Anthony Mann
Road House (1948) Jean Negulesco
The Secret Fury (1950) Mel Ferrer
Shock (1946) Alfred L. Werker
Strange Illusion (1945) Edgar G. Ulmer
Strangers in the Night (1944) Anthony Mann
They Made Me a Killer (1946) William C. Thomas
Tight Spot (1955) Phil Karlson
The Unseen (1945) Lewis Allen
The Window (1949) Ted Tetzlaff
Witness to Murder (1954) Roy Rowland
The Wrong Man (1957) Alfred Hitchcock

MELODRAMAS
(THE PSYCHOLOGICAL AND SOCIAL DRAMA)

Sleeping with the Enemy

The Amazing Mr. X (1948) Bernard Vorhaus
The Big Bluff (1955) W. Lee Wilder
Caught (1949) Max Ophuls
Female on the Beach (1955) Joseph Pevney
The House on Telegraph Hill (1951) Robert Wise
Julie (1956) Andrew L. Stone
Rage in Heaven (1941) W. S. Van Dyke
Secret Beyond the Door (1948) Fritz Lang
Shadow of a Woman (1946) Joseph Santley
Sleep My Love (1948) Douglas Sirk
Sudden Fear (1952) David Miller
The Two Mrs. Carrolls (1947) Peter Godfrey
Woman in Hiding (1950) Michael Gordon

Psychological and Moral Disturbances

Blind Alley (1939) Charles Vidor
Born to be Bad (1950) Nicholas Ray
Don't Bother to Knock (1952) Roy Baker
Fourteen Hours (1951) Henry Hathaway
Guest in the House (1944) John Brahm
The Lady Gambles (1949) Michael Gordon
The Locket (1946) John Brahm
The Mask of Diijon (1946) Lew Landers
Night into Morning (1951) Fletcher Markle
Queen Bee (1955) Ranald MacDougall
The Snake Pit (1948) Anatole Litvak

Social Issues

City Across the River (1949) Maxwell Shane
Edge of the City (1957) Martin Ritt
The Fallen Sparrow (1943) Richard Wallace
Storm Warning (1951) Stuart Heisler
Thieves' Highway (1949) Jules Dassin
The Well (1951) Leo C. Popkin & Russell Rouse

Anatomies of a Corrupt Society

The Boss (1956) Byron Haskin
The Strange Love of Martha Ivers (1946) Lewis Milestone
The Sweet Smell of Success (1957) Alexander MacKendrick
Underworld Story (1950) Cy Endfield

Miscellaneous Melodramas

Alias Nick Beal (1949) John Farrow
The Breaking Point (1950) Michael Curtiz
Clash by Night (1952) Fritz Lang
The Company She Keeps (1951) John Cromwell
Crisis (1950) Richard Brooks
Desert Fury (1947) Lewis Allen
Detective Story (1957) William Wyler
The House Across the Bay (1940) Archie Mayo
House of Strangers (1949) Joseph L. Mankiewicz
Jeopardy (1953) John Sturges
Out of the Fog (1941) Anatole Litvak
Over Exposed (1956) Lewis Seiler
The Red House (1947) Delmer Daves
The River's Edge (1957) Allan Dwan
Second Chance (1953) Rudolph Maté
Shanghai Gesture (1941) Josef von Sternberg
Strange Fascination (1952) Hugo Haas
Strange Impersonation (1946) Anthony Mann
Swamp Fire (1946) William H. Pine
Tomorrow Is Forever (1946) Irving Pichel
Whistle Stop (1946) Léonide Moguy
A Woman's Secret (1949) Nicholas Ray

Works Cited

Abel, Richard. "*Notorious*: Perversion par Excellence." In *A Hitchcock Reader*, 2nd ed., edited by Marshall Deutelbaum and Leland Poague. Chichester, UK: Wiley-Blackwell, 2009.
Altman, Rick. *Film/Genre*. London: British Film Institute, 1999.
Alton, John. *Painting with Light*. Berkeley: University of California Press, 1995 [1949].
Aulier, Dan. *Vertigo: The Making of a Hitchcock Classic*. New York: St. Martin's Press, 1998.
Bazin, André. "Mort d'Humphry Bogart." In *Cahiers du Cinema: The 1950s, Neo-Realism, Hollywood, New Wave*, edited by Jim Hillier. Cambridge: Harvard University Press, 1985 [1957].
———. *Qu'est-ce Que Le Cinema?* Vol. 1, *Ontologie e Langage*. Paris: Les Editions Du Cerf, 1958.
Biesen, Sheri Chinen. *Blackout: World War II and the Origin of Film Noir*. Baltimore: Johns Hopkins University Press, 2005
Blackmur, R. P. *Eleven Essays in the European Novel*. New York: Harcourt, Brace & World, 1964.
Borde, Raymond, and Etienne Chaumenton. *A Panorama of American Film Noir, 1941–1953*. San Francisco: City Light Books, 2002 [1955].
Bordwell, David, Janet Staiger, and Kristin Thompson. *The Classical Hollywood Cinema: Film Style & Mode of Production to 1960*. New York: Columbia University Press, 1985.
Brill, Lesley. "Hitchcock's *The Lodger*." In *A Hitchcock Reader*, 2nd ed., edited by Marshall Deutelbaum and Leland Poague. Chichester, UK: Wiley-Blackwell, 2009.
Broe, Dennis. *Film Noir, American Workers, and Postwar Hollywood*. Gainesville: University Press of Florida, 2009.
Brook, Vincent. *Driven to Darkness: Jewish Émigré Directors and the Rise of Film Noir*. New Brunswick: Rutgers University Press, 2009.

Buhle, Paul and David Wagner. *Radical Hollywood: The Untold Story Behind America's Favorite Movies*. New York: New Press, 2002.

Cantor, Paul A. "Film Noir and the Frankfort School: America as Wasteland in Edgar Ulmer's *Detour*." In *The Philosophy of Film Noir*, edited by Mark T. Conard. Lexington: University Press of Kentucky, 2006.

Cavell, Stanley. *Contesting Tears*. Chicago: University of Chicago Press, 1996.

Chandler, Raymond. *The Simple Art of Murder*. New York: Vintage Books, 1988 [1944].

Chopra-Gant, Mike. *Hollywood Genre and Postwar America: Masculinity, Family and Nation in Popular Movies and Film Noir*. London: I. B. Tauris, Publisher, 2006.

Conard, Mark T. *The Philosophy of Film Noir*. Lexington: University Press of Kentucky, 2006.

Copjec, Joan, ed. *Shades of Noir*. London: Verso, 1993.

Cowie, Elizabeth. "Film Noir and Women." In *Shades of Noir*, edited by Joan Copjec. London: Verso, 1993.

Crouch, Stanley. "Noir America." *Slate*. March 15, 2007. Available at www.slate.com/id/2161815/.

Damico, James. "Film Noir: A Modest Proposal." In *Film Noir Reader*, 6th edition, edited by Alain Silver and James Ursini. New York: Limelight Editions, 2000 [1978].

Deming, Barbara. "The Artlessness of Walt Disney." *Partisan Review* 12 (1945): 231.

———. *Running Away from Myself*. New York: Grossman Publishers, 1969.

Doherty, Thomas. *Hollywood Censor*. New York: Columbia University Press, 2007.

Duncan, Paul. *Film Noir: Films of Trust and Betrayal*. Harpendon, UK: Pocket Essentials, 2006.

Durgnat, Raymond. "Paint it Black: The Family Tree of Film Noir." In *Film Noir Reader*, 6th ed., edited by Alain Silver and James Ursini. New York: Limelight Editions, 2000 [1970].

———. *The Strange Case of Alfred Hitchcock: Or the Plain Man's Hitchcock*. London: Faber and Faber, 1974.

Dyer, Richard. *The Matter of Images: Essays on Representation*. London: Routledge, 1993.

Edwards, James. *The Plain Sense of Things: The Fate of Religion in an Age of Normal Nihilism*. University Park: Pennsylvania State University Press, 1997.

Elsaesser, Thomas. "Too Big and Too Close: Alfred Hitchcock and Fritz Lang." In *The Hitchcock Annual Anthology*, edited by Stanley Gottlieb and Richard Allen. London: Wallflower Press, 2009.

———. *Weimar Cinema and After: Germany's Historic Imaginary*. London: Routledge, 2000.

Empson, William. "Tom Jones." *Kenyon Review* 20 (1958): 217–49.

Erickson, Todd. "Kill Me Again: Movement Becomes Genre." In *Film Noir Reader*, 6th ed., edited by Alain Silver and James Ursini. New York: Limelight Editions, 2000.

Farber, Manny. *Negative Space*. New York: Praeger, 1971.

Fay, Jennifer, and Justus Nieland. *Film Noir: Hard-Boiled Modernity and the Cultures of Globalization*. London: Routledge, 2010.
Flory, Dan. *Philosophy, Black Film, Film Noir*. University Park: Pennsylvania State University Press, 2008.
Frank, Nino. "A New Kind of Police Drama: The Criminal Adventure." In *Film Noir Reader 2*, edited by Alain Silver and James Ursini. New York: Limelight Editions, 1999 [1946].
Frye, Northrop. *Anatomy of Criticism*. Princeton: Princeton University Press, 1957.
Gaines, Philip. "Noir 101." In *Film Noir Reader 2*, edited by Alain Silver and James Ursini. New York: Limelight Editions, 1999.
Gardiner, Dorothy, and Kathrine Sorley Walker. *Raymond Chandler Speaking*. Plainview, NY: Books for Libraries Press, 1971.
Gunning, Tom. "The Desire and Pursuit of the Hole: Cinema's Obscure Object of Desire." In *Erotikon*, edited by Shadi Bartsch and Thomas Bartscherer. Chicago: Chicago University Press, 2005.
Harvey, James. *Movie Love in the Fifties*. New York: Alfred A. Knopf, 2001.
Haskell, Molly. *From Reverence to Rape: The Treatment of Women in the Movies*. New York: Holt, Rinehart and Winston, 1974.
Hauser, Arnold. "Style and Its Changes." In *The Philosophy of Art History*. Cleveland, OH: World Publishing Company, 1963.
Hibbs, Thomas S. *Arts of Darkness: American Noir and the Quest for Redemption*. Dallas, TX: Spence Publishing Company, 2008.
Hinkson, Jake. "Hearing Voices: The Varieties of Film Noir Narration," *Noir City Sentinel* 5 (2010): 43.
———. "The Lord of Godless Town." *Noir City Sentinel, Annual #2: The Best of the Noir City Sentinel*. San Francisco: Film Noir Foundation, 2009.
Hirsch, Foster. *The Dark Side of the Screen*. 3rd ed., Cambridge, MA: Da Capo Press, 2008 [1981].
———. *Detours and Lost Highways: A Map of Neo-Noir*. New York: Limelight Editions, 1999.
Hodges, Daniel M. "The Rise and Fall of the War Noir." In *Film Noir Reader 4: The Crucial Films and Themes*, edited by Alain Silver and James Ursini. New Jersey: Limelight Editions, 2004.
Irwin, John T. *Unless the Threat of Death Is Behind Them: Hard-Boiled Fiction and Film Noir*. Baltimore: Johns Hopkins University Press, 2006.
Kael, Pauline. *Kiss Kiss Bang Bang*. New York: Bantam Books, 1969.
Karimi, A. M. *Toward a Definition of the American Film Noir (1941–1949)*. New York: Arno Press, 1976.
Keaney, Michael J. *Film Noir Guide: 745 Films of the Classical Era, 1940–1959*. Jefferson, NC: McFarland & Company Publishers, 2003.
Keene, Marian E. "A Closer Look at Scopophilia: Mulvey, Hitchcock, and *Vertigo*." In A *Hitchcock Reader*, 2nd ed., edited by Marshall Deutelbaum and Leland Poague. Chichester, UK: Wiley-Blackwell, 2009.
Kracauer, Siegfried. "Hollywood's Terror Films: Do They Reflect an American State of Mind?" *Commentary* 2 (1946): 132–36.

Kolker, Robert Philip. *A Cinema of Loneliness: Penn, Kubrick, Scorsese, Spielberg, Altman.* 2nd ed. New York: Oxford University Press, 1988.

Krutnik, Frank. *In a Lonely Street: Film Noir, Genre, Masculinity.* London: Routledge, 1991.

Leff, Leonard, and Jerold L. Simmons. *The Dame in the Kimono: Hollywood Censorship, and the Production Code from the 1920s to the 1960s.* New York: Grove Weidenfeld, 1990.

Luhr, William. *The Maltese Falcon.* New Brunswick, NJ: Rutgers University Press, 1996.

Lyons, Arthur. *Death on the Cheap: The Lost B Movies of Film Noir.* New York; Da Capo, Press, 2000.

Markos, Louis. "In the Mind of a Madman: How Film Noir Got Its Look." *American Arts Quarterly* (Winter, 2007): 32.

McArthur, Colin. *Underworld USA.* London: Secker & Warburg, British Film Institute, 1972.

McLaughlin, James M. "All in the Family: Alfred Hitchcock's *Shadow of a Doubt.*" In *A Hitchcock Reader*, 2nd ed., edited by Marshall Deutelbaum and Leland Poague. Chichester, UK: Wiley-Blackwell, 2009.

Metz, Christian. *Film Language: A Semiotics of the Cinema.* New York: Oxford University Press, 1974.

Minturn, Kent. "*Peinture Noire:* Abstract Expressionism and *Film Noir.*" In *Film Noir Reader 2*, edited by Alain Silver and James Ursini. New York: Limelight Editions, 1999.

Morris, Christopher D. *The Hanging Figure: On Suspense and the Films of Alfred Hitchcock.* Westport, CT: Praeger, 2002.

Muller, Eddie. *Dark City: The Lost World of Film Noir.* New York: St. Martin's Press, 1998.

———. "Dateline Buenos Aires." *Noir City Sentinel* 4 (2009): 2.

———. "Noir for a New Century." *Noir City Sentinel, Annual #2: The Best of the Film Noir Sentinel.* San Francisco: Film Noir Foundation, 2009.

Mulvey, Laura. "Visual Pleasure and Narrative Cinema." In *Film Theory and Criticism: Introductory Readings*, edited by Leo Braudy and Marshall Cohen. New York: Oxford University Press, 1999 [1975].

Muscio, Giuliana. *Hollywood's New Deal.* Philadelphia: Temple University Press, 1996.

Naremore, James. "Hitchcock at the Margins of Noir." In *Alfred Hitchcock: Centenary Essays*, edited by Richard Allen and S. Ishli-Gonzalez. London: BFI Publishing, 1999.

———. *More than Night: Film Noir in Its Contexts.* Updated and expanded edition. Berkeley: University of California Press, 2008 [1998].

Neale, Steve. *Genre and Hollywood.* London: Routledge, 2000.

Palmer, R. Barton. *Hollywood's Dark Cinema: The American Film Noir.* New York: Twayne Publisher, 1994.

———. "Moral Man in the Dark City." In *The Philosophy of Film Noir*, edited by Mark T. Conard. Lexington: University Press of Kentucky, 2006.

Park, William. *The Idea of Rococo*. Newark: University of Delaware Press, 1992.

———. "The Losing of the West." *The Velvet Light Trap* 12 (1974): 2–5.

———. "The Police State." *Journal of Popular Film* 3 (1978): 229–37.

———. *Pure Cinema*. Essays by Sarah Lawrence Faculty [No.1]. Bronxville: Sarah Lawrence College, 1972.

Perez, Gilberto. *The Material Ghost*. Baltimore: Johns Hopkins University Press, 1998.

Place, Janey, and Lowell Peterson. "Some Visual Motifs of *Film Noir*." In *Film Noir Reader*, 6th ed., edited by Alain Silver and James Ursini. New York: Limelight Editions, 1996.

Polan, Dana. *Power and Paranoia: History, Narrative, and the American Cinema, 1940–1950*. New York: Columbia University Press, 1986.

Pope, Alexander. *Pastoral Poetry and An Essay on Criticism*. Edited by E. Audry and Aubrey Williams. New Haven, CT: Yale University Press, 1961.

Porfiro, Robert. "*The Killers*: Expressionism of Sound and Image in Film Noir." In *Film Noir Reader*, 6th ed., edited by Alain Silver and James Ursini. New York: Limelight Editions, 1996.

———. "No Way Out: Existential Motifs in *Film Noir*." In *Film Noir Reader*, 6th ed., edited by Alain Silver and James Ursini. New York: Limelight Editions, 1996 [1976].

———. "The Noir Title Sequence." In *Film Noir Reader 4: The Crucial Films and Theme*, edited by Alain Silver and James Ursini. New Jersey: Limelight Editions, 2004.

Rabinowitz, Paula. *Black & White & Noir: America's Pulp Modernism*. New York: Columbia University Press, 2002.

Ray, Robert B. *A Certain Tendency of the Hollywood Cinema*. Princeton: Princeton University Press, 1985.

Rich, Nathaniel. *San Francisco Noir*. New York: Little Bookroom, 2005.

Richardson, Carl. *Autopsy: An Element of Realism in Film Noir*. Metuchen, NJ: Scarecrow Press, 1992.

Root. Jane. "Film Noir." In *The Cinema Book*, edited by Pam Cook. New York: Pantheon Books, 1985.

Jonathan Rosenbaum, "Introduction to the Chinese edition of *More than Night*." JonathanRosenbaum.com. Available at www.jonathanrosenbaum.com/?p=15842 (accessed June 11, 2009).

Rosenbladt, Bettina. "Doubles and Doubts in Hitchcock: The German Connection." In *Hitchcock: Past and Future*, edited by Richard Allen and Sam Ishi-Gonzalez. London: Routledge, 2004.

Saada, Nicholas. "The Noir Style." In *Film Noir Reader 4: The Crucial Films and Themes*, edited by Alain Silver and James Ursini. New Jersey: Limelight Editions, 2004.

Santos, Marlisa. *Dark Mirror: Psychiatry and Film Noir*. Lanham, MD: Lexington Books, 2010.

Sarris, Andrew. *The American Cinema: Directors and Directions, 1929–1968*. New York: Dutton, 1968.

Schapiro, Meyer. "Style." In *Anthropology Today*, edited by A.L. Kroeber. Chicago: University of Chicago Press, 1953.

Schatz, Thomas. *Boom and Bust: The American Cinema in the 1940s*. New York: Charles Scribner's Sons, 1997.

———. *Hollywood Genres: Formulas, Filmmaking, and the Studio System*. Boston: McGraw Hill, 1981.

Schorske, Carl. *Fin-De-Siecle Vienna: Politics and Culture*. New York: Vintage Books, 1981.

Schrader, Paul. "Notes on Film Noir." In *Film Noir Reader*, 6th edition, edited by Alain Silver and James Ursini. New York: Limelight Editions, 2000 [1972].

Scott, A. O. "Review of *The Last Station*." *New York Times*. December 4, 2009, C19.

Shadoian, Jack. *Dreams and Dead Ends: The American Gangster Film*, 2nd ed. New York: Oxford University Press, 2003.

Silet, Charles L. P. "Through a Woman's Eyes: Sexuality and Memory in *The 39 Steps*." In *A Hitchcock Reader*, 2nd ed., edited by Marshall Deutelbaum and Leland Poague. Chichester, UK: Wiley-Blackwell, 2009.

Silver, Alain, and Elizabeth Ward, eds. *Film Noir: An Encyclopedic Reference to the American Style*. 3rd ed. Woodstock, NY: Overlook Press, 1992.

Silver, Alain, Elizabeth Ward, James Ursini, Robert Porfirio and Coeditor: Carl Macek. *Film Noir: The Encyclopedia*. 4th ed. New York: Overlook Duckworth, 2010.

Silver, Alain, and James Ursini, eds. *Film Noir Reader*, 6th edition. New York: Limelight Editions, 2000 [1996].

———. *Film Noir Reader 2*. New York: Limelight Editions, 1999.

———. *Film Noir Reader 3: Interviews with Filmmakers of the Classic Noir Period*. New York: Limelight Editions, 2001.

———. *Film Noir Reader 4: The Crucial Films and Themes*. New Jersey: Limelight Editions, 2004.

Sklar, Robert. *Movie-Made America*. New York: Random House, 1975.

Skoble, Aeon J. "Moral Clarity and Practical Reason in Film Noir." In *The Philosophy of Film Noir*, edited by Mark T. Conard. Lexington: University Press of Kentucky, 2006.

Sobchack, Vivian. "Lounge Time: Postwar Crises and the Chronotype of Film Noir." In *Refiguring American Film Genres*, edited by Nick Browne. Berkeley: University of California Press, 1998.

Somer, Eric. "The Noir Horror of *Cat People* (1942)." In *Film Noir Reader 4: The Crucial Films and Themes*, edited by Alain Silver and James Ursini. New Jersey: Limelight Editions, 2004.

Spicer, Andrew, ed. *European Film Noir*. Manchester, UK: Manchester University Press, 2007.

Sussman, Warren. "Did Success Spoil the United States? Dual Representations in Postwar America." In *Recasting America: Culture and Politics in the Age of the Cold War*, edited by Larry May. Chicago: University of Chicago Press, 1989.

Telotte, J. P. "Voices from the Deep: Film Noir *as* Psychodrama." In *Film Noir Reader 4: The Crucial Films and Themes*, edited by Alain Silver and James Ursini. New Jersey: Limelight Editions, 2004.

Trumpener, Katie. "Fragments of the Mirror: Self Reverence, Mise en Abyme, *Vertigo*." In *Hitchcock's Rereleased Films: From Rope to Vertigo*, edited by Walter Raubicheck and Walter Srebnick. Detroit, MI: Wayne University Press, 1991.
Ursini, James. "Noir Westerns." In *Film Noir Reader 4: The Crucial Films and Themes*, edited by Alain Silver and James Ursini. New Jersey: Limelight Editions, 2004.
Wager, Jans B. *Dames in the Driver's Seat*. Austin: University of Texas Press, 2005.
Walker, Michael. "Film Noir: An Introduction. In *The Book of Film Noir*, edited by Ian Cameron. New York: Continuum, 1992.
Ward, Barbara. Commentary on the DVD of *Tension* (1949).
Warshow, Robert. "Movie Chronicle: The Westerner." In *The Immediate Experience*. New York: Atheneum, 1972 [1954].
Wolfflin, Heinrich. *Principles of Art History*. New York: Dover, 1950 [1915].
Wood, Robin. *Hitchcock's Films*. New York: A. S. Barnes, 1969.
———. "*Rancho Notorious* (1952): A Noir Western in Color." In *Film Noir Reader 4*, edited by Alain Silver and James Ursini. New Jersey: Limelight Editions, 2004.
Žižek, Slavoj. "In His Bold Gaze My Ruin Is Writ Large." In *Everything You Wanted to Know* about *Lacan (But Were Afraid to Ask Hitchcock)*, edited by Slavoj Zizek. London: Verso, 1992.1

Index

Adams, Cleve F., 68
Agamemnon, 122
Agar, John, 151, 164
Aherne, Brian, 151
Albertson, Frank, 112
Alda, Robert, 158
Aldrich, Robert, *33*, 34, 139, 154, 171
Allen, Lewis, 131, 151, 179, 181, 182, 184
Altman, Rick, 1, 6, 21, 39; his theory of genre, 12–18, 31, 63, 135
Alton, John, 56, 62, 139, 143, 150, 160, 162, 165, 167
Ambler, Eric, 156
American Film Institute, 72, 89
Andrews, Dana, 24, 77, 79, 85, 138, 147, 154, 170
anti-Semitism, 51, 143
Aristophanes, 112
Aristotle, 13, 127
Armstrong, Louis, 166
Arness, James, 160
Arnold, Edward, 78, 142
Ashcroft, Peggy, 97
Astaire, Fred, 5, 35, 56, 72, 81, 82, 120, 123
Astor, Mary, 137, 154, 156
Ayres, Lew, 49, 145, 168

Bacall, Lauren, 51, 79, 129, 139, 145
Backus, Jim, 144
Ball, Lucille, 120, 145
Ballard, Lucien, 175
Bari, Lynn, 176
baroque, 27, 31, 65, 66, 67, 70, 128, 168
Barrymore, Ethel, 102, 156, 159
Barthes, Roland, 4
Basehart, Richard, 24, 42, 62, 150, 167
Baxter, Anne, 24, 49, 78, 103, 120, 140, 151
Bazin, André, 4, 5–6, 7, 12, 19, 41, 51, 59
Beavers, Louise, 117
Beddoe, Don, *32*
Begley, Ed, 159, 162
Bel Geddes, Barbara, 109, 155, 169
Belafonte, Harry, 159
Belita, 24, 167
Belloc Lowndes, 92
Benchley, Robert, 83
Bendix, William, 140, 150, 155, 161, 169
Bennett, Bruce, 45, 49, 144, 156, 158
Bennett, Joan, 12, 126, 150, 162, 163, 170, 177

Bergman, Ingrid, 42, 45, 48, 76, 77, 101, 104, 123, 150, 158, 165
Bernhard, Jack, 140, 146
Bernhardt, Curtis, 49, 142, 150, 160
Berry, John, 150, 167
Bezzerides, A. I., 159
Bickford, Charles, 147, 170
Biesen, Sheri Chinen, 23, 34, 68, 69
Biograph, 55
Bitzer, Billy, 55
Blackmer, Sidney, 138
Blackmur, R. P., 131
Blackout: World War II and the Origen of Film Noir, 34, 68
Blondell, Joan, 27, 176
Blore, Eric, 123
Blyth, Ann, 45, 156
Boetticher, Budd, 153, 180
Bogart, Humphrey, 6, 24, 77, 79, 124, 126; Bazin's view of, 7; as hard-boiled detective, 21, 50–51; notes on his films, 139, 142, 145, 152, 174, 175
Boileau, Pierre, 110
Boland, Mary, 149
Bonanova, Fortunio, *121*, 122
Bond, James, 2
Bond, Ward, 159
Boone, Richard, 169
Borde, Raymond, 1, 21, 33, 35, 37, 60, 78
Bordwell, David, 40, 41, 55, 67, 92
Bowers, William, 160
Boyer, Charles, 42
Brady, Scott, 150
Brahm, John, 174, 175, 183
Brandon, Henry, 76
Breen, Joseph, 8, 36–37, 41, 68, 124
Brennan, Walter, 158
Brent, George, 43
Brian, David, 144
Bridges, Lloyd, 156, 168, 178
Brill, Lesley, 92
Brodie, Steve, 24, 146
Brook, Vincent, 85, 96

Brooks, Geraldine, 162
Brooks, Leslie, 140, 163
Brooks, Richard, 180, 184
Buchanan, Edgar, 155
Bugs Bunny, 81
Buhle, Paul, 124
Burckhardt, Jacob, 67
Burr, Raymond, 104, 105, 140, 143, 146, 150, 160, 162, 177

Cahiers du Cinema, 7, 89
Cahn, Edward I., 146
Cain, James M., 1, 35, 41, 45, 68, 85, 147, 156, 165
Calhern, Louis, 138
Calthrope, Donald, 94
Camus, Albert, 86
Cantor, Paul, 85
Capra, Frank, 20, 78, 124
Carey, Harry, 137, 138
Carey, Macdonald, 100, 164
Carey, Philip, 161, 163, 178
Carey, Timothy, 153
Carlson, Richard, 178
Carmichael, Hoagy, 129, 154
Carnovsky, Morris, 123, 145, 146
Carroll, Leo G., 102, 123, 159, 165
Carroll, Madeleine, 97
Carson, Jack, 45, 80, 156
Carter, Janis, 148, 157
Catcher in the Rye, 83
Cavell, Stanley, 22, 44, 80, 97
Cervantes, Miguel, 32
Chan, Charlie, 20
Chandler, Raymond, 90, 102, 127; as a source of film noir, 1, 3, 22–23, 68, 85; his novels as films, 35, 50–51, 58, 130; notes on films related to him, 139, 140, 147, 149, 154, 157, 174
Chaplin, Charlie, 73, 81
Charisse, Cyd, 35, 167, 176
Chaumenton, Etienne, 1, 21, 33, 35, 37, 60, 78
Chekov, Michael, 123

Chopra-Gant, Mike, 67, 81–82
Christie, Agatha, 90
Clarissa, 33
Clark, Dane, 49, 150, 156
Clark, Mae, 119
Clift, Montgomery, 24, 103, 151, 160
Clothier, William, 175
Clouzot, Henri-Georges, 110
Clurman, Harold, 145
Clytemnestra, 122
Cobb, Lee J., 123, 147, 153, 176, 177
Coburn, Charles, 102, 152, 159
Cochran, Steve, 141, 161
Colbert, Claudette, 71, 120
Cole, Nat King, 129
Coleman, Ronald, 12, 147
Collins, Ray, 142
Conard, Mark T., 22, 85
Conrad, William, 159
Conte, Richard, 138, 140, 165, 170, 174, 177
Cook, Elisha, Jr., *48*, 68, 70, 140, 147, 148, 151, 153, 160, 166
Cooper, Gary, 7, 17, 72, 78
Coppell, Alec, 111
Corey, Wendell, 46, 137, 139, 148, 149, 151, 153
Cortese, Valentina, 42
Cortez, Ricardo, 20
Cotten, Joseph, 40, 42, 85, 100, 140, 153, 157, 164, 168, 178
Cowie, Elizabeth, 66
Craig, James, 164, 166, 170
Crain, Jeanne, 117, 169
Crawford, Broderick, 24, 139, 150, 163
Crawford, Joan, 44, *44*, 45, 79, 120, 144, 156, 160
Cregar, Laird, 72, 151, 167, 169, 174, 175
Crime and Punishment, 26, 130–31, 177
Cromwell, John, 145, 180, 181, 184
Cronjager, Edward, 70
Cronyn, Hume, 100
Crosby, Bing, 75, 82, 147
Crouch, Stanley, 116

Cukor, George, 72, 147, 175
Cummings, Robert, 46, 137, 141, 146
Curtis, Alan, 152, 160
Curtiz, Michael, 156, 182, 184

Da Silva, Howard, 177
Daffy Duck, 81
Dahl, Arlene, 158, 165, 178
Dali, Salvador, 123, 165
Dall, John, 24, 102, 149, 162
Damico, James, 22, 38
Daniell, Henry, 177
Daniels, Bebe, 20
Dassin, Jules, 176, 180, 181, 183
Daves, Delmer, 145, 184
Davis, Bette, 20, 43, 49, 71, 78, 79, 145, 155
Davis, Nancy, 164
Day, Doris, 80, 104
Day, Laraine, 151
De Carlo, Yvonne, 142
de Havilland, Olivia, 42, 49, 145
de Kooning, Willem, 83
De Toth, André, 143, 160, 182
Dean, James, 83
Death of a Salesman, 83
Decline and Fall of the Roman Empire, 65
Defore, Don, 80, 168
Dekker, Albert, 48, 137, 138, 146, 167
Deming, Barbara, 4, 8, 34, 81
D'entre les morts, 110
Derek, John, 25, 147, 163, 175
Derrida, Jacques, 4
Dick, Douglas, *47*
Dieterle, William, 137, 144, 168
Dix, Richard, 163
Dodd, Claire, 27
Doherty, Thomas, 36, 37
Domergue, Faith, 170
Don Quixote, 32, 33
Donald Duck, 81
Donat, Robert, 97
Donlevy, Brian, 24, 138, 149, 152
Dostoyevsky, Fyodor, 131

Douglas, Gordon, 173
Douglas, Kirk, 108, 151, 159
Douglas, Melvyn, 45
Dowling, Constance, 139
Downs, Cathy, 75
Drake, Betsy, 163
Drew, Ellen, 143, 153
Driscoll, Bobby, 39
Driven to Darkness, 85
Duff, Howard, 161, 170
Duncan, Paul, 135
Dunne, Irene, 27, 71
Durbin, Deanna, 78, 128, *130*, *141*
Durgnat, Raymond, 66
Duryea, Dan, *57*, 126, 139, 141, 142, 144, 149, 156, 159, 163, 168, 170, 171
Dvorak, Ann, 155
Dwan, Allan, 165, 194
Dyer, Richard, 124
Dymytrk, Edward, 140, 142, 157

Ebert, Roger, 24
Eddy, Nelson, 82
Edwards, James, 117, 153
Ekberg, Anita, 163, 175
Elsaesser, Thomas, 2, 97, 115
Emerson, Faye, 144, 149, 150, 156, 158
Empson, William, 13
Enfield, Cy, 168
Erdman, Richard, 143
Erickson, Todd, 27, 66
Exemplary Novels, 32

Farber, Manny, 4, 34
Farewell My Lovely, 50, 157
Farrow, John, 138, 150, 158, 170, 184
Faulkner, William, 51
Faye, Alice, 71, 147
Felton, Earl, 178
Fenton, Frank, 178
Ferguson, Otis, 4
Ferrer, Jose, 170
Ferrer, Mel, 117
Fielding, Henry, 15, 32, 52

Film/Genre, 12
film noir, defined, 25; not an afterthought, 31–37; not too amorphous, 39–40; its canon, 37–38; docu-noirs and police procedurals, 60–62; and other genres, 76–81; and the hard-boiled detective, 50–51; nothing new, 40–41; and painting, 83; and women's films, 42, 49
Film Noir Guide, 13, 35, 40, 135
Film Noir: An Encyclopedic Reference to the American Style, 135
Film Noir: Films of Trust and Betrayal, 135
Film Noir: The Dark Side of the Screen, 24, 135
Fisher, Steve, 70, 145, 149
Fitzgerald, Geraldine, 153, 165
Fleischer, Richard, 142, 176, 178, 179
Fleming, Rhonda, 79, 143, 153, 159, 165, 170
Florey, Robert, 143, 144, 181
Fonda, Henry, 75, 105, 155, 171
Fontaine, Joan, 42, 138, 154
Ford, Glenn, 49, 79, 124, 139, 148, 150, 173
Ford, Wallace, 100, 150
Forrest, Sally, 166, 170
Forrest, Steve, 162
Foster, Preston, 174, 152, 165
Foucault, Michel, 4
Frank, Nino, 1, 26, 34, 37
Franz, Arthur, 165
Freudianism, 5, 34, 42, 89, 199, 100, 101, 121, 123, 141, 165, 170, 177
From Reverence to Rape, 119
Frye, Northrop, 4, 13–18, 126
Fuller, Sam, 143, 160, 164, 175, 179

Gabin, Jean, 175
Gaines, Philip, 38
Gam, Rita, 167
Gardner, Ava, 140, 153, 174
Garfield, John, 35, 117, 148, 150, 158, 161

Gargan, William, 157, 171
Garland, Judy, 82
Garmes, Lee, 59, 102, 176
Garner, Peggy Ann, 139
Garnett, Tay, 161, 174
Gavin, John, 112
Genn, Leo, 169
Gibbon, Edward, 65
Gifford, Frances, 138
Gomez, Thomas, 148, 151, 153
Gone with the Wind, 43
Goodis, David, 141, 158, 168
Goulding, 175
Grable, Betty, 70, *71*, 151
Grahame, Gloria, 51, 79, *119*, 124, 126, 139, 143, 150, 152, 155, 157, 159
Granger, Farley, 24, 102, 147, 162, 164, 166, 177
Grant, Cary, 44, 101, 111, 158
Granville, Bonita, 78, 149
Gray, Coleen, 174, 177
Greene, Graham, 3, 85
Greenstreet, Sidney, 123, 142, 156, 169
Greer, Jane, 79, 108, 159, 167
Griffith, D. W., 51, 55, 96
Guild, Nancy, 165, 174

Hadley, Reed, 61, 150
Hagen, Jean, 138, 158
Hamlet, 26
Hammett, Dashiell, 1, 3, 68, 85, 90, 149, 156; and the crime novel, 20–22
Hardwicke, Cedric, 102
Harris, Theresa, *116*
Harrison, Rex, 80
Haskell, Molly, 119
Haskin, Byron, 151, 168, 184
Hasso, Signe, 147, 165
Hatfield, Hurd, 48, 146
Hathaway, Henry, 145, 157, 179, 180
Hauser, Arnold, 67
Havoc, June, 141
Hawks, Howard, 51, 139
Hayden, Sterling, *79*, 126, 138, 143, 153, 156, 157

Hayes Office, 19. *See also* Production Code Administration
Hayward, Susan, 137, 145, 167
Hayworth, Rita, 80, 124, 129, 148, 154, 173
Hearst, William Randolph, 60
Hecht, Ben, 100, 102, 162, 165, 170
Heflin, Van, 44, 124, 137, 139, 160, 161, 174
Heisler, Stuart, 137, 149, 181, 183
Helmore, Tom, 105, 164
Hendrix, Wanda, 162
Henreid, Paul, 43, 145, 150
Hepburn, Katharine, 71, 72, 79, 80, 175, 178
Hernandez, Juano, 117
Herrmann, Bernard, 108, 111, 112, 128, 159, 169, 174
Heston, Charlton, 70, 144, 168
Heywood, Eddie, 129
Hibbs, Thomas, 125, 127
High Window, 34, 50, 174
Highsmith, Patricia, 103
Hinkson, Jake, 59
Hirsch, Foster, 24, 105
Hitchcock, Alfred, 38, 42, 58, 74, 86, 123, 124, 130, 133; achievements, 111–13; *Blackmail*, 92–97; films in the context of film noir, 97–105; *The Lodger*, 91–92; Naremore's view of, 89–90; notes on his films, 146, 151, 158, 159, 162, 164, 165, 166, 169, 177, 182; *Vertigo*, 105–11
Hodiak, John, 25, 138, 140, 160, 165, 175
Holden, William, *43*, 62, 166, 168
Hollywood's Censor, 36
Holmes, Sherlock, 20, 21
Homer, 13, 102, 112
Homier, Skip, 144
Homolka, Oscar, 98
homosexuality, 123–24
Hope, Bob, 35, *36*, 82, 157
Horace, 13, 127
Horton, Edward Everett, 123

HUAC (House Un-American Activities Committee), 124
Hughes, Mary Beth, 149, 152
Humberstone, H. Bruce, 70, 151
Hume, David, 11, 127
Hunt, Marsha, 162
Hunter, Jeffrey, 153
Hunter, Kim, 169
Hurt, William, 130
Huston, John, 21, 73, 130, 138, 156, 174, 181
Huston, Virginia, 59, 159, 176
Hyer, Martha, 144

Iliad, 122
Ireland, John, 176

Jackson, Patrick, 164
Jaffe, Sam, 138
Jagger, Dean, 144, 169
James, Henry, 59
Jane Eyre, 43
Jergens, Adele, 147
Jordan, Dorothy, 76
Johnson, Nunnally, 139
Johnson, Samuel, 32, 65
Joseph Andrews, 32
Jourdan, Louis, 102, 159

Kael, Pauline, 13
Kardos, Laszlo, 166
Karimi, A. M., 21
Karlson, Phil, 78, 137, 140, 163, 174, 180, 182
Karns, Roscoe, 120
Keaney, Michael F., 35, 40, 63
Keaton, Buster, 166
Keeler, Ruby, 166
Keen, Malcolm, 92
Kelly, Grace, 104, 120, 146, 177
Kelly, Paul, 51, 143, 148, 164
Kennedy, Arthur, 74, 141, 168
Kern, Jerome, 80
Keyes, Evelyn, 137, 149, 153, 161
Kiss, Kiss, Bang, Bang, 13

Kline, Franz, 83
Knowles, Patric, 171
Kolker, Robert Philip, 70
Korngold, Erich Wolfgang, 145
Kroeger, Berry, 175
Krutnik, Frank, 21, 66
Kubrick, Stanley, 153

Lacan, Jacques, 4
Ladd, Alan, 35, *36*, 62, 140, 141, 149, 167
Lake, Veronica, 128, 140, 149, 167
Lamarr, Hedy, 120, 123, 146, 175
Lamour, Dorothy, 36, 156, 157
Lancaster, Burt, 17, 23, 143, 151, 153, 154
Landis, Carole, 70, *71*, 72, 120, 151
Lang, Fritz, 39, 124; and Hitchcock, 91, 96–97; notes on his films, 138, 139, 140, 150, 163, 170, 171, 177; as an originator of film noir, 2, 26, 133
Laughton, Charles, 102, 124, 138, 156, 159, 177
Lawrence, Marc, 152
Lazarillo de Tormes, 32
Le Paysan Parvenu, 32
Leachman, Cloris, 154
Lee, Gypsy Rose, 163
Leigh, Janet, 70, 112, 137, 162, 168
Leisen, Mitchell, 158
Leith, Virginia, 153–54
Leja, Michael, 83
Leonard, Robert Z., 140
Leslie, Joan, 174
Levin, Henry, 147, 157, 181
Lévi-Strauss, Claude, 4
Lewis, Joseph H., 138, 149, 175, 179, 180, 182
Lindfors, Viveca, 144
Litel, John, 149
Litvak, Anatole, 155, 182, 183, 184
Lockhart, Gene, 170
Loder, John, 98, 146
Lombard, Carole, 71
London, Julie, 173

Long Day's Journey into Night, 83
Longden, John, 92–93
Longinus, 127
Losey, Joseph, 161, 182
Louise, Tina, 177
Lovejoy, Frank, 168
Loy, Myrna, 20
Luhr, William, 21, 55
Lukas, Paul, 145
Lund, John, 80, 158
Lupino, Ida, 139, 159, 161, 170, 173, 174, 175, 181
Lynn, Diana, 160
Lynn, Jeffrey, 165
Lyons, Arthur, 19

MacDonald, Jeanette, 82
MacDougall, Ranald, 156, 183
Mackenzie, Joyce, 48, 146
MacMurray, Fred, 24, 59, 108, *121*, 146, 161
Macready, George, 124, 138, 148, 154, 175
Mad Men, 82
Malden, Karl, 103, 151, 170
Malone, Dorothy, 148, 155, 161
Mankiewicz, Herman, 141
Mankiewicz, Joseph L., 117, 165, 176, 184
Mann, Anthony, 74, 76, 146, 149, 162, 164, 179, 182, 184
Mansfield, Jayne, 141, 151
March, Fredric, 77
Marianne, 32
Marin, Edwin L., 161, 176, 179
Markos, Louis, 21
Marlowe, Hugh, 151
Marlowe, Philip, 22, 23, 50, 51, 110, 127, 139, 151, 154, 157, 174
Marshall, Herbert, 43, 138, 142, 150, 155, 178
Marshan, D., 34
Marvin, Lee, *119*, 139
Marx Brothers, 5, 16
Marx, Karl, and Marxism, 4, 84, 121

Mason, James, 46, 111, 159, 162, 174
Mason, Perry, 20
Massen, Osa, 45
Massey, Raymond, 44, 160
Maté, Rudolph, 144, 180, 181, 184
Mature, Victor, 54n27, 70, 72, 75, 76, 79, 151, 154, 174
Maxwell, Marilyn, 161
Maybeck, Bernard, 110
Mayo, Archie, 175, 184
Mayo, Virginia, 78, 148, 162
Mazurki, Mike, 175
McArthur, Colin, 121
McCarthy, Joseph and McCarthyism, 3, 59, 73, 84, 124
McCarthy, Kevin, 147
McDaniel, Hattie, 117
McGavin, Darren, 141
McGraw, Charles, *32*, 121, 155, 162, 176
McGuire, Dorothy, 155
McLaglen, Andrew, 175
McNally, Stephen, 142, 155
Mears, Martha, 128
Meeker, Ralph, 154
Menjou, Adolphe, 165
Meredith, Burgess, 156, 166
Merrie Melodies, 81
Merrill, Gary, 140, 170
Metz, Christian, 12
Meyers, Abram F., 36
MGM, 34, 72, 140, 161, 167
Milland, Ray, 24, 138, 146, 167
Miller, Laurence, 123
Minturn, Kent, 83
Mitchell, Thomas, 49, 145, 170, 175
Mitchum, Robert, *52*, 59, 79, 108, *116*, 138, 143, 150, 154, 155, 159, 169, 178
Modleski, Tania, 103
Moll Flanders, 32
Monogram, 16, 149
Monroe, Marilyn, 138, 157
Montgomery, George, 50, 174
Montgomery, Robert, 50, 154, 162

Moorehead, Agnes, 145
Morales, Esy, 129
More Than Night, 3, 89
Morgan, Harry, 161, 165
Morgan, Julia, 60
Morgan, Michele, 141
Morris, Chester, 23, 50, 139
Muller, Eddie, 24, 59, 85
Mulvey, Laura, 103, 107
Murphy, George, 138, 158
Musuraca, Nicholas, 50, 56, 145, 166

Narcejac, Thomas, 110
Naremore, James, 13, 22, 25, 31; on Bazin, 7–8; on Hitchcock, 89–91, 105; on noir style, 56–57; on period, 83–85
Neal, Tom, 24, 126, 146, 152
Neale, Steve, 2, 21, 31, 34, 37, 41, 43, 44, 51, 66, 76
Negulesco, Jean, 156, 158, 182
Neo-realism, 2
New Deal, 19, 59, 83, 84, 123
Newman, Paul, 17
Nietzschean, 22, 84, 85, 102, 125
Nilsson, Ann Q., 166
Nolan, Lloyd, 50, 61, 154, 165
Novak, Kim, 106, *107*, 161, 169
novel: its rise into consciousness, 32–33
Novello, Ivor, *91*, 92
Nugent, Elliot, 157

Oberon, Merle, 175
O'Brien, Edmond, 23, *25*, 62, 143, 144, 147, 153, 164, 168, 169, 173
O'Brien, Pat, 24, 142, 144
O'Connor, Flannery, 125
O'Donnell, Cathy, 164, 177
Oedipus Rex, 26
Office of War Information, 68
O'Keefe, Dennis, 62, 146, 162, 167
On the Road, 83
Ondra, Anny, 92, *93*, *95*
Orestes, 122

Oswald, Gerd, 142, 153, 163
Our Town, 100

Paget, Debra, 174
Paglia, Camille, 130
Paige, Janis, 80, 140
Painting with Light, 56
Pallette, Eugene, 16
Palmer, R. Barton, 66, 125, 127
Pamela, 32, 68
Panama, Norman, 177
Pangborn, Franklin, 123
Panorama du film noir americain, 1, *33*
Paramount, 34, 35
Pascal, Blaise, 125
Patrick, Gail, 109
Payne, John, 25, 79, 137, 143, 165, 174
PCA. *See* Production Code Administration
Pearson, Beatrice, 148
Pechter, William, 4
Peck, Gregory, 17, 48, 101, 102, 123, 159, 165
Perez, Gilberto, 6, 12, 75
Perreau, Gigi, 164
Peters, Jean, 140, 157, 160, 169
Peterson, Lowell, 55–56
Phaedo, 11
Pichel, Irving, 161, 167, 184
Pitt, Brad, 121
Place, Janey, 55–56
Plato, 112
Platt, Louise, 166
Poe, Edgar Allen, 21
Poitier, Sidney, 117
Pollack, Jackson, 83
Polonsky, Abe, 148
Pope, Alexander, 13–14
Porfirio, Robert, 9n13, 22, 39, 63, 125
Porter, Cole, 82
Powell, Dick, 24, 50, *58*, 78, 79, 82, 127, 142, 153, 157, 160, 181
Powell, William, 20
Power, Tyrone, 17, 78, 176
pre-Code, 1, 20, 119

Preminger, Otto, 2, 61, 138, 147, 154, 170, 182
Presley, Elvis, 5
Preston, Robert, 167
Price, Vincent, 42, 49, 140, 150, 154, 155, 169, 170
Production Code Administration, 1, 8, 20, 22, 41, 62, 75, 76, 161; effect of World War II on, 68; film noir's subversion of, 84; Hitchcock and the Code, 101–3, 112; Neo-noir and "post" code, 133; and the New Deal, 19; its relation to moral clarity, 125, 129; its response to film noir, 36–37; weakening of the Code, 84, 116, 119, 123, 134

Queen, Ellery, 20
Quine, Richard, 142, 147, 161

Rabinowitz, Paula, 84, 115–16
Raft, George, 21, 144, 155, 161, 162, 176
Raines, Ella, 24, 48, 144, 152, 160, 165, 169, 177
Rains, Claude, 77, 101, 145, 158, 170, 175
Raksin, David, 155
Rapper, Irving, 145
Ray, Nicholas, 152, 155, 159, 175, 176, 177, 183, 184
Ray, Robert, 70
Redgrave, Michael, 177
Reed, Carol, 85
Reed, Donna, 141, 163
Reframing Abstract Expressionism, 83
Republic, 16
Revere, Ann, 177
Reville, Alma, 102
Rich, Nathaniel, 1, 2, 105, 122
Richardson, Samuel, 15, 32, 33, 68
Ritchard, Cyril, 93
Ritter, Thelma, 104, 160, 177
RKO, 50, 69, 70, 76, 157
Robinson Crusoe, 32

Robinson, Edward G., 23, 24, 59, *121*, 122, 126, 146, 151, 163, 170
Robinson, Jackie, 117
Rococo, 27, 31, 66, 67
Rogers, Ginger, 5, 71, 72, 78, 80, 109, 139
Rogers, Kasey, 102
Roman, Ruth, 103
Rooney, Mickey, 24, 78, 147, 161, 166
Roosevelt, Eleanor, 19
Root, Jane, 66
Rosenbladt, Bettina, 92
Rothko, Mark, 83
Rouse, Russell, 167, 181, 183
Rousseau, Jean-Jacques, 4
Rozsa, Miklos, 123, 128, 154, 165
Ruggles, Charles, 49
Running Away from Myself, 34
Russell, Gail, 156, 158
Russell, Jane, 129, 150, 154, 155
Russell, Rosalind, 169
Rutherford, Ann, 78, 152
Ryan, Robert, 24, *52*, 74, 79, 137, 143, 151, 159, 170, 173

Saada, Nicholas, 38
Sanders, George, 50, 78, 165, 170, 174, 175
Santos, Marlisa, 123
Sarris, Andrew, 73, 89
Sartre, Jean-Paul, 86
Savage, Ann, 146
Schatz, Thomas, 21, 55, 66, 69
Schorske, Carl, 84
Schrader, Paul, 22, 63, 66
Scott, Lizabeth, 79, 144, 145, 151, 160, 168
Scott, Martha, 165
Scott, Randolph, 72
Scourby, Alexander, 139, 173
Seiter, William A., 155, 179
Sekeley, Steve, 150
Selznick, David, 102, 111
Shadoian, Jack, 124
Shakespeare, William, 38, 89, 112

Shamroy, Leon, 49
Shane, Maxwell, 148, 182, 183
Shaw, Anabel, 42
Shearer, Lloyd, 34, 68
Sherman, George, 163, 177, 181
Sherman, Vincent, 144, 158, 168, 173, 182
Shirley, Anne, 127, 157
Sidney, Sylvia, *98*, 113n17, 171
Siegel, Don, 76, 161, 179, 181, 182
Silly Symphonies, 81
Silver, Alain, 37, 38, 39, 63, 135
Silvers, Phil, 80
Simmons, Jean, 138
Simple Art of Murder, 23
Siodmak, Robert, 2, 49, 86, 124; notes on his films, 141, 142, 145, 148, 153, 160, 165, 174, 177, 180, 182
Skelton, Red, 81
Skipworth, Alison, 20
Sklar, Robert, 66
Skoble, Aeon, 126
Slezak, Walter, 140, 142
Smith, Alexis, 62, 142, 168
Smith, Kent, 24, 144, 158
Sobchack, Vivian, 72
Socrates, 11
Sondergaard, Gale, 141
Songs in film noir, 128–29
Sophocles, 112
Sothern, Ann, 78, 140, 164
Spade, Sam, 20–23, 50, 105, 110, 126
Staiger, Janet, 40, 41, 55
Stanley, Fred, 35
Stanwyck, Barbara, 43, 47, 71, 78, 108, 120, 142, 146, 148, 158, 174
Steiger, Rod, 139
Stevens, George, 160
Stevens, Mark, 79, 120, 144, 145, 173
Stevenson, Robert, 146, 151, 154, 178
Stewart, Donald Ogden, 45
Stewart, James, 74, 102, 104, 105, 162, 169, 177
Stewart, Paul, 147, 155, 178
Stone, Sharon, 130

Storm, Gale, 173
Streetcar Named Desire, 83
Strudwick, Shepperd, 46, 162, 166
Sturges, Preston, 80
Sullivan, Barry, 78, 148, 155, 158, 167, 168, 174
Sussman, Warren, 83
Swanson, Gloria, *43*, 166
Symposium, 112
Sypher, Wylie, 67

Talman, William, 142
Tarzan, 2
Taylor, Elizabeth, 160
Taylor, Robert, 78, 124, 140, 150, 162, 176, 178
Taylor, Samuel, 111
Telotte, J. P., 123
Temple, Shirley, 19
Tester, Desmond, 98
Tetzlaff, Ted, 144, 182
Thaxter, Phyllis, 137, 158
The Princess of Cleves, 32
Thompson, Kristin, 40, 41, 55
Thorpe, Richard, 168
Tierney, Gene, 49, 103, 120, 127, 154, 170, 176
Tierney, Lawrence, 140
Todd, Ann, 102, 159
Tom Jones, 33
Tone, Franchot, 152, 156, 160
Totter, Audrey, 31, 150, 154, 167
Tourneur, Jacques, 76, 158, 159, 180
Towers, Constance, 175
Tracy, Spencer, 72, 80, 160, 175
Travers, Henry, 100, 164
Treacher, Arthur, 20
Trevor, Claire, 140, 142, 162, 166, 169
Trumpener, Katie, 109, 110
Tufts, Sonny, 143
Tully, Tom, 62
Turner, Kathleen, 130
Turner, Lana, 35, 71, 161
Tuttle, Frank, 143, 167
Twentieth Century Fox, 34, 70

Ulmer, Edgar G., 2, 86, 146, 157, 182, 186
Ursini, James, 38, 74, 76

Valentino, Rudolph, 121
Valli, Alida, 102, 159, 178
Vance, Philo, 20
Veidt, Conrad, 45
Vickers, Martha, 141
Vidor, Charles, 148, 183
Vincent, June, *57*, 139
Von Sternberg, Josef, 155, 184
Von Stroheim, Erich, 149, 166

Wagner, David, 124
Walker, Helen, 123, 152, 176
Walker, Robert, 102, 166
Walker, Vernon, 145, 166
Wallace, Jean, 138, 152
Walsh, Raoul, 174, 181
Ward, Barbara, 39, 63
Warner Brothers (Warners), 5, 20, 34, 35, 70, 81, 117, 156
Warner, H. B., 166
Warshow, Robert, 4, 16, 19, 129
Webb, Clifton, 127, 145, 154,
Weegee, 60
Welles, Orson, 154, 168, 180; *Citizen Kane* and film noir, 41, 69–70, 96, 134; on framing the period, 90, 91; role in *The Third Man*, 90–91
Werker, Alfred L., 150, 180, 182
West, Mae, 19

Widmark, Richard, 54n27, 118, 160, 176, 177
Wilde, Cornel, 138
Wilder, Billy, 2, 80, 91, 146, 166, 181
Wilder, Thornton, 100
William, Warren, 20
Williams, Bill, 142, 144, 145
Williams, Esther, 5, 81
Windsor, Marie, 31, *32*, 79, 121, 142, 148, 149, 153, 165, 176
Winters, Shelley, 139, 147, 150, 159, 160
Wittgenstein, Ludwig, 15
Wood, Edward D., Jr., 102, 140, 146, 152
Wood, Natalie, 76, 143
Wood, Robin, 2, 89, 97
Woodward, Joanne, 113n17, 153
Woolrich, Cornell, 1, 39, 85, 104, 107; notes on films based on his work, 139, 141, 145, 147, 148, 149, 158, 160, 166, 169, 177
Wright, Teresa, 78, 100, 164
Wyatt, Jane, 160
Wyler, William, 155, 184

Young, Gig, 24, 152
Young, Loretta, 24, 46, *47*, 137, 174
Young, Robert, *52*, 143, 163, 167

Ziegfeld, Flo, 82
Zinnemann, Fred, 137, 182

Index of Cited Films
See Appendix C for Additional Listings

The 3rd Voice, 173
The 39 Steps, 97
99 River Street, 40, 137
The Accused, 24, 46, *47*, 49, 137
Act of Violence, 25, 122, 137
Adam's Rib, 80
Affair in Trinidad, 173
Air Force, 73
All About Eve, 49, 73, 78
Among the Living, 137
Angel Face, 38, 138
Apache, 17
Appointment with Danger, 62
The Arnelo Affair, 138
Arsenic and Old Lace, 78
The Asphalt Jungle, 37, 58, 61, 73, *79*, 119, 126, 138
Attack, 34

Back Street, 6
Badlands, 27
The Band Wagon, 35
Basic Instinct, 27, 130
Bataan, 73
The Beautiful Blonde from Bashful Bend, 16
Behave Yourself, 53n14
The Bells of St. Mary's, 76, 82
Bend of the River, 74

The Benny Goodman Story, 39
The Best Years of Our Lives, 73, 77–78
Between Midnight and Dawn, 173
Beware My Lovely, 173
Beyond a Reasonable Doubt, 38, 138
The Big Clock, 24, 119, 124, 138
The Big Combo, 38, 58, 138
The Big Heat, 38, 58, *119*, 129, 130
The Big Night, 38, 139
The Big Sleep, 34, 37, 38, 51, 58, 73, 127, 129, 139
The Birds, 112
The Birth of a Nation, 96
Black Angel, 57, 139
Black Widow, 78, 139
Blackmail, 92–96, *93*, *95*, 98, 112
Blind Spot, 23, 139
Blonde Ice, 140
Blonde Venus, 44, 56
Blood on the Moon, 74
The Blue Dahlia, 5, 34, 38, 140
The Blue Gardenia, 24, 120, 129, 140
Blue Skies, 82
Blue Velvet, 27
Blueprint for Murder, 149
Body Heat, 27, 130
Border Incident, 37, 38

Born to Be Bad, 48
Born to Kill, 140
The Brasher Doubloon, 34, 50, 174
The Bribe, 140
The Breaking Point, 117, *118*
Broken Arrow, 16, 76
Broken Blossoms, 51,
The Brothers Rico, 140
Brute Force, 38
Bullitt, 20
The Burglar, 141

The Cabinet of Dr. Caligari, 92
Call Northside 777, 63
Casablanca, 73, 77, 102
The Case Against Brooklyn, 141
Cat Ballou, 16
Cat People, 76
Caught, 38
Cause for Alarm, 47, 174
The Chase, 141
Chicago Deadline, 37, 141
Chinatown, 27, 130
Christmas Holiday, 69, 128, *130*, 141
Citizen Kane, 7, 21, 23, 58, 59–60, *69*, 73, 96, 100, 128, 134; and the birth of film noir, 67–72
City That Never Sleeps, 24, 142
Clash by Night, 5, 39
The Clay Pigeon, 142
Conflict, 34, 48, 123, 142
Cornered, 25, 142
Cover Girl, 80
The Covered Wagon, 17
Crack-Up, 24, 142
Crime of Passion, 47, 142
Crime Wave, 125, 143
The Crimson Kimono, 143
Criss Cross, 22, 38, 126, 129, 143
The Crooked Way, 25, 37, 122, 143
Crossfire, 5, 24, 42, 51–52, 143
Cry Danger, 24, 143
Cry in the Night, 143
Cry of the City, 174
Cry Vengeance, 144

D.O.A., 22, 23, 26, 38, 105, 126, 128, 144
The Damned Don't Cry, 129, 144
Dances with Wolves, 17
Danger Signal, 144
A Dangerous Profession, 144
Dark City, 129, 144
The Dark Corner, 34, 58, 118, 120, 129, 145
The Dark Mirror, 38, *49*, *123*, *145*
Dark Passage, *129*, *145*
The Dark Past, 38, *59*, *123*
Dead Reckoning, 25, *129*, *145*
Deadline at Dawn, 145
Deception, 129, 145
Decoy, 39, 146
Desperate, 24, 125, 146
Destination Murder, 48, 120, 146
Destry Rides Again, 17
Detour, 5, 21, 24, 38, 126, 129, 146
Devil in a Blue Dress, 28
Devil's Doorway, 78
Diabolique, 110
Dial M for Murder, 104, 105, 120, 146
Dirty Harry, 20
Dishonored Lady, 120, 123, 146
Double Indemnity, 21,22, 24, 58–59, 73, 90, 91, 100, 108, 124, 125, 126, 128, 146; bringing the genre into consciousness, 34–35, 41, 49, 68–69, 133; in the canon, 37–38; and class, *121–22*; as essential to film noir, 1, 23, 39
A Double Life, 23, 81, 147
Down Argentine Way, 17
Dr. Jekyll and Mr. Hyde, 5
Drive a Crooked Road, 78, 147
Duel in the Sun, 74, 82

East Side West Side, 129, 174
Edge of Doom, 147
The Egg and I, 81

The Falcon Takes Over, 50
Fall Guy, *147*

Fallen Angel, 24, 37, 38, 71, 147
Falling Down, 27
Family Secret, 147
Fargo, 28
Fatal Attraction, 113n7
Fear in the Night, 148
The File on Thelma Jordan, 37, 61, 125, 148
Flaxy Martin, 148
Follow the Fleet, 56, 70, 123
Force of Evil, 124, 148
Foreign Affair, 80
Foreign Correspondent, 99
Forever Amber, 81, 82
Fort Apache, 75
Framed, 148
Frankenstein, 5
The French Connection, 20
The Fuller Brush Girl, 53n14

Gaslight, 42–43
The Gay Divorcee, 70
Gentleman's Agreement, 51
Gilda, 37, 124, 129, 148
The Glass Key, 149
Go West, 16
Golden Boy, 40
Gone with the Wind, 43–44
The Great Dictator, 81
The Great Flamarion, 149
The Great Train Robbery, 16
Green Dolphin Street, 81
The Green Years, 82
The Grifters, 27
Guest in the House, 49
The Guilty, 149
Guilty Bystander, 149
Gun Crazy, 22, 24, 37, 38, 126, 129, 149
The Gunfighter, 17

Hangover Square, 174
Harriet Craig, 49
Hell's Half Acre, 120, 149
He Ran All the Way, 150

Her Kind of Man, 150
He Walked by Night, 37, *61*–62, 150
High Noon, 75
High Sierra, 7, 174
High Wall, 37, 159
His Kind of Woman, 150
Hollow Triumph, 150
Home of the Brave, 117
The House on Telegraph Hill, 42
The Hucksters, 82
Human Desire, 150

I Am a Fugitive from a Chain Gang, 5
I Confess, 24, 103, 125, 151
I Died a Thousand Times, 174
I Married a Communist, 125, 151
I Wake Up Screaming, 23, 58, *71*, 120, 128, 151; its relation to *Citizen Kane*, 69–72
I Walk Alone, 129, 151
Illegal, 24, 151
Imitation of Life, 51
Impact, *24*, 122, 152
In a Lonely Place, 24, 38, 119, 124, 126, 129, 152
The Informer, 5, 56
Inner Sanctum, 152
Inside Job, 78, 152
Invasion of the Body Snatchers, 76
The Invisible Man, 5
The Iron Horse, 16, 76
It Happened One Night, 120
It's a Wonderful Life, 78, 129
It's Always Fair Weather, 81
It's in the Bag, 53n14

Jail Bait, 102
Jesse James, 17
Jezebel, 5
Jigsaw, 152
Johnny Eager, 124
Johnny O'Clock, 153
Jolson Sings Again, 81
The Jolson Story, 81, 82
Junior Bonner, 16

Kansas City Confidential, 174
Keeper of the Flame, 72, 175
The Killer is Loose, 153
The Killers, 21, 23, *25*, 37, 38, 73, 126, 127, 153
Killer's Kiss, 153
The Killing, 38, 126, 153
Kill Me Again, 27, 130
A Kiss Before Dying, 113n17, 153
Kiss Me Deadly, 5, 34, 38, 115, 154
Kiss of Death, 37, 40, 154
Kiss the Blood Off My Hands, 154
Klute, 27
Knock on Any Door, 175

L.A. Confidential, 20
The Lady from Shanghai, 37, 38, 154
The Lady Gambles, 47, 120
The Lady in the Lake, 34, 37, 50–51, 61, 154
A Lady without a Passport, 175
The Las Vegas Story, 129, 154
Laura, 5, 22, 23, 24, 38, 119, 127, 129, 154
Leave Her to Heaven, 82, 103, 105, 120; why it is a borderline film noir, 49
Left Handed Gun, 17
The Lemon Drop Kid, 53n14
The Leopard Man, 76
The Letter, 155
Life with Father, 81
Lifeboat, 99
Little Big Man, 17
Little Caesar, 19
The Loan Shark, 155
The Lodger (1927), *91*–92, 96, 111
The Lodger (1944), 175
Lonely Are the Brave, 16
The Long Goodbye, 130
Loophole, 155
Lost Boundaries, 51, 117
Love Letters, 40, 62
The Lusty Men, 16

M, 26, 90
Macao, 155
Make Haste to Live, 120, 155
The Maltese Falcon (1931), 20
The Maltese Falcon (1941), *6*, 35, 41, 55, 58, 70, 73, 90, 100, 113, 126, 156; adaptations of Hammett's novel, 20–23; in the canon, 37, 38; as an early film noir, 1, 3, 7, 66, 68–70, 115
The Manchurian Candidate, 3
Manhandled, *156*
The Man in the Vault, 175
The Man on the Eiffel Tower, 156
The Man Who Knew Too Much, 99
Marnie, 112
The Mask of Dimitrios, 156
McCabe and Mrs. Miller, 17
Meet John Doe, 78
Mildred Pierce, 23, 35, 38, *46*, 119, 126, 156
Monsieur Verdoux, 81
Moonrise, 156
Moontide, 128, 175
Mr. & Mrs. Smith, 99
Mr. Deeds Goes to Town, 123
Mr. Smith Goes to Washington, 5
Mulholland Dr., 10
Murder He Says, 53n14
Murder Is My Beat, 157
Murder, My Sweet, 34, 38, 50, *58*, 68, 127, 157
My Darling Clementine, 74–75
My Favorite Brunette, 35–36, 157
My Name is Julia Ross, 120

Naked Alibi, 157
Naked City, 38, 60–67
The Naked Kiss, 175
The Naked Spur, 17, 74
The Narrow Margin, *32*, 121, 176
Neptune's Daughter, 81
Niagara, 157
Night and Day, 82
Night and the City, 37, 38, 176

Index of Cited Films

Night Editor, 157
Nightfall, 158
Night Has a Thousand Eyes, 158
Nightmare, 129
Nightmare Alley, 78, 123, 176
Nobody Lives Forever, 38, 158
No Country for Old Men, 27
Nocturne, 176
No Man of Her Own, 120, 158
Nora Prentiss, 24, 122, 158
No Questions Asked, 158
North by North West, 111
Nosferatu, 92
Notorious, 73, 101, 102, 158
No Way Out, 117, 176

Odds Against Tomorrow, 159
On Dangerous Ground, 51, 159
One False Move, 27
One Way Street, 159
The Other Woman, 159
Ossesione, 161
Out of the Past, 22, 23, 39, 73, 106, 129, 159; in the canon, 38; as an essential film noir, 1, 49; its noir style and conventions, 55–56, 59, 128; as tragedy, 126; its treatment of race, 116–17
Out of Time, 130
The Ox-Bow Incident, 17, 74

Panic in the Streets, 38
The Paradine Case, 102, 159
Party Girl, 176
The People Against O'Hara, 160
Phantom Lady, 23, 24, 38, 48, 69, 119, 128, 160
Pick-Up on South Street, 124, 160
Pinky, 51, 117
Pitfall, 38, 160
A Place in the Sun, 160
The Plainsman, 17
Point Blank, 27
Portrait in Smoke, 178
Possessed, 42, 44–45, 120, 160

The Postman Always Rings Twice, 22, 34, 35, 38, 55, 161
Private Hell 36, 161
The Prowler, 51, 161
Psycho, 111–12
Public Enemy, 19
Pulp Fiction, 27
Pursued, 17, 74
Pushover, 161

Queen Kelly, 166
Quicksand, 24, 78, 161

Race Street, 161
Ramrod, 74
Rashomon, 85
Raw Deal, 74, 162
The Razor's Edge, 81, 82
Rear Window, 104–5
Rebecca, 42, 177
The Reckless Moment, 24, 46, 119, 162
Red Light, 37, 162
Ride the Pink Horse, 37, 38, 162
The River's Edge, 129
Roadblock, 162
Road to Utopia, 82
Rogue Cop, 51, 162
Romance on the High Seas, 80
Rope, 37, 102, 105, 119, 162
Roxie Hart, 80

Sabotage, 98–99
Saboteur, 99
Samson and Delilah, 76
Satan Met a Lady, 20
Scandal Sheet, 24, 25, 121, 163
Scarface, 5, 19, 39, 56
Scarlet Street, 23, 38, 58, 126, 163
Screaming Mimi, 163
Se7en, 130
The Searchers, 76
The Second Woman, 120, 163
Secret Beyond the Door, 177
The Secret of the Whistler, 163
Serenade, 34, 35

The Set-Up, 37, 40
Seven Brides for Seven Brothers, 16
Shadow of a Doubt, 38, 69, *99*, 100, 113, 164
Shadow on the Wall, 78, 164
The Shanghai Gesture, 37
Shield for Murder, 51, 164
Shock, 42
Shockproof, 164
The Shootist, 17
Shoot to Kill, 164
Side Street, 59, 129, 164
Slightly Scarlet, 165
The Sleeping City, 177
The Snake Pit, 42
The Sniper, 165
Somewhere in the Night, 37, 165
The Song of Bernadette, 76, 77
Spellbound, 48, 82, 100–101, 123, 165
Stage Fright, 99
Stagecoach, 5, 40
A Stolen Life, 49
Storm Warning, 78
The Strange Affair of Uncle Harry, 165
Strange Bargain, 165
The Strange Love of Martha Ivers, 124
Stranger on the Third Floor, 68–69, 166
Strangers on a Train, 24, 38, 90, 102–3, 119, 166
Strange Triangle, 166
Street of Chance, 166
The Strip, 78, 129, 166
Sunset Boulevard, 22, 38, 42–43, 75, 126, 166
The Suspect, 177
Suspense, 24, 166, 167
Suspicion, 42, 177,
Sweet Dreams, 39

Taxi Driver, 27
Tension, 24, 122, 125, 167
Thelma & Louise, 27
They Died with Their Boots On, 75
They Live by Night, 22, 177
They Won't Believe Me, 167

The Thief, 24, 167
The Thin Man, 20
The Third Man, 5, 62, 73, 85
This Gun for Hire, 37, 38, 58, 69, 119, 128, 167
The Three Caballeros, 81
The Thrill of Brazil, 80
Tight Spot, 78
Till the Clouds Roll By, 82
Time to Kill, 50, 128
T-Men, 37, 38, 62, 168
To Catch a Thief, 99
Too Late for Tears, 168
Top Hat, 120, 123
Touch of Evil, 1, 38, 42, 58, 66, 115, 168
Transsiberian, 28
The Trap, 177
Trapped, 178
The Treasure of the Sierra Madre, 73
The Trouble with Harry, 99
Try and Get Me, 124, 168
The Turning Point, 62, 168
The Two Mrs. Carrolls, 38

Unconquered, 81
Under Capricorn, 99
Undercurrent, 35, 178
Unfaithful, 47, 120, 168
Unfaithfully Yours, 80
Union Pacific, 16, 76
The Unknown Man, 169
The Unsuspected, 38

The Velvet Touch, 169
Vertigo, 23, 38, 73, *107*, 122, 128, 135, 169; as the ultimate film noir, 105–12
Vicki, 129, 169
The Virginian, 16

Waikiki Wedding, 168
Walk Softly, Stranger, 178
Way Out West, 16
The Web, 169
Welcome Stranger, 81

Western Union, 16
When Strangers Marry, 169
Where Danger Lives, 170
Where the Sidewalk Ends, 37, 51, 61, 170
While the City Sleeps, 170
Whirlpool, 170
White Heat, 37, 38, 39
The Window, 39–40, 63
The Woman in the Window, 38, 58, 73, 170

A Woman's Face, 45
The Woman on the Beach, 170
World for Ransom, 171
The Wrong Man, 105

The Yearling, 81
You Only Live Once, 26, 113n17, 171

Ziegfeld Follies, 5, 82

About the Author

William Park received his AB from Princeton and his PhD from Columbia. He has taught at Hamilton College, Columbia, and for thirty-eight years at Sarah Lawrence College, where he cofounded the film program. He is the coeditor of *The College Anthology of English and American Poetry*; the editor of *Newman on the Bible*; and the author of *The Idea of Rococo* and *Hollywood: An Epic Production*. He has written extensively on the eighteenth-century novel, and his articles on film have appeared in *The Hudson Review*, *The Velvet Light Trap*, *The Journal of Popular Film*, and *Crisis*. He now lives in Santa Cruz, California.